الموجز

في التصريف

علي عبد الرشيد

الموجز

في التصريف

مؤلف:

علي عبد الرشيد

AL-MUJAZ

A Summary Of Tasreef

A Concise Treatise
On The Morphology Of
The Arabic Word

By
Ali Abdur-Rasheed

AL-MUJAZ
A Summary Of Tasreef

By

Ali Abdur-Rasheed

Copyright © 2006 Ali Abdur-Rasheed
Second Edition
Madani E-Publications
aliarasheed@gmail.com

TABLE OF CONTENTS

AUTHOR'S PREFACE

بسمه تعالى

و له الحمد و هو مستعان و الصلاة و السلام على خيرته من خلقه محمد سيد المرسلين

و آله الطاهرين المعصومين صلوات الله عليهم أجمعين

al-Mujaz: A Summary Of Tasreef-is a compilation of the rules of *Tasreef*, one of the fundamental branches of Arabic grammar. *Tasreef*, essentially, is the study of the Arabic word. *al-Mujaz* is a summary based on the traditional organization of this branch of Arabic grammar. Particular attention is focused on verb conjugation, the process of derivation and the meanings associated with particular word patterns.

al-Mujaz, as a publication, is an outgrowth of my experiences as a student and teacher in an Islamic seminary. I began my seminary studies in 1987 in a new seminary just opening in a small village called Medina in upstate New York. The seminary, the Islamic Seminary Of North America, was under the capable guidance of Shaikh Amir Mukhtar Fa'ezi of Pakistan. He gave students a uniquely traditional seminary education with a particular focus on the Arabic language. We will always remain indebted to him for setting us aright on the path of Islamic Studies in America.

I completed my first course in *Tasreef* under the instruction of Sayyid Tilmeez Hasnain, a well-known lecturer and language teacher from Pakistan. I initiated my Persian studies with Sayyid Hasnain as well. After completing the course in Tasreef, I was requested to prepare myself to teach the course to new incoming students, as was the traditional method in seminaries. Our primary course was the books found in the seminary student's handbook of preliminary studies known as *Jaami' al-Muqaddimaat (The Collection Of Preliminary Books)*. Most notably, the Book of Tasreef and the book of its commentary were the centerpieces of the course.

Tasreef proved a challenging subject to teach as American students were unfamiliar with the rigorous memorization that our course required. In the beginning we used Persian text books borrowed from the seminaries in Iran and later translated. After graduating, I joined the teaching staff and we prioritized developing English introductory texts for the various courses we offered.

This publication, then, is the culmination of my involvement in developing an English text book on the topic of *Tasreef*. In 1998, I decided to rewrite the text that we had used for several years with the intent of improving its language and content. I put the project aside for about a year while searching for the proper word processing software for the project. I renewed the project in the fall of 1999 and worked on it sporadically until completion at the end of the year 2000.

The resulting work, *al-Mujaz-A Summary Of Tasreef*-is a comprehensive compilation of the rules and patterns related to the Arabic word presented in a summary format. While following a traditional approach, I intended from the onset to make this publication more of an aid for self-study as opposed to a classroom text. It is a six month course compressed into 450 pages of text and tables.

This first edition of this book is being published as an electronic document in the Adobe® PDF format. It is provided without cost to individuals and educational institutes with the aim of furthering the development of Islamic studies in English speaking societies. I pray that those who read and study it will benefit from it.

Ali Abdur-Rasheed
29 Ramadhaan 1421 Hijri
December 26, 2000

The second electronic edition of this book is being published after minor revisions. It is being released in celebration of the birthday of the Prophet of Islam, Muhammad, peace be upon him and his noble family.

Ali Abdur-Rasheed
17 Rabial-Awwal 1427 Hijri
April 16, 2006

A SUMMARY OF TASREEF

الجزء الأوّل: الفعل

PART ONE: THE VERB

INTRODUCTION

Before delving into the study of *Tasreef*, a number of preliminary matters must be introduced beginning with the definition of *Tasreef*, the organization of this study and some terminology that will be useful during the course of this study.

▶ DEFINITION OF TASREEF

In the 'Arabic Language, **Tasreef** literally means to spend, change, to use and more. As a technical term of linguistics, *Tasreef* is the process of changing the patterns and forms of words in order to derive different meanings. A synonym of *Tasreef* is **Sarf** (صَرْف). *Tasreef* is also called the morphology of 'Arabic. The study of *Tasreef* involves the study of the hundreds of patterns and forms of words found in the 'Arab language with regard to their origin, derivation, construction and meaning.

The majority of words in 'Arabic can undergo a prolific process of derivation whereby one root word can become the source of literally hundreds of derivative words. These derivative words have their own particular pattern and form which distinguish them from their respective root words. To exemplify the point, from this one root word: عِلْمٌ (Knowledge), the rules of *Tasreef* can be applied to produce the following forms of verbs:

عَلِمَ، يَعْلَمُ، إِعْلَمْ، عُلِمَ، يُعْلَمُ، لِيُعْلَمْ

The meaning changes to: *He knew s.th.; He knows s.th.; Know!; It was known; It is known and Be it known,* respectively. Without making any significant changes, six new words have been formed all of which are verbs. The root word was a Noun and from it both Nouns and Verbs can be derived. Most of these forms of verbs also can be further conjugated according to the Subject and number. In the final analysis more than 76 other forms of these verbs can be derived from these six verbs alone.

This process of derivation also occurs in the Noun, although to a lesser extent than with the Verb. For example, the word: رَجُلٌ (A Man) can be changed in form thereby changing its meaning to the Plural, the Dual and the Diminutive:

رَجُلٌ، رَجُلانِ، رِجالٌ، رُجَيلٌ   A man, Two Men, Men, A little man

▶ THE BENEFIT OF THE STUDY OF TASREEF

The Arabic language has a very organized system of derivation. It is imperative to engage in the study of *Tasreef* in order to become thoroughly familiar with the Arabic word and the nuances of its meaning. Tasreef is the foundation a student first establishes in his quest for mastery of the Arabic language. With careful study, memorization and practice, a strong knowledge of the Arabic word is an objective well within reach. With this foundation the study of syntax or Nahw, the next level of grammar, will be made easier. With these two branches of grammar, a student can gain a comprehensive knowledge of the Arabic language.

▶ THE TOPIC OF TASREEF

The topic of the study of *Tasreef* is the 'Arabic word or the **Kalimah** (كَلِمَةٌ). *In Tasreef*, the *Kalimah* is examined from the viewpoint of its origin, construction and its particularities in usage and meaning.

▶ DEFINITION OF THE KALIMAH

Whenever man speaks, his expressions (أَلْفاظٌ) are either meaningful or unmeaningful. The *Kalimah* is a singular expression signifying a particular meaning. The Kalimah is a singular expression in that it is a word as opposed to a sentence. In *Tasreef*, a meaningful expression is called an expression in usage (لَفْظٌ مُسْتَعْمَلٌ).

▶ THE DIVISIONS OF THE KALIMAH

'Arabic words are like words in many other languages in that they can be divided into three groups:

▷ The Noun or **Ism** (الإِسْمُ) is a Kalimah that signifies an independent meaning without being associated with a tense of time (i.e., the past, present or future), for example: عِلْمٌ Knowledge: مَالٌ Wealth.

▷ The Verb or **Fi'l** (الفِعْلُ) is a Kalimah that signifies an independent meaning in association with one of the tenses of time, meaning the Past (الماضِيُ) Present (الحالُ) and future (المُسْتَقْبَلُ), for example ذَهَبَ (He left-Past Tense), يَذْهَبُ (He is leaving-Present Tense), إذْهَبْ (Leave!-Present Tense Command Verb).

▷ The Particle or **Harf** (الحَرْفُ) is a Kalimah that does not signify an independent meaning in itself, rather, it links other Kalimah together and its meaning is interpreted through this linkage, as seen by the Particle (فِي) in the following sentence: دَخَلْتُ في المَدْرَسَةِ (I entered into the school) and the Particle (مِنْ) in the sentence: خَرَجْتُ مِنَ الدَّارِ (I emerged from the house).

▶ PRIMARY WORDS AND DERIVATIVES

The *Kalimah* can either be a **Substantive Word** (الجامِدُ) or a **Derivative Word** (المُشْتَقُّ). The *Substantive Word* is that word which is not derived from another word. Its original letters are not derived from other words, such as: فِيلٌ، سَيْفٌ، تَمْرٌ (Elephant, sword and a date, resp.).

The *Derivative* word is derived from another word, as in: عَالِمٌ، مَذْهَبٌ، إِسْلَامٌ (A learned person, a sect and Islam, resp.). The word from which the *Derivative Word* is taken is the Root Word (الأَصْلُ). From the Root Word, many derivatives can be formed and both (the Root Word and the Derivative Word) are said to be of the same genus or *Jins* (الجِنْسُ). The Root Word can be one of two kinds:

Masdar (المَصْدَرُ) and the **Non-Masdar** or Ghairul-*Masdar* (غَيْرُ المَصْدَرِ)

The *Masdar* is a type of word from which derivative words are formed while the Non-*Masdar* words are not found having derivatives. The Non-*Masdar* are primarily Particles and a limited number of Nouns that do not form derivatives, like: فَأْرَةٌ، آيَةٌ (a mouse, a verse).

▶ ORIGINAL LETTERS AND ADDITIONAL LETTERS

▷ The letters of a root word that are also found in its derivatives are referred to as the **Original Letters** (الأَحْرُفُ الأَصْلِيُّ).

▷ The letters that are found only in some of the Derivative Words are called **Additional Letters** (الأَحْرُفُ الزَّائِدَةُ).

For example, in the words: عِلْمٌ، عَالِمٌ، مَعْلُومٌ، أَعْلَمَ, the three letters: (علم) are the *Original Letters* since they are found in its Root Word (عِلْمٌ) and each of the subsequent words. The remaining letters are *Additional Letters* because they are only found in some of these words, all of which are *Derivative Words* (المُشْتَقَّاتُ).

▶ CONSTRUCTION OF THE KALIMAH

Based on its Original Letters, the *Kalimah* has three types of construction:

▷ The Kalimah comprised of three Original Letters is called **Thulaathi** (الثُّلَاثِيُّ) or three-lettered.

▷ The Kalimah comprised of four Original Letters is called **Rubaa'i** (الرُّبَاعِيُّ) or four-lettered.

▷ The Kalimah comprised of five Original Letters is called **Khumaasi** (الخُمَاسِيُّ).

In addition, each of these three constructions also has two subdivisions:

‣ **Mujarrad** (المُجَرَّدُ)   ‣ **Mazeed Fihi** (المَزِيدُ فِيهِ)

If the Kalimah contains only the Original Letters, it is referred to as **Mujarrad**. Literally, *Mujarrad* means to be bare, devoid of or free of something. The word that is referred to as *Mujarrad* is free of any Additional Letters and only contains the Original Letters of the Root Word. In our study, we will refer to *Mujarrad* as Primary Words.

The Kalimah having Additional Letters aside from the *Original Letters* is known as **Mazeed Fihi**, meaning having additions in it. We will refer to *Mazeed Fihi* as Derivative Words.

All together the Kalimah has six divisions:

▷ **The Three Letter Word** (الثُّلَاثِيُّ)

‣ **The Three Letter Primary Word** (الثُّلَاثِيُّ المُجَرَّدُ): عَلِمَ *To know;* رَجُلٌ *A man.*

‣ **The Three Letter Derivative Word** (الثُّلَاثِيُّ المَزِيدُ فِيهِ): أَعلَمَ *To inform s.o.;* رِجَالٌ *Men.*

▷ **The Four Letter Word** (الرُّباعِيُّ)

 › The Four Letter Primary Word (الرُّباعِيُّ المُجَرَّدُ) : دَحْرَجَ *To roll*; جَعْفَرٌ *A small stream.*

 › The Four Letter Derivative Word (الرُّباعِيُّ المَزِيدُ فِيهِ) : تَدَحْرَجَ *To roll something*; جعافِرٌ *Small streams.*

▷ **The Five Letter Word** (الخُماسِيُّ)

 › The Five Letter Primary Word (الخُماسِيُّ المُجَرَّدُ): سَفَرْجَلٌ *A Quince.*

 › The Five Letter Derivative Word (الخُماسِيُّ المَزِيدُ فِيهِ): خُنْدَرِسٌ *An ancient Greek wine.*

▶ **PATTERNS AND THEIR RULES**

A particular pattern or **Wazn** (الوَزْنُ) is utilized in Tasreef to distinguish the Original Letters from the Additional Letters. Three letters: ف، ع، ل are used in the place of the first, second and third Original Letters, respectively. For example, we say: كَتَبَ is on the pattern of: فَعَلَ and عَلِمَ is on the pattern of: فَعِلَ and so forth. When constructing a pattern for a Kalimah, the following rules should be noted:

The Letter (ف) represents the first Original Letter of the Root word. The letter (ع) represents the second Original Letter and the letter (ل) represents the third Original Letter. If the Kalimah has more than three letters, the letter (ل) will be repeated. According to this, the pattern of the Thulaathi word has one letter (ل), as in: سَأَلَ on the pattern of فَعَلَ.

The pattern of the *Rubaa'i* word will have the letter (ل) repeated twice, for example: دَحْرَجَ
on the pattern of فَعْلَلَ. The pattern of the *Khumaasi* word will have the letter (ل) repeated
three times as in: سَفَرْجَلٌّ on the pattern of: فَعَلْلَلٌ.

As previously mentioned, in the pattern (فعل), the three letters represent the first, second
and third Original Letters, respectively. The first Original Letter is referred to as (فاءُ الكَلِمَةِ),
the second Original Letter is referred to as: (عَينُ الكَلِمَةِ) and the third Original Letter is
called: (لامُ الكَلِمَةِ). If the word contains four Original Letters instead of three, the fourth
letter is referred to as: (لامُ الكَلِمَةِ الثَّانِيُ) The Second Lam, as in فَعْلَلَ and if the word has
five Original Letters, the fifth letter is called: (لامُ الكَلِمَةِ الثَّالِثُ) The Third Lam, as in:
فَعَلْلَلٌ.

Sometimes, the Original Letters of a Kalimah are repeated, as in: سَلَّمَ and جِلْبَبٌ , where
the second and third letters respectively are doubled. This being the case, the letters (فعل)
are repeated to indicate the repetition of an Original Letter, for example: سَلَّمَ is on the
pattern of: فَعَّلَ and: جِلْبَبٌ is on the pattern of: فِعْلَلٌ.

Additional Letters, however, exist in a pattern just as they are found in the word. For
example, take the words: عالِمٌ and: مَعْلُومٌ, the word has added an Additional Letter Alif (ا)
to the pattern (فاعِلٌ). The word مَعْلُومٌ has added two Additional Letters (م, و) to the pattern
(مَفْعُولٌ). These Additional Letters are repeated in the pattern in the same manner that they
are found in the word. In this manner, it becomes clear which letters are original and which
are additional.

The vowels or **Harakaat** (حَرَكاتٌ) on each of the letters in the pattern must correspond
with the vowels of each letter in the word upon which the pattern is based.

The word that is formed according to a particular pattern is termed **Mauzoon** (الْمَوْزُونُ).

Based on this, when we say that عَلِمَ is on the pattern of: فَعِلَ, it means that the first letter is voweled with Fathah, the second with Kasrah and the third with Fathah.

This is the case except when the vowel has been changed due to the rules governing the conversion of weak letters or other rules in which the vowels are altered. For example, the word: قَالَ (He said) is on the pattern of: فَعَلَ because, originally, it was قَوَلَ, although it could not remain in that form due to the rules of conversion of weak letters. Likewise, we say مَدَّ is on the pattern of: فَعَلَ because it was مَدَدَ originally but the similar letters were contracted in writing.

If the letter has a **Shaddah** (ّ), it is counted that there are actually two letters of the same kind. One must refer to the Kalimah to see if the two letters are both Original Letters or both Additional Letters or one is an Original Letter and the other is an Additional Letter.

In the first instance, the pattern will be without the Shaddah, for example مَرَّ which we will say is on the pattern of: فَعَلَ (the doubled letters are both Original Letters). In the second instance, the Shaddah in the pattern is written upon letters that are additional. This Shaddah is reproduced in the pattern, for example: إِجْلَوَّازَ is one the pattern of: إِفْعَوَّالَ (in which the Shaddah is doubling a letter that is an Additional Letter).

In the third instance, whenever it cannot be distinguished whether the first letter of the two is an Additional Letter or an Original Letter, then, each letter of the pattern, i.e. (فعل) which represents that doubled letter will become **Mushaddad** (الْمُشَدَّد) or doubled with Shaddah. For example, the word عَمَّار is on the pattern of: فَعَّال.

Whenever it is known which of the doubled letter is an Original Letter and which is an Additional Letter, the pattern is made without Shaddah, for example, we will say that the word: سَيِّدٌ is on the pattern of: فَعْيِلٌ and the word: عَلِيٌّ is on the pattern of: فَعِيلٌ.

If, due to the application of the rules of alteration of Weak Letters or **I'laal** (الإِعْلال) or other rules, the Original Letter is elided or removed, the letter representing the Original Letter will also be removed from the pattern. For example, we say: قُلْ (*Say!*) which is taken from the verb: قَالَ يَقُولُ, is on the pattern of فُلْ. The word هَبْ (*Bestow!*), taken from وَهَبَ يَهَبُ, is on the pattern of: عَلْ and the word: فِ (*Fulfill!*) is taken from the word: وَفَى يَفِي, and is on the pattern of: عِ.

If Conversion or **Qalb** (القَلْبُ) occurs in a word, meaning that the sequence of the Original Letters (فعل) is disrupted, the pattern will reflect that conversion, as in:, we say: جاه is on the pattern of: عَفَلَ, because in referring to words which are derived from the same root, we know that other derivitives are: وَجْهٌ، وَجِيهٌ، وَجاهَةٌ and the letter (ج) is the second letter of the root represented by: (ع). The letter Alif (ا) is converted from the letter Waw (و) which is the first letter of the root.

The benefit of knowing the pattern of a Kalimah is the ability to distinguish the Original Letters from the Additional Letters. In doing so, it becomes easier to recognized what type of word it is and its construction.

▶ SOUND, WEAK AND DOUBLED LETTERED WORDS

Viewing the *Kalimah* from the perspective of the similarities and differences of its root letters, there are three categories:

▷ Sound And Weak Words الصَّحِيحُ وَ المُعْتَلُّ

The word in which none of its Original Letters are Weak Letters (الْحَرْفُ العِلَّةُ), is called a Sound Word or **Saheeh** (الصَّحِيحُ). *The word in which one or more of its Original Letters is a Weak Letter is called a Weak Word or **Mu'tall*** (المُعْتَلُّ). The Weak Letters are only: و، ي، ى (Waw, Yaa and *Alif* Maqsoorah).

Mu'tall has seven divisions:

› *Mu'tall* of the 1st *Original Letter* (مُعْتَلُّ الفاءِ) is called **Mithaal** (المِثالُ) as in: يَسَرَ، وَقْتٌ.

› *Mu'tall* of the 2nd *Original Letter* (مُعْتَلُّ العَيْنِ) is called **Ajwaf** (الأَجْوَفُ) as in: خافَ، بَيْعٌ

› *Mu'tall* of the 3rd *Original Letter* (مُعْتَلُّ اللاَّمِ) is called **Naaqis** (النَّاقِصُ) for example: دَعا، رَمَى.

› *Mu'tall* of the first and third *Original Letter* (مُعْتَلُّ الفاءِ وَ اللاَّمِ) is called **Lafeef Mafrooq** (اللَّفِيفُ المَفْرُوقُ), as in: وَفَى، وَحِيَ.

› *Mu'tall* of the second and third *Original Letter* (مُعْتَلُّ العَيْنِ وَ اللاَّمِ) is called **Lafeef Maqroon** (اللَّفِيفُ المَقْرُونُ), for example: لَوَى، حَيَّ.

- *Mu'tall* of the first and second *Original Letter* (مُعْتَلُّ الفاءِ وَ العَيْنِ) is called **Lafeef Maqroon** also, for example وَيْلٌ.

- *Mu'tall* of all three *Original Letters* (مُعْتَلُّ الفاءِ وَ العَيْنِ وَ اللَّامِ), for example وَاوٌ، ياءٌ, whose original was وَوَوٌ، يَيْيِ.

▷ **Mahmooz** المَهْمُوزُ

The Kalimah in which one or more of its Original Letters is Hamzah is called **Mahmooz** (المَهْمُوزُ) for example: أَمَرَ، سَأَلَ، بَرِئَ. *Mahmooz* has three types:

- If the *Hamzah* is found in the first Original Letter (فاءُ اكَلِمَةِ), it is called **Mahmoozul-Faa'** (مَهْمُوزُ الفاءِ) , as in: أَمَرَ، أمِرٌ.

- If the *Hamzah* occurs in the second Original Letter (عَيْنُ الكَلِمَةِ), it is called **Mahmoozul-'Ayn** (مَهْمُوزُ العَيْنِ), for example: سَأَلَ، سائِلٌ.

- If the *Hamzah* is found in the third Original Letter (لامُ الكَلِمَةِ), it is called **Mahmoozul-Lam** (مَهْمُوزُ اللَّامِ), for example: بَرَأَ، بَرِئَ.

▷ **Mudhaa'af** المُضاعَفُ

The Three Letter Kalimah whose second Original Letter and third Original Letter are of the same type is called **Mudhaa'af** (المُضاعَفُ), as in: حَجَّ، بَرَ. The Four Letter Kalimah is not found with its doubled letters existing side by side. The *Mudhaa'af* in the Four Letter Kalimah will have its letters repeated in the same sequence, for example:

$$ زَلْزَلَةٌ، قَهْقَهَةٌ، جَعْجَعَ، نَعْنَعٌ $$

► CONCLUDING NOTES

▷ The sound *Kalimah* which is not *Mu'tall* nor *Mahmooz* nor *Mudhaa'af* is called **Saalim** (السَّالِمُ), as in: ضَرَبَ، بَقَـرٌ. It is possible for a word to be both Sound and *Mahmooz* (الصَّحِيحُ وَ المَهْمُوزُ), as in: أَمَرَ، سَـأَلَ or it is possible for a word to be both Sound and *Mudhaa'af* (الصَّحِيحُ وَ المُضاعَفُ), for example: مَدَّ، دَدَنْ. Similarly, it is possible for a Kalimah to be both *Mu'tall* and *Mahmooz* (المُعْتَلُّ وَ المَهْمُوزُ), as in: يَئِسَ، أَبَى. Likewise, a Kalimah *can be both Mu'tall and Mudhaa'af* (المُعْتَلُّ وَ المُضاعَفُ), as in: حَيِيَ، وَدَّ. It is also possible for a word to be *Mahmooz* and *Mudhaa'af* (المَهْمُوزُ وَ المُضاعَفُ), as in: أَنَّ، أَزَّ.

▷ If the Weak Letter (الحَرْفُ العِلَّةِ) has no vowel or is **Saakin** (ساكِنٌ), it is termed **Harf al-Lain** (حَرْفُ اللَّيِنِ), as in: قَوْلٌ، بَيْعٌ. If the vowel preceding the Weak Letter is similar to the Weak Letter, is called *Harf al-Madd* (حَرْفُ المَدِّ), i.e., a long vowel, as in: دَازٌ، أَمِيْرٌ.

▷ The *Mudhaa'af* in the three letter word (الثُّلاثِيُّ) exhibits a type of contraction or **Idghaam** (الإِدْغام). *Idghaam* occurs when two letters are to be spoken from the same point of pronunciation (مَخْرَجٌ), the words are pronounced in such a way that there is no separation between them.

The first letter is referred to as **Mudgham** (المُدْغَمُ) and the second letter is called **Mudgham Fihi** (المُدْغَمُ فِيهِ). Most often, the two letters are written in the form of one letter that possesses the sign of *Shaddah* to indicate its *Idghaam* or contraction. For example: مَدَد مَدَّ الرَّجُلُ الرَّجُلَ.

▷ *Hamzah* and Weak Letters exhibit alterations at times. The alteration of the *Hamzah* is called **Takhfeef** (التَّخْفِيفُ), meaning to lessen, lighten. *Takhfeef* is of two types: Conversion (القَلْبُ) and Elision (الحَذْفُ). Whenever a vowelless Hamzah follows a voweled *Hamzah*, the voweled *Hamzah* will be converted to a long vowel or *Harful-Madd* and the other *Hamzah* is elided. This conversion of the *Hamzah* is called **Takhfeef al-Qalbi** (التَّخْفِيفُ القَلْبِيُّ), For example:

أَءْمَنَ آمَنَ،   أُءْمُرْ أُوْمُرْ،   إِءْمان إِيْمان

If the vowelless *Hamzah* occurs after a voweled letter which is not another *Hamzah*, the changing to a *Harf al-Madd* is permissible, although not obligatory, for example:

رَأْسٌ – رَاسٌ، شُؤْمٌ – شُومٌ، ذِئْبٌ – ذِيبٌ

There are other words, however, that are not found to be converted in this manner at all. Their construction is established according to usage (السَّماعِيُّ), for example, these conversions are never found:

أَئِمَّةٌ أَيِمَّةٌ، نَبِئٌ نَبِيٌّ،   بَرِئٌ بَرِي،   نَبُوءَةٌ نَبُوَّةٌ

The second type of alteration is called Elision or **Hazhf** (الحَذْفُ). The rules of Elision are established according to usage as opposed to specific rules of grammar, for example:

أُوْخُذْ خُذْ   أُوْكُلْ كُلْ

The alteration that occurs in Weak Letters is called **I'laal** (الإِعْلالُ). There are three types of I'laal: *Sukoon* (الإِعْلالُ السُّكُونِيُّ), *Conversion* (الإِعْلالُ القَلْبِيُّ) and *Elision* (الإِعْلالُ الحَذْفِيُّ). The rules governing *I'laal* in weak letters are quite extensive and will be mentioned where appropriate.

PART ONE

THE VERB

الفِعْلُ

The first part of this Book is devoted to the study of the Verb. The second part will focus on the Noun. Since *Tasreef* does not occur in the Particle to any extent, the Particle will be mentioned only as it relates to either the Verb or Noun. A more comprehensive study of the Particle can usually be found in books of 'Arabic grammar and syntax.

The study of the verb is divided into the following sub-sections:

› The Three Letter Primary Verb (الفِعْلُ الثُّلَاثِيُّ المُجَرَّدُ)

› The un-sound verb (الفِعْلُ غَيرُ السَّالِمِ)

› The Weak Verb (الفِعْلُ المُعْتَلُّ)

› The Three Letter Derivative Verb (الفِعْلُ الثُّلَاثِيُّ المَزِيدُ فِيهِ)

› The 4 Letter Verb (Primary and Derivative) (الفِعْلُ الرُّباعِيُّ المُجَرَّدُ وَ المَزِيدُ فِيهِ)

› The states of the verb (أَحْوَالُ الفِعْلِ)

› Miscellaneous Verbs: (الأَفْعَالُ الشَّتَّى): the Artificial Verb (الفِعْلُ الصَّناعِيُّ), the Defective Verb (الفِعْلُ غَيرُ المُتَصَرِّفِ) and the Verbal Noun (إِسْمُ الفِعْلِ)

A PREFACE TO PART ONE

THE VERB

▶ **DEFINITION AND DIVISIONS OF THE VERB** تَعْرِيفُ الفِعْلِ وَ أَقْسَامُهُ

The Verb (الفِعْلُ) is a Kalimah that signifies the occurrence of an action or the existence of a state in association with the past, present or future tense. The signification of the occurrence of an action is referred to as **Hadath** (الحَدَثُ), like: ضَرَبَ *He hit*, يَضْرِبُ *He is hitting* and إِضْرِبْ *Hit!* (the Past, Present and Command Verb, respectively). The signification of a state is referred to as **Haalah** (الحَالَةُ), for example: حَسُنَ *He was good*, يَحْسُنُ *He is good* and أُحْسُنْ *Be good!*

There are three types of Verbs (the details of each will be mentioned shortly):

· **Maadhi** (الماضِيُّ) · **Mudhaari'** (المُضارِعُ) · **Amr** (الأَمْرُ)

▷ **Maadhi** is the Past Tense Verb. It signifies the occurrence of an action or a state in the time before speaking or the past (الماضِيُّ), as in: *He struck* ضَرَبَ and حَسُنَ *He was good*.

▷ **Mudhaari'** is the Present Tense Verb. It signifies the occurrence of an action or state in the present tense (الحالُ) or the future tense (المُسْتَقْبَلُ), like: يَضْرِبُ *He is hitting* and: يَحْسُنُ *He is good* or *He will hit* or *He will be good*. The Future tense is understood from the context of the verb's usage in the sentence since the form for both the Present and Future Tense Verb are identical.

▷ **Amr** is the Command Verb. It signifies that the speaker is seeking to initiate an action or state, such as إِضْرِبْ *Strike!* and أُحْسُنْ *Be good!*

▶ THE ORIGIN OF THE VERB - THE MASDAR أَصْلُ الفِعْلِ هُوَ المَصْدَرُ

The Verb is derived from the **Masdar** (المَصْدَرُ). The *Masdar* is a Noun that signifies the occurrence of an action or a state, without association with a tense of time. The Masdar is similar to the English Infinitive Noun, as in: خُرُوج *Exiting* and حُسن *Goodness*. The Past Tense Verb (الفِعْلُ الماضِيُ) is derived directly from the *Masdar*. The Present Tense Verb (الفِعْلُ المُضارِع) is derived from the Past Tense Verb. The Command Verb (الفِعْلُ الأَمْرُ) is derived from the Present Tense Verb. The method of derivation is as follows:

Masdar > Past Tense Verb > Present Tense Verb > Command Verb

▶ ACTIVE VOICE AND PASSIVE VOICE المَعْلُومُ وَ المَجْهُولُ

Verbs are found either in the **Active Voice** (المَعْلُومُ) or the **Passive Voice** (المَجْهُولُ). The *Active Voice Verb* (الفِعْلُ المَعْلُومُ) is that Verb whose Subject (الفاعِلُ) is mentioned in a sentence, as in: ضَرَبَ زَيْدٌ بَكْراً *Zaid Struck Bakr*. Zaid is the Subject while Bakr is the Object. In some instances, the Subject is referred to but not written, as in: ضَرَبَ بَكْراً *He (Zaid) struck Bakr*. Here, the verb's concealed pronoun refers to the unwritten Subject.

The *Passive Voice Verb* is that Verb whose Subject is not mentioned in the sentence nor referred to (by the Subject's pronoun), for example: ضُرِبَ بَكْرٌ *Bakr was struck*. The Subject of the Active Voice (Zaid) is removed and the Active Voice's Object (Bakr) occupies the place of the Subject. For this reason, the displaced Object is referred to as the **Proxy Subject** (نائِبُ الفاعِلِ).

Accordingly, every Verb either has a Subject (written or referred to) and is in the Active Voice or it has a Proxy Subject and is in the Passive Voice.

It should be noted that the *Passive Voice Verb* is not derived directly from the *Masdar* like the *Active Voice Verb*. Rather, the *Past Tense Passive Voice Verb* (الفِعْلُ الماضِيُ المَجْهُولُ) is derived directly from the *Past Tense Active Voice* (الفِعْلُ الماضِيُ المَعْلُومُ). Likewise, the *Present Tense Passive Voice Verb* (الفِعْلُ المُضارِعُ المَجْهُولُ) is derived from the *Present Tense Active Voice Verb* (الفِعْلُ المُضارِعُ المَعْلُومُ). However, the *Passive Voice Command Verb* (الفِعْلُ الأَمْرُ المَجْهُولُ) is derived directly from the *Present Tense Passive Voice Verb* (الفِعْلُ المُضارِعُ المَجْهُولُ). The method of derivation is as follows:

P.T. Active Voice Verb > P.T. Passive Voice Verb.

الماضِيُ المَعْلُومُ > الماضِيُ المَجْهُولُ

Pr.T. Active Voice Verb > Pr.T. Passive Voice Verb > Passive Voice Command Verb

المُضارِعُ المَعْلُومُ > المُضارِعُ المَجْهُولُ > الأَمْرُ المَجْهُولُ

▶ FORMS OF THE VERB صِيغُ الفِعْلِ

Every Active Voice Verb has a Subject that is the actual performer of the action or the one possessing the state which the verb signifies. Sometimes, the Subject is mentioned directly in the sentence or, at other times, a reference is made to the Subject by the Pronoun that is signified in the form of the verb. The Subject of Verbs in the Active Voice is called Faa'il (الفاعِل). Verbs in the Passive Voice will have a Proxy Subject or **Naa'ib al-Faa'il** (نائِبُ الفاعِل). The Subject/Proxy Subject will be either in the Third Person (الغائِبُ) or Second Person (المُخاطَبُ) or First Person (المُتَكَلِّمُ).

The Verb will be appropriately named according to the category of the Subject as a Third Person Verb, a Second Person Verb or a First Person Verb, respectively.

The Subject/*Proxy Subject* of the Third Person and the Second Person will be either **Masculine** (المُذَكَّرُ) or **Feminine** (المُؤَنَّثُ). The Subject/Proxy Subject will also be either **Singular** (المُفْرَدُ), **Dual** (المُثَنَّى) or **Plural** (الجَمْعُ). The First Person is only Singular (المُفْرَدُ) and Plural (الجَمْعُ). Each change in the Subject/Proxy Subject necessitates a change of form in the Verb. Each form that the Verb is changed into is called a **Seeghah** (الصِّيغَةُ). Each *Seeghah* is based on its Subject/Proxy Subject.

Each *Seeghah* is named according to its Subject or Proxy Subject, for example:

(صِيغَةُ المُفْرَدِ المُذَكَّرِ الغَائِبِ) The *Seeghah* of the Third Person Masculine Singular

(صِيغَةُ المُثَنَّى المُذَكَّرِ الغَائِبِ) The *Seeghah* of the Third Person Masculine Dual and

(صِيغَةُ الجَمْعِ المُذَكَّرِ الغَائِبِ) The *Seeghah* of the Third Person Masculine Plural ...etc.

The Third Person Verb has six *Seeghah* (three Masculine and three Feminine); the Second Person Verb also has six *Seeghah* (three Masculine and three Feminine) and the First Person Verb only has two *Seeghah* (without signifying gender). As a result, each Verb has fourteen *Seeghah*. The names of these fourteen *Seeghah* are given below:

▷ **The Third Person** (الغَائِبُ)

- › 1 Third Person Masculine Singular   (المُفْرَدُ المُذَكَّرُ الغَائِبُ)
- › 2 Third Person Masculine Dual   (المُثَنَّى المُذَكَّرُ الغَائِبُ)
- › 3 Third Person Masculine Plural   (الجَمْعُ المُذَكَّرُ الغَائِبُ)
- › 4 Third Person Feminine Singular   (المُفْرَدَةُ المُؤَنَّثُ الغَائِبَةُ)
- › 5 Third Person Feminine Dual   (المُثَنَّى المُؤَنَّثُ الغَائِبَةُ)
- › 6 Third Person Feminine Plural   (الجَمْعُ المُؤَنَّثُ الغَائِبَةُ)

▷ **The Second Person** (المُخَاطَبُ)

   › 7 Second Person Masculine Singular   (المُفْرَدُ المُذَكَّرُ المُخَاطَبُ)

   › 8 Second Person Masculine Dual   (المُثَنَّى المُذَكَّرُ المُخَاطَبُ)

   › 9 Second Person Masculine Plural   (الجَمْعُ المُذَكَّرُ المُخَاطَبُ)

   › 10 Second Person Feminine Singular   (المُفْرَدَةُ المُؤَنَّثُ المُخَاطَبَةُ)

   › 11 Second Person Feminine Dual   (االمُثَنَّى لمُؤَنَّثُ المخَاطَبَةُ)

   › 12 Second Person Feminine Plural   (الجَمْعُ المُؤَنَّثُ المُخاطَبَةُ)

▷ **The First Person** (المُتَكَلِّمُ)

   › 13 The First Person Singular   (المُتَكَلِّمُ وَحْدَهُ)

   › 14 The First Person Plural   (المُتَكَلِّم مَعَ غَيْرِه)

CHAPTER ONE

THE THREE LETTER PRIMARY VERB
الفعل الثلاثي المجرّد

SECTION ONE

THE ACTIVE VOICE VERB

الفِعلُ المَعلُومُ

The Past Tense Active Voice Verb

الماضِيُ المَعلُومُ

The Active Voice form of the Past Tense Three Letter Primary Verb (المَاضِيُ المَعلُومُ) is derived from the Masdar. In order to derive the Past Tense Verb from the Masdar, any additional letters found in the Masdar are removed. The first Original Letter (فاءُ الكَلِمَةِ) and the third Original Letter (لامُ الكَلِمَةِ) are made **Maftooh** (مَفتُوحٌ), meaning that they are voweled with *Fathah*. The second Original Letter (عينُ الكَلِمَةِ) may be voweled with *Fathah*, *Kasrah* or *Dhammah* (i.e. **Maftooh, Maksoor** (مَكسُورٌ) or **Madhmoom** (مَضمُومٌ), respectively). The Active Voice Verb's vowelization patterns are established according to usage (السَّماعِيُّ).

With this being the case, any Past Tense Active Voice Three Letter Primary Verb will have one of following three patterns: فَعَلَ، فَعِلَ، فَعُلَ. Note the following examples of verbs with their respective root words (Masdar): ذَهَبَ (ذَهابٌ) *He left* (*leaving*); عَلِمَ (عِلمٌ) *He knew* (*Knowledge*); حَسُنَ (حُسنٌ) *He was good* (*Goodness*).

▶ THE FORMS OF THE PAST TENSE ACTIVE VOICE VERB صِيَغُ الماضِيِّ المَعْلُوم

▷ 1st Seeghah/Third Person Masculine Singular (المُفْرَدُ المُذَكَّرُ الغائِبُ)

According to what was mentioned above, the first Seeghah is derived from the Masdar. Each of the three patterns shown above are in this same first Seeghah. This Seeghah will have only the three Original Letters of the root: (فَعَلَ) .

▷ 2nd Seeghah/Third Person Masculine Dual (المُثَنَّى المُذَكَّرُ الغائِبُ)

This Seeghah is derived from the 1st Seeghah. It is formed by simply adding an Alif (ا) to the end of the 1st Seeghah which forms a long vowel: (فَعَلَ + ا = فَعَلا).

▷ 3rd Seeghah/Third Person Masculine Plural (الجَمْعُ المُذَكَّرُ الغائِبُ)

This Seeghah is also derived from the 1st Seeghah. It is formed by removing the *Fathah* on the third Original Letter and replacing it with *Dhammah,* then, the letter Waw (و) is added to the end of the verb forming a long vowel: (فَعَلُ + و = فَعَلُو). Then, the letter Alif is written after the letter Waw: (فَعَلُو + ا= فَعَلُوا). This Alif has no vowel and is not is not pronounced. Its sole purpose is to separate the Verb from any word that may follow it. This Alif is called the **Separating Alif** (الأَلِفُ الفاصِلَةُ).

▷ 4th Seeghah/Third Person Feminine Singular (المُفْرَدَةُ المُؤَنَّثُ الغائِبَةُ)

This Seeghah is formed from the first Seeghah as well. The Letter Taa' with *Sukoon* or **Taa' As-Saakinah** (تاءُ السَّاكِنَة) is added to the end of 1st Seeghah: (فَعَلَ + تْ = فَعَلَتْ). *Taa' As-Saakinah* is the sign of the Feminine in the Third Person.

▷ **5th Seeghah/Third Person Feminine Dual** (المُثَنَّى المُؤَنَّثُ الغَائِبَةُ)

This Seeghah is derived from the 4th Seeghah by removing the Sukoon on the Taa' and adding the Letter Alif to the end of the word forming a long vowel: (فَعَلَتَا = ا + فَعَلَتْ). As in the 4th Seeghah, the Taa' is the sign of the feminine.

▷ **6th Seeghah/Third Person Feminine Plural** (الجَمْعُ المُؤَنَّثُ الغَائِبَةُ)

This Seeghah is derived from the 1st Seeghah by making the third Original Letter **Saakin** (meaning to make it vowelless with Sukoon) and adding the letter Noon with Fathah (نَ) to the end of the Verb (فَعَلْنَ = نَ + فَعَلْ). In this Seeghah and all that follow, the third Original Letter will be *Saakin* as a rule.

▷ **7th Seeghah/Second Person Masculine Singular** (المُفْرَدُ المُذَكَّرُ المُخَاطَبُ)

This Seeghah is derived from the 1st Seeghah by making the third Original Letter *Saakin* and adding the Taa' voweled with Fathah or **Taa' Maftoohah** (تَاءُ المَفْتُوحَةِ) to the end of the Verb: (فَعَلْتَ = تَ + فَعَلْ).

▷ **8th Seeghah/Second Person Masculine Dual** (المُثَنَّى المُذَكَّرُ المُخَاطَبُ)

Likewise, this Seeghah is formed from the 1st Seeghah by making the third Original Letter *Saakin* and adding the suffix (تُما) to the end of the Verb: (فَعَلْتُما = تُما + فَعَلْ).

▷ **9th Seeghah/Second Person Masculine Plural** (الجَمْعُ المُذَكَّرُ المُخَاطَبُ)

This Seeghah is also formed from the 1st by making the third Original Letter *Saakin* and adding the suffix (تُم) to the end of the Verb: (فَعَلْتُم = تُم + فَعَلْ).

▷ **10th Seeghah/Second Person Feminine Singular** (الْمُفْرَدَةُ الْمُؤَنَّثُ الْمُخَاطَبَةُ)

As with the three forms of the Second Person Masculine, the three forms Second Person Feminine are also formed from the 1st Seeghah by making the third Original Letter *Saakin*. In this Seeghah, the Taa' with Kasrah (تِ)also known as **Taa' Maksoorah** (تَا ءُ الْمَكْسُورَة) is added to the end of the Verb: (فَعَلْتِ = تِ + فَعَلْ).

▷ **11th Seeghah/Second Person Feminine Dual** (الْمُثَنَّى لِمُؤَنَّثُ الْمُخَاطَبَةُ)

This Seeghah is formed from the 1st Seeghah after making the third Original Letter *Saakin*, then, the suffix (تُما) is added to form this Seeghah: (فَعَلْتُما = تُما + فَعَلْ).

▷ **12th Seeghah/Second Person Feminine Plural** (الْجَمْعُ الْمُؤَنَّثُ الْمُخَاطَبَةُ)

Likewise, this Seeghah is formed from the 1st Seeghah by adding the suffix (تُنَّ) to the end of the Verb after making the third Original Letter *Saakin*: (فَعَلْتُنَّ = تُنَّ + فَعَلْ).

▷ **13th Seeghah/First Person Singular** (الْمُتَكَلِّمُ وَحْدَهُ)

The two forms of the first person are also formed from the 1st Seeghah. The third Original Letter is made Saakin, then, **Taa' Madhmoomah** (تَا ءُ الْمَضْمُومَة) or Taa' with Dhammah (تُ), is added to the end of the Verb: (فَعَلْتُ = تُ + فَعَلْ).

▷ **14th Seeghah/First Person Plural** (الْمُتَكَلِّمُ مَعَ غَيْرِهِ)

After making the third Original Letter of the 1st Seeghah *Saakin*, Noon and Alif (نا) are added to the end of the Verb: (فَعَلْنا = نا + فَعَلْ).

The following table provides the complete conjugation of the Past Tense Active Voice Verb:

Table 1.1 - The Patterns Of The Active Voice Three Letter Primary Verb: Past Tense

الجَمْع	المُثَنَّى	المُفْرَد	الماضي المَعْلُوم
فَعَلُوا	فَعَلا	فَعَلَ	الغائِب:
فَعَلْنَ	فَعَلَتَا	فَعَلَتْ	الغائِبَة:
فَعَلْتُمْ	فَعَلْتُما	فَعَلْتَ	المُخَاطَب:
فَعَلْتُنَّ	فَعَلْتُما	فَعَلْتِ	المُخَاطَبَة:
فَعَلْنا		فَعَلْتُ	المُتَكَلِّم:

There are only three possible vowel patterns for Past Tense Active Voice Verb:

$$ \text{فَعَلَ، فَعِلَ، فَعُلَ} $$

The Seeghah of verbs found on the two other patterns (فَعِلَ، فَعُلَ) will be formed in a similar manner to what has been mentioned above. The only difference being the vowel on the 2nd Original Letter (عينُ الكَلِمَة), the vowel will either be Kasrah or Dhammah.

The Active Voice Verb is conjugated according its Subject or **Faa'Il** (الفَاعِلُ). The Subject is represented in the form of a Pronoun or **Dhameer** (الضَّمِيْر). This type of Pronoun is called the **Pronoun of the Subject** (الضَّمِيْرُ الفَاعِلِيْ). Each of the fourteen Seeghah has a different Subject/Pronoun based on person, number and gender. The suffixes attached to the Verb in most of the Seeghah are, in fact, Pronouns of the Subject.

Therefore, most Seeghah of the verb will have obvious indicators that signify particular Pronouns. These indicators are signs of the Pronoun of the Subject (عَلامَةُ الضَّمِيْرِ الفَاعِلِي). The Seeghah having obvious indicators are as follows:

2) ا	3) و	5) ا
6) نَ	7) تَ	8) تُما
9) تُمْ	10) تِ	11) تُما
12) تُنَّ	13) تُ	14) نا

In two Seeghah (1&4), there is no obvious indicator of the Pronoun. Therefore, in these Seeghah, the Pronoun is estimated (المُقَدَّرُ), meaning that the Pronoun has no apparent sign and is known only by the Seeghah. An estimated Pronoun is called a **Concealed Indicator** (العَلامَاتُ المُسْتَتِر), due to its lack of displaying an indicator for the Pronoun of the Subject. The Seeghah mentioned above, all have a visible indicators for the Pronoun of the Subject and they are called **Visible Indicators** (العَلامَاتُ البَارِز).

The Pronoun is a type of Kalimah which stands in the place of a Noun. Therefore, the Pronoun is only mentioned in place of the actual Subject. At times, a Verb will have a Subject that is written. This Subject is said to be apparent (الظَّاهِرُ). When the Subject is apparent, the usage of the Pronoun of the Subject is unnecessary. For example, in the following Sentence the Subject (Zaid or Fatimah) is written and apparent:

ذَهَبَ زَيْدٌ إِلَى السُوقِ أَوْ ذَهَبَتْ فاطِمَةُ *Zaid (or Fatimah) went to the market*

When the Subject is unwritten, the Pronoun of the Subject stands in place of that Subject to which it refers. This type of Subject is said to be concealed or **Mudhmar** (المُضْمَرُ). For example, in the following sentence, the same Subjects are only referred to by the Pronouns estimated from the Seeghah of the Verb. These Pronouns refer to the Subjects that are unwritten:

ذَهَبَ إِلَى السُوقِ أَوْ ذَهَبَتْ *He (Zaid) or she (Fatimah) went to the market*

A chart indicating the Pronouns of the Subject for each of the fourteen Seeghah is as follows:

Table 1.2 - Pronouns Of The Subject

الجَمْع	المُثَنَّى	المُفْرَد	الضَّمائِرُ الفاعِلِي
هُمْ	هُما	هُوَ	الغائِب:
هُنَّ	هُما	هِيَ	الغائِبَة:
أَنْتُمْ	أَنْتُما	أَنْتَ	المُخاطَب:
أَنْتُنَّ	أَنْتُما	أَنْتِ	المُخاطَبَة:
نَحْنُ		أَنا	المُتَكَلِّم:

THE PRESENT TENSE
ACTIVE VOICE VERB

المُضارِعُ المَعْلُومُ

The Present Tense Active Voice Primary Verb (الفِعْلُ الثُّلاثِيُّ المُجَرَّدُ المُضارِعُ المَعْلُومُ) is derived from the Past Tense Active Voice Verb (الفِعْلُ الثُّلاثِيُّ المُجَرَّدُ الماضِيُ المَعْلُومُ) in this manner: To begin with, the letter Yaa' with Fathah (يَـ) or **Yaa' Maftoohah** (يَاءُ المَفْتُوحَةِ) is prefixed to the first Seeghah of the past Tense Verb (يَـ + فَعَلَ). Then, the Fathah on the first Original Letter is removed and the replaced with a Sukoon (يَفْعَلَ). Then, the vowel on the third Original Letter is changed from Fathah to Dhammah, meaning it becomes Madhmoom (يَفْعَلُ).

The vowel on the second Original Letter varies and is known according to usage (السَّماعِيُّ). It is possible for it to be found voweled with Fathah, Kasrah or Dhammah. According to this, the Present Tense Active Voice Primary Verb has three basic patterns يَفْعَلُ، يَفْعِلُ، يَفْعُلُ. For example:

(ذَهَبَ) يَذْهَبُ، (ضَرَبَ) يَضْرِبُ، (قَتَلَ) يَقْتُلُ

▶ The Forms Of The Present Tense Active Voice Verb صِيَغُ المُضارِع المَعْلُوم

▷ **1st Seeghah/The Third Person Masculine Singular** (المُفْرَدُ المُذَكَّرُ الغائِبُ)

The first Seeghah *of the Third Person Masculine Singular is derived from the first Seeghah* of the Past Tense Active Voice Verb as described above. The letter prefixed to the beginning of the Verb is called the **Particle of the Present Tense**(حَرْفُ المُضارِع). All together, there are four Particles of the Present Tense: *Yaa* ' (ي), *Taa*' (ت), *Alif* (أ) and *Noon* (ن). In this form of the Verb, meaning the Three Letter Primary Active Voice Verb, the Particle of the Present Tense will always be voweled with *Fathah*. The usage of these Particles will be explained as we examine each *Seeghah*.

▷ **2nd Seeghah/The Third Person Masculine Dual** (المُثَنَّى المُذَكَّرُ الغائِبُ)

The 2nd Seeghah is derived from the first Seeghah by annexing the *Alif* and *Noon* with *Kasrah* (الأَلِفُ وَ النُّونُ المَكْسُورَةُ) to the end of the 1st Seeghah after removing the *Dhammah* on the 3rd Original Letter and making it *Maftooh*: (يَفْعَلُ + انِ = يَفْعَلانِ).

▷ **3rd Seeghah/The Third Person Masculine Plural** (الجَمْعُ المُذَكَّرُ الغائِبُ)

The 3rd Seeghah is also derived from the 1st. The *Dhammah* will remain at the end of the Verb and the Letters Waw and *Noon* voweled with *Fathah* (الواوُ وَ النُّونُ المَفْتُوحَةُ) are added to the end: (يَفْعَلُ + ونَ = يَفْعَلُونَ).

▷ **4th Seeghah/Third Person Feminine Singular** (المُفْرَدَةُ المُؤَنَّثُ الغائِبَةُ)

This Seeghah is, likewise, derived from the 1st Seeghah. The Particle of the Present Tense, namely *Yaa*' (ي), is changed to *Taa*' voweled with *Fathah* (تَ) and everything else remains as is: (يَفْعَلُ = تَفْعَلُ).

▷ **5th Seeghah/Third Person Feminine Dual** (الْمُفْرَدَةُ الْمُؤَنَّثُ الْغَائِبَةُ)

This Seeghah is derived from the 1st Seeghah. The letter *Taa'*, the Particle of the Present Tense, is substituted for the letter *Yaa'* of the 1st Seeghah. The *Dhammah* at the end of the Verb is removed (يَفْعَلُ – تَفْعَلُ), then, the letters *Alif* and *Noon* with *Kasrah* (انِ) are added to the end Verb: (تَفْعَل + انِ = تَفْعَلَانِ).

▷ **6th Seeghah/Third Person Feminine Plural** (الْجَمْعُ الْمُؤَنَّثُ الْغَائِبَةُ)

This Seeghah is derived from the 1st Seeghah by making the third Original Letter *Saakin* or vowelless and suffixing the letter *Noon* voweled with *Fathah* (نَ) to the end of the Verb: (يَفْعَلْ + نَ = يَفْعَلْنَ).

▷ **7th Seeghah/Second Person Masculine Singular** (الْمُفْرَدُ الْمُذَكَّرُ الْمُخَاطَبُ)

This *Seeghah* is derived from the 1st by changing the *Particle of the Present Tense* from Yaa' voweled with *Fathah* (يَ) to Taa' voweled with *Fathah*: (تَ): (يَفْعَلُ – تَفْعَلُ).

▷ **8th Seeghah/Second Person Masculine Dual** (الْمُثَنَّى الْمُذَكَّرُ الْمُخَاطَبُ)

This Seeghah is derived from the 7th Seeghah. The third Original Letter becomes *Maftooh* and *Alif* and *Noon* voweled with *Kasrah* (انِ) are both added to the end of the verb: (تَفْعَلُ – تَفْعَل + انِ = تَفْعَلَانِ).

▷ **9th Seeghah/Second Person Masculine Plural** (الْجَمْعُ الْمُذَكَّرُ الْمُخَاطَبُ)

Likewise, this Seeghah is also derived from the 1st Seeghah, then, the Particle of the Present Tense is changed to Taa' voweled with *Fathah*. The letters *Waw* (*Saakin*) and *Noon* voweled with *Fathah* (ونَ) are added to the end the verb whose 3rd Original Letter is already *Madhmoom*: (يَفْعَلُ – تَفْعَلُ + ونَ = تَفْعَلُونَ).

▷ **10th Seeghah/Second Person Feminine Singular** (الْمُفْرَدَةُ الْمُؤَنَّثُ الْمُخَاطَبَةُ)

The Feminine Singular Seeghah is derived from the 1st Seeghah. The Particle of the Present Tense, *Taa'* voweled with *Fathah*, is substituted for the prefix of the 1st Seeghah. The 3rd Original Letter is made *Maksoor* or voweled with *Kasrah*, then *Yaa'* and *Noon* with *Fathah* are added to the end: (يَفْعَلُ – تَفْعَل + ينَ = تَفْعَلِينَ).

▷ **11th Seeghah/Second Person Feminine Dual** (االْمُثَنَّى لِمُؤَنَّثُ الْمُخَاطَبَةُ)

This *Seeghah* is derived from the 1st Seeghah. After the Particle of the Present Tense is changed to *Taa'*, the 3rd Original Letter is made *Maftooh* or voweled with *Fathah* and *Alif* and *Noon* with *Kasrah* (انِ) are suffixed to the end: (يَفْعَلُ – تَفْعَلَ + انِ = تَفْعَلانِ).

▷ **12th Seeghah/Second Person Feminine Plural** (الْجَمْعُ الْمُؤَنَّثُ الْمُخَاطَبَةُ)

This Seeghah *is also derived from the 1st by changing the Particle of the Present Tense to Taa'* voweled with *Fathah*. The 3rd Original Letter is made *Saakin*, then the letter *Noon* voweled with *Fathah* is added to the end of the verb: (يَفْعَلُ – تَفْعَلْ + نَ = تَفْعَلْنَ).

▷ **13th Seeghah/First Person Singular** (الْمُتَكَلِّمُ وَحْدَهُ)

Hamzah voweled with *Fathah* (أَ) is substituted as the Particle of the Present Tense for the first Seeghah in order to derive this form: (يَفْعَلُ – أَفْعَلُ).

▷ **14th Seeghah/First Person Plural** (الْمُتَكَلِّمُ مَعَ غَيْرِهِ)

The *Noon* voweled with *Fathah* (نَ) is substituted for the Particle of the Present Tense of the first Seeghah: (يَفْعَلُ نَفْعَلُ).

The letters which are prefixed to the beginning of the *Seeghah* of the Present Tense Verb
are called the **Particles of the Present Tense** (أَحْرُفُ المُضَارِعِ) or, sometimes, the **Signs of
the Present Tense** (عَلَامَاتُ المُضَارِعِ). These Particles will be voweled with *Fathah* when the
Past Tense Verb is three lettered (الثُّلَاثِيُ المُجَرَّدُ). According to this, the conjugation of the
Present Tense Active Voice Primary Verb is as follows:

Table 1.3 - The Patterns Of The Active Voice Three Letter Primary Verb: Present Tense

الجَمْع	المُثَنَّى	المُفْرَد	المُضَارِعُ المَعْلُوم
يَفْعُلُونَ	يَفْعُلَانِ	يَفْعُلُ	الغَائِب:
يَفْعَلْنَ	تَفْعُلَانِ	تَفْعُلُ	الغَائِبة:
تَفْعُلُونَ	تَفْعُلَانِ	تَفْعُلُ	المُخَاطَب:
تَفْعَلْنَ	تَفْعُلَانِ	تَفْعَلِينَ	المُخَاطَبة:
نَفْعَلُ		أَفْعَلُ	المُتَكَلِّم:

Note that the Second Original Letter can accept any of the three vowels, namely Fathah,
Kasrah and Dhammah.

▶ PRONOUNS OF THE PRESENT TENSE ACTIVE VOICE VERB ضَمائِرُ المُضارِعِ المَعْلُوم

The indicators of the Pronouns of the Subject are *Alif* (ا) in all the Dual forms (المُثَنَّى), *Waw* (و) in the Masculine Plurals (الجَمْعُ المُذَكَّرُ), *Noon* (ن) in the Feminine Plurals (الجَمْعُ المُؤَنَّث) and *Yaa'* (ي) in the Second Person Feminine Singular (المُفْرَدَةُ المُؤَنَّثُ المُخاطَبَةُ). These are all Visible Indicators (العَلاماتُ البارِزُ). In the Seeghah 1, 4, 7, 13, 14, the indicators of the Pronouns of the Subject are Concealed (العَلاماتُ المُسْتَتِرُ). In the 1st Seeghah the Concealed Pronoun is (هُوَ); in the 4th Seeghah the Concealed Pronoun is: (هِيَ); in the 7th Seeghah the Concealed Pronoun is (أَنتَ); in the 13th Seeghah the Concealed Pronoun is (أَنا) and in the 14th Seeghah the Concealed Pronoun is: (نَحْنُ).

In the Present Tense Verb, two Seeghah (6&12), namely the feminine plurals, are **Mabniy** (المَبْنِي) meaning that they have a permanently fixed ending, while the remaining Seeghah are **Mu'rab** (المُعْرَب), meaning that they have changeable endings which reflect any changes in the verb's grammatical state. Normally, the Present Tense Verb is in the state of **Raf'** (الرَّفْعُ) or is said to be *Marfoo'* (المَرَفُوعُ). The sign of the state of *Raf'* in 1st, 4th, 7th, 13th and 14th Seeghah is the *Dhammah* on the 3rd Original Letter.

In the Seeghah of the Duals (المُثَنَّى), the Masculine Plurals (الجَمْعُ المُذَكَّرُ) and the 2nd Person Feminine Singular (المُفْرَدَةُ المُؤَنَّثُ المُخاطَبَةُ), the sign of *Raf'* is the letter *Noon* with *Fathah* (نَ) in the Masculine Plurals and the 2nd person Feminine Singular and *Noon* with *Kasrah* in the Dual. This indicator of *Raf'* is called the **Noon of I'raab** (النُّونُ الإعْرابِي). Note that in the 6th and 12th Seeghah, the Feminine Plurals(الجَمْعُ المُؤَنَّثُ), its *Noon* voweled with *Fathah* (نَ) is the Pronoun of the Subject, not a sign of *Raf'*.

When the Past Tense Verb is on the pattern of: (فَعَلَ), the Present Tense can be one of three possible patterns: (يَفْعُلُ، يَفْعِلُ، يَفْعَلُ). The Past Tense of the Verb on the pattern of: (فَعِلَ) has two possible patterns for the Present Tense: (يَفْعَلُ، يَفْعِلُ). The Past Tense Verb on the pattern of: (فَعُلَ) has only one possible pattern for the Present Tense: (يَفْعُلُ). The combination of the patterns for the Past Tense Verb and the Present Tense Verb is referred to as a **Baab**, the singular of **Abwaab** (بَابٌ، أَبْوَابٌ). In the terminology of Tasreef, the Active Voice Three Letter Primary Verb has six *Abwaab* or six basic pattern groups:

Table 1.4 - The Basic Patterns Of The Active Voice Three Letter Primary Verb

المَعْنى	المِثَال	البَاب
Meaning	Example	Pattern
To help, assist	نَصَرَ يَنْصُرُ	(١) فَعَلَ يَفْعُلُ
To strike, hit s.th.	ضَرَبَ يَضْرِبُ	(٢) فَعَلَ يَفْعِلُ
To block, prevent	مَنَعَ يَمْنَعُ	(٣) فَعَلَ يَفْعَلُ
To hear	سَمِعَ يَسْمَعُ	(٤) فَعِلَ يَفْعَلُ
To figure, reckon	حَسِبَ يَحْسِبُ	(٥) فَعِلَ يَفْعِلُ
To be generous	كَرُمَ يَكْرُمُ	(٦) فَعُلَ يَفْعُلُ

SECTION TWO

The Command Verb

الفِعْلُ الأَمرُ

The Command Verb is that verb that seeks the initiation of an action or state in an imperative manner, particularly when the speaker is of greater distinction than the person who is being addressed.

Two types of Command Verbs are derived from the Active Voice Verb

▷ **Second Person Command Verb** (الأَمرُ الحاضِرُ)

▷ **Active Voice Command Verb** (الأَمرُ المَغلُومُ)

Both types of Command Verbs are derived from the Present Tense of the Active Voice Verb (المُضارِعُ المُغلُومُ), however, their method of derivation differs from the Present Tense Verb. As opposed to being derived from one Seeghah, each Seeghah of the Command Verb is derived from the corresponding Seeghah of the Present Tense Verb. The Second Person Command Verb is derived from the six Seeghah of the second person and the Active Voice Command Verb is derived from the remaining eight Seeghah.

▶ THE SECOND PERSON COMMAND VERB (الأَمرُ الحاضرُ)

The Second Person Command Verb are six verbs derived from the six Seeghah of the Second Person (المُخاطَبُ). This type of Command Verb is also referred to as **Haadhir** (الحاضرُ), meaning to be present. This is due to the fact that the Subject (*You*) is always present when speaking in the Second Person.

The rules for forming the six Seeghah of the Second Person Command Verb are summarized in the following four steps:

1 The Particle of the Present Tense (حرفُ المُضارع) is removed from the beginning of the verb (تَفْعَلُ > فْعَلُ) .

2 After removing the Particle of the Present Tense, if the 1st Original Letter is *Saakin*, a *Hamzah* is prefixed to the beginning of the verb replacing the Particle of the Present Tense (فْعَلُ > افْعَلُ). By necessity, this *Hamzah* is voweled. In some types of the Primary Verb, like the weak or doubled consonant verbs, the 1st Original Letter is vowelled. The Command Verb of these verbs will be mentioned in the appropriate place. When the verb is sound, the 1st Original Letter is *Saakin.* The Hamzah's vowel is determined according to the rules in the following paragraph.

3 The vowel on the *Hamzah* is determined by the vowel on the 2nd Original Letter. If the vowel on the 2nd Original Letter is *Madhmoom* or voweled with *Dhammah*, the *Hamzah* must also be voweled with *Dhammah* (افْعُلُ > أُفْعُلُ). If the 2nd Original Letter is *Maftooh* or *Maksoor* (i.e. voweled with *Fathah* or *Kasrah*, resp.), the *Hamzah* is voweled with Kasrah (افْعَلُ > إِفْعَلُ). Accordingly, this *Hamzah* is never voweled with *Fathah* in the Command Verb of the Three Letter Active Voice Primary Verb.

4 The sign of I'raab is removed from the end of the Seeghah. In the singular Seeghah (Seeghah 7), the sign of I'raab is Dhammah. The Dhammah is replaced with a Sukoon (إفْعَلُ > إفْعَلْ). In the Seeghah of the Dual (Seeghah 8& 11) and the Masculine Plural (Seeghah 9) and the Feminine Singular (Seeghah 10), the sign of I'raab is the Noon of I'raab (النُّونُ الإعْرابِي). This Noon of I'raab, as an indicator or I'raab, must be elided as a rule (إفْعَلا > إفْعَلانِ); (إفْعَلُوا > إفْعَلُونَ) and (إفْعَلي > إفَعَلِينَ) respectively.

As previously mentioned, the Seeghah of the Feminine Plural of the Present Tense is Mabniy and, therefore, does not possess a sign of I'raab. Therefore, in this Seeghah there is nothing to remove as a sign of I'raab (إفْعَلْنَ > إفْعَلْنَ).

According to these rules we derive the Second Person Command Verb in the following manner:

(Table 1.5)

(٤)	(٣)	(٢)	(١)	الفِعْل	الصِّيغَة
Step 4	Step 3	Step 2	Step 1	Verb	Seeghah
إفْعَلْ	إفْعَلُ	افْعَلُ	فْعَلُ	تَفْعَلُ	(٧)
إفْعَلا	إفْعَلانِ	افْعَلانِ	فْعَلانِ	تَفْعَلانِ	(٨)
إفْعَلُوا	إفْعَلُونَ	افْعَلُونَ	فْعَلُونَ	تَفْعَلُونَ	(٩)
إفْعَلي	إفْعَلِينَ	افْعَلِينَ	فْعَلِينَ	تَفْعَلِينَ	(١٠)
إفْعَلا	إفْعَلانِ	افْعَلانِ	فْعَلانِ	تَفْعَلانِ	(١١)
إفْعَلْنَ	إفْعَلْنَ	افْعَلْنَ	فْعَلْنَ	تَفْعَلْنَ	(١٢)

According to this, the Second Person Command Verb derived from the six Seeghah of the Second Person are as follows:

إِفْعَلْ، إِفْعَلا، إِفْعَلُوا، إِفْعَلِي، إِفْعَلا، إِفْعَلْنَ

This pattern is used when the Present Tense Verb is on the patterns of: (يَفْعَلُ) and (يَفْعِلُ).

According to rule 3, Verbs on the pattern of: (يَفْعُلُ) will have the following patterns of Command Verbs (The *Hamzah* being vowelled with *Dhammah*):

أُفْعُلْ، أُفْعُلا، أُفْعُلُوا، أُفْعُلِي، أُفْعُلا، أُفْعُلْنَ

Below are examples of Command Verbs (with their corresponding Seeghah in the Present Tense) on each of the three patterns:

مَنَعَ – يَمْنَعُ (فَعَلَ – يَفْعَلُ)

إِمْنَعْ (تَمْنَعُ)، إِمْنَعَا (تَمْنَعَانِ)، إِمْنَعُوا (تَمْنَعُونَ) إِمْنَعِي (تَمْنَعِينَ)، إِمْنَعَا (تَمْنَعَانِ)، إِمْنَعْنَ (تَمْنَعْنَ)

ضَرَبَ – يَضْرِبُ (فَعَلَ – يَفْعِلُ)

إِضْرِبْ (تَضْرِبُ)، إِضْرِبا (تَضْرِبانِ)، إِضْرِبُوا (تَضْرِبونَ)، إِضْرِبِي (تَضْرِبِينَ)، إِضْرِبا (تَضْرِبانِ)، إِضْرِبْنَ (تَضْرِبْنَ)

نَصَرَ – يَنْصُرُ (فَعَلَ – يَفْعُلُ)

أُنْصُرْ (تَنْصُرُ)، أُنْصُرا (تَنْصُرَانِ)، أُنْصُرُوا (تَنْصُرُونَ)، أُنْصُرِي (تَنْصُرِينَ)، أُنْصُرا (تَنْصُرَانِ)، أُنْصُرْنَ (تَنْصُرْنَ)

▶ THE ACTIVE VOICE COMMAND VERB الأَمْرُ المَعْلُومُ

The Active Voice Command Verbs are derived from the six Seeghah of the Third Person (الغَائِبُ) and the two Seeghah of the First Person (المُتَكَلِّمُ). The verb is formed by prefixing a Particle to the Present Tense Active Voice Verb. The Particle which is prefixed to the Verb is called *Lamul-Amr* (لامُ الأَمْرِ) which is the letter Lam voweled with *Kasrah* (لِ).

As previously mentioned, the Present Tense Verb is in the state of *Raf'* by default. This Particle, *Lamul-Amr*, will change the state of the Present Tense Verb from *Raf'* to Jazm. Therefore, in each Seeghah *the sign of I'raab* must be removed and replaced by the sign of Jazm.

Jazm has two signs: first is the *Sukoon* (السُّكُونُ), the second is the removal of the Noon of I'raab (حَذْفُ النُّونِ الإِعْرابِي), which is the sign of *Raf'* in some forms. The *Seeghah* in which *Dhammah* is the sign of *Raf'* (*Seeghah* 1, 4, 13, 14), the *Dhammah* will be replaced with *Sukoon*. The *Seeghah* in which the Noon of *I'raab* is the sign of *Raf'* (*Seeghah* 2, 3, 5), the *Noon* itself is elided. Again, the *Seeghah* of the Feminine Plural (*Seeghah* 12) is *Mabniy* and has no sign of *I'raab* and, therefore, remains unchanged. The eight *Seeghah* of the Active Voice Command Verb are derived from their respective *Seeghah* as follows:

Table 1.6 - The Active Voice Command Verb

الأَمْرُ المَعْلُوم	لامُ الأَمْرِ	المُضارِعُ المَعْلُوم	الصِّيغَة
Command Verb	Particle	Pres. Tense	Seeghah
لِيَفْعَلْ	لِ	يَفْعَلُ	(١)
لِيَفْعَلا	لِ	يَفْعَلانِ	(٢)
لِيَفْعَلُوا	لِ	يَفْعَلُونَ	(٣)
لِتَفْعَلْ	لِ	تَفْعَلُ	(٤)
لِتَفْعَلا	لِ	تَفْعَلانِ	(٥)
لِيَفْعَلْنَ	لِ	يَفْعَلْنَ	(٦)
لأَفْعَلْ	لِ	أَفْعَلُ	(١٣)
لِنَفْعَلْ	لِ	نَفْعَلُ	(١٤)

Here are the Active Voice Command Verbs of three model verbs:

(مَنَعَ يَمْنَعُ)

لِيَمْنَعْ، لِيَمْنَعا، لِيَمْنَعُوا، لِتَمْنَعْ، لِتَمْنَعا، لِيَمْنَعْنَ، لأَمْنَعْ، لِنَمْنَعْ

(ضَرَبَ يَضْرِبُ)

لِيَضْرِبْ، لِيَضْرِبا، لِيَضْرِبُوا، لِتَضْرِبْ، لِتَضْرِبا، لِيَضْرِبْنَ، لأَضْرِبْ، لِنَضْرِبْ

(نَصَرَ يَنْصُرُ)

لِيَنْصُرْ، لِيَنْصُرا، لِيَنْصُرُوا، لِتَنْصُرْ، لِتَنْصُرا، لِيَنْصُرْنَ، لأَنْصُرْ، لِنَنْصُرْ

Table 1.7-Active Voice Command Verbs Derived From Verbs On The Wazn Of: (يَفْعَلُ يَفْعِلُ)

الجَمْع	المُثَنَّى	المُفْرَد	الأَمْرُ المَعْلُوم
لِيَفْعِلُوا	لِيَفْعِلا	لِيَفْعِلْ	الغائب:
لِيَفْعِلْنَ	لِتَفْعِلا	لِتَفْعِلْ	الغائبة:
إفْعِلُوا	إفْعِلا	إفْعِلْ	المُخاطَب:
إفْعِلْنَ	إفْعِلا	إفْعِلي	المُخاطَبة:
لِنَفْعِلْ		لأَفْعِلْ	المُتَكَلِّم:

Table 1.8 - Patterns Of Active Voice Command Verbs From Verbs On The Wazn Of: (يَفْعُلُ)

الجَمْع	المُثَنَّى	المُفْرَد	الأَمْرُ المَعْلُوم
لِيَفْعُلُوا	لِيَفْعُلا	لِيَفْعُلْ	الغائب:
لِيَفْعُلْنَ	لِتَفْعُلا	لِتَفْعُلْ	الغائبة:
أُفْعُلُوا	أُفْعُلا	أُفْعُلْ	المُخاطَب:
أُفْعُلْنَ	أُفْعُلا	أُفْعُلي	المُخاطَبة:
لِنَفْعُلْ		لأَفْعُلْ	المُتَكَلِّم:

► CONCLUDING NOTES

▷ Whenever the Noon of I'raab is removed from the Seeghah of the Masculine Plural the *Separating Alif* (الأَلِفُ الفاصِلَةُ) will be inserted after the letter Waw. This is the same type of Alif that was mentioned in regards to the Third Person Masculine Plural Seeghah of the Past Tense Verb, for example:

$$\text{تَفْعَلُونَ} > \text{إِفْعَلُوا، } \quad \text{يَفْعَلُونَ} > \text{لِيَفْعَلُوا}$$

▷ One common element in all forms of Command Verbs is that all are *Saakin* at their endings. These *Saakin* endings, however, are not all resultant from the same causes. All of the Seeghah of the Active Voice Command Verb are *Mu'rab* (except the feminine plural), meaning that they indicate different grammatical states. By prefixing the the Particle *Lam*, the verb is changed from the state of *Raf'* to the state of *Jazm*. As a result, the indicators of the state of *Raf'* are elided and the verb becomes *Saakin* indicating the state of *Jazm*. On the other hand, all of the Seeghah of the Second Person Command Verb are *Mabniy*. Their being *Saakin*, therefore, is not an indicator of the state of *Jazm*.

▷ Whenever the *Particle of the Command* (لاَمُ الأَمْرِ) is preceded by the following words: (وَ، فَ، ثُمَّ), the Particle can be made *Saakin*, for example:

59:19 ﴿وَ لْتَنْظُرْ نَفْسٌ ما قَدَّمَتْ لِغَدٍ﴾

106:3 ﴿فَلْيَعْبُدُوا رَبَّ هَذا البَيْتِ﴾

22:29 ﴿ثُمَّ لِيَقْضُوا تَفَثَهُمْ وَ لْيُوفُوا نُذُورَهُمْ وَ لْيَطَّوَّفُوا بِالبَيْتِ العَتِيقِ﴾

▷ Both the Second Person Command Verb and the Active Voice Command Verb are derived from the Active Voice Verb. A third type of Command Verb, the Passive Voice Command Verb, is derived from the Passive Voice Verb which will be examined in the next section.

SECTION THREE

THE PASSIVE VOICE VERB

الفِعلُ المَجْهُولُ

▶ PAST TENSE PASSIVE VOICE VERB الماضِيُ المَجْهُولُ

The Past Tense Passive Voice Verb is not derived directly from the *Masdar* like the Past Tense Active Voice Verb. Rather, the Passive Voice Verb is derived directly from the Past Tense Active Voice Verb. As previously mentioned, the first and second Original Letters in the Active Voice Verb will always be found voweled with *Fathah*. Only the second Original Letter has any variance in its vowels in the Active Voice Verb. To convert the Past Tense Active Voice to the Past Tense Passive Voice Verb, the vowel on the first Original Letter will be changed from *Fathah* to *Dhammah* (فَعَلَ < فُعَلَ).

It has also been mentioned that the vowel of the second Original Letter is variable, meaning that it can be found voweled with *Fathah*, *Kasrah* or *Dhammah*, according to its *Baab*. The second step is to change that vowel of the second Original Letter to *Kasrah* (فُعَلَ < فُعِلَ). The second Original Letter will always be the voweled or *Mutaharrik* (المُتَحَرِّكُ) letter precedes the last letter of the verb (in the first *Seeghah*) whether the verb is a Primary Verb or a Derivative Verb. The vowel on the third Original Letter will remain *Fathah*. Observe the conversion in the following verbs:

مَنَعَ مُنِعَ، ضَرَبَ ضُرِبَ، نَصَرَ نُصِرَ

According to this, the Past Tense Passive Voice Verb has only this one pattern: (فُعِلَ). Each Seeghah of the Past Tense Passive Voice Verb is derived from its respective *Seeghah* in the Past Tense Active Voice Verb.

The difference between the Active Voice and Passive Voice verbs is that the Passive Voice Verb is not conjugated according to the Subject (الفَاعِلُ) like the Active Voice Verb. Rather, it is conjugated according to the Proxy Subject (نَائِبُ الفَاعِلِ). For example, in the following sentence, Ja'far is the subject and Fatimah is the Object:

نَصَرَ جَعْفَرُ فَاطِمَةَ   *Ja'far helped Fatimah*

Below , the sentence is converted to the Passive Voice.

نُصِرَتْ فَاطِمَةُ   *Fatimah was helped*

Observe three changes in this sentence when changed from the Active to Passive Voice:

› First, the Subject (Ja'far) is removed.

› Second, that the verb has been changed from the Masculine Singular (1st Seeghah) to the Feminine Singular (4th Seeghah). This is what is intended when it is said that the Passive Voice Verb is conjugated according to the Proxy Subject. The Subject is removed and the Object (Fatimah) now becomes the Proxy Subject, occupying the place of the Subject . As a result of this change, the Passive Voice Verb now has to be conjugated to reflect the feminine gender of its Proxy Subject.

› The third change to observe is that as the word Fatimah changed from the Object to the Proxy Subject, its grammatical state changed from *Nasb* to *Raf'* as seen by the change in the Sign Of *I'raab* from *Fathah* to *Dhammah*. Below are the conjugated patterns for the Past Tense Passive Voice Verb:

Table 1.9 - The Patterns Of The Past Tense Passive Voice Verb

الجَمْع	المُثَنَّى	المُفْرَد	الماضيُ المَغلُوم
فُعِلُوا	فُعِلا	فُعِلَ	الغائب:
فُعِلْنَ	فُعِلَتا	فُعِلَتْ	الغائبة:
فُعِلْتُم	فُعِلْتُما	فُعِلْتَ	المُخاطَب:
فُعِلْتُنَّ	فُعِلْتُما	فُعِلْتِ	المُخاطَبة:
فُعِلْنا		فُعِلْتُ	المُتَكَلِّم:

▶ **PRESENT TENSE PASSIVE VOICE VERB** المُضارعُ المَجْهُولُ

The Present Tense Passive Voice Verb is derived from the Present Tense Active Voice Verb in a similar manner as mentioned for the Past Tense. To convert the Active Voice Verb to the Passive Voice Verb, first make the Particle of the Present Tense (حَرْفُ المُضارعِ)

Madhmoom or voweled with *Dhammah* (يُفْعَلُ > يَفْعَلُ), then, make the second Original Letter *Maftooh*. For example:

يَمْنَعُ يُمْنَعُ، يَضْرِبُ يُضْرَبُ، يَنْصُرُ يُنْصَرُ

Like the Past Tense, the Present Tense Passive Verb has only one pattern or *Wazn* (يُفْعَلُ).

Therefore, there is only one *Baab* associated with the Passive Voice Verb: (فُعِلَ يُفْعَلُ). The conjugated patterns of the Present Tense Passive Voice Verb are as follows:

Table 1.10 - Patterns Of The Present Tense Passive Voice Verb

الجَمْع	المُثَنَّى	المُفْرَد	المُضارِعُ المَعْلُوم
يُفْعَلُونَ	يُفْعَلانِ	يُفْعَلُ	الغائب:
تُفْعَلْنَ	تُفْعَلانِ	تُفْعَلُ	الغائبَة:
تُفْعَلُونَ	تُفْعَلانِ	تُفْعَلُ	المُخاطَب:
تُفْعَلْنَ	تُفْعَلانِ	تُفْعَلِينَ	المُخاطَبَة:
نُفْعَلُ		أُفْعَلُ	المُتَكَلِّم:

▶ THE PASSIVE VOICE COMMAND VERB الأَمْرُ المَجْهُولُ

The Passive Voice Command Verb is derived Seeghah by Seeghah from the Present Tense Passive Voice Verb. The method of deriving the Command Verb is to prefix the Particle of the Command (لامُ الأَمْرِ) to each Seeghah of the Present Tense Passive Voice Verb. The Particle of the Command or Lamul-Amr is Maksoor or voweled with Kasrah. Since this Particle is one of the Jawaazim (الجَوازِمُ), meaning that it changes a verb to the state of Jazm, the signs of Raf' are removed from the end of the verb.

As mentioned, the sign of Raf' in the Present Tense is either the Dhammah at the end of some Seeghah or the Noon of I'raab found at the end of others. These signs must be removed now that the verb is in the state of Jazm. The Dhammah will be replaced with Sukoon. Thus, the two signs of Jazm in the Present Tense Verb are Sukoon (السُّكُونُ) and the removal of the Noon of I'raab (حَذْفُ النُّونِ الإِعْرابِي). Observe the change in the following examples:

يُمْنَعُ لِيُمْنَعْ،   يُضْرَبُ لِيُضْرَبْ،   يُنْصَرُ لِيُنْصَرْ

Accordingly, the Passive Voice Command Verb utilizes the *Lamul-Amr* in each *Seeghah* and is conjugated in the following manner:

لِيُفْعَلْ، لِيُفْعَلَا، لِيُفْعَلُوا، لِتُفْعَلْ، لِتُفْعَلَا، لِيُفْعَلْنَ،

لِتُفْعَلْ، لِتُفْعَلَا، لِتُفْعَلُوا، لِتُفْعَلِي، لِتُفْعَلَا، لِتُفْعَلْنَ، لِأُفْعَلْ، لِنُفْعَلْ

▶ THE PASSIVE VOICE OF THE INTRANSITIVE VERB

As previously mentioned, the Passive Voice eliminates the Verb's Subject and requires that the Verb's Object follow the verb as its Proxy Subject. For this reason, the Passive Voice is derived from the Transitive Verb (الفِعْلُ المُتَعَدِّي). A Transitive Verb is that verb which requires an Object in order to complete its meaning. Therefore, the Passive Voice Verb cannot be derived from the Intransitive Verb (الفِعْلُ اللَّازِمُ) as it has no need of an Object.

To convert a Intransitive Verb to the Passive Voice, the Intransitive Verb must first be made Transitive. Verbs are either Transitive in and of themselves (المُتَعَدِّي بِنَفْسِها) or they become Transitive by means of linking a Preposition to it (المُتَعَدِّي بِحَرْفِ الجَرِّ). Meaning that the verb will exert its influence on its Object directly, making it *Mansoob* or it will indirectly link itself to another word by way of a Preposition. Observe the manner of the Intransitive Verb in the following sentence:

ذَهَبَ زَيْدٌ *Zaid left*

To transform the Intransitive Verb to a Transitive Verb, a Preposition and its direct object is linked with the verb:

ذَهَبَ زَيْدٌ بِكِتَابٍ *Zaid took a Book (i.e. Zaid left with a book)*

Now the verb has connected to the word: (كِتَاب) *A book*, by means of the Preposition (بِ). After linking with the Preposition's direct object, the verb can be transformed into the Passive Voice. Then, the Subject is removed and the Preposition and its direct object will be put in the place of the Subject:

ذُهِبَ بِكِتَابٍ *A book was taken*

The main difference between the Passive Voice Verb that is derived from the Transitive Verb and that which is derived from the Intransitive Verb is that the Transitive Verb will have a Proxy Subject when converted to the Passive Voice. This Proxy Subject is always in the state of *Raf'*.

The Intransitive Verb, on the other hand, will not have a Proxy Subject when converted to the Passive Voice. The verb will be connected to the Preposition's direct object which is a noun in the state of *Jarr*. For example in the above sentence: ذُهِبَ بِكِتَابٍ, we have the Passive Voice Verb (ذُهِبَ), the Preposition (بِ) and the *Majroor* Noun (كِتَاب) or the Noun in the state of *Jarr* (the Preposition's direct object).

The Passive Voice Verb (derived from the Transitive Verb) is conjugated according to the Proxy Subject. However, the Passive Voice Verb that is derived from the Intransitive Verb is conjugated according to the *Majroor* Noun attached to the Preposition. The verb itself will only be conjugated in the first Seeghah.

Often, the *Majroor* Noun will be a Pronoun, however, in the Third Person, a regular Noun may be attached to the verb as seen in the sentence above. For example:

ذُهِبَ بِكِتَابٍ أَوْ ذُهِبَ بِهِ

According to this, the Past Tense Passive Voice that is made Transitive by a Preposition is conjugated in the following manner:

Table 1.11 - Conjugation Of the Past Tense Passive Voice Verb With A Preposition

الجَمْع	المُثَنَّى	المُفْرَد	الماضِي
فُعِلَ بِهِمْ	فُعِلَ بِهِما	فُعِلَ بِهِ	الغائِب:
فُعِلَ بِهِنَّ	فُعِلَ بِهِما	فُعِلَ بِها	الغائِبة:
فُعِلَ بِكُمْ	فُعِلَ بِكُما	فُعِلَ بِكَ	المُخاطَب:
فُعِلَ بِكُنَّ	فُعِلَ بِكُما	فُعِلَ بِكِ	المُخاطَبة:
فُعِلَ بِنا		فُعِلَ بِي	المُتَكَلِّم:

The Present Tense Passive Voice is conjugated in a similar manner.

▶ PRONOUNS OF THE PASSIVE VOICE VERB DERIVED FROM THE INTRANSITIVE VERB

The Passive Voice Verb that has been made Transitive by means of a Preposition are a different type of Pronoun than the types which we have examined thus far. Up to this point, the Pronouns that we have mentioned are called **Independent Pronouns** (الضَّمائِرُ المُنْفَصِلُ). The type of Pronoun that this Passive Voice Verb uses is called **Dependent Pronouns** (الضَّمائِرُ المُتَّصِلُ). These Pronouns are all attached to the Preposition itself (or a noun) and never written independently, they are as follows:

Table 1.12 - The Dependent Pronouns

الجَمْع	المُثَنَّى	المُفْرَد	الضَّمائِرُ المُنْفَصِل
هُمْ	هُما	هُ	الغائِب:
هُمْ	هُما	ها	الغائِبَة:
كُمْ	كُما	كَ	المُخاطَب:
كُنَّ	كُما	كِ	المُخاطَبَة:
نا		يْ	المُتَكَلِّم:

These Pronouns will be found attached to different Prepositions in the same manner as outlined above, for example, if the Preposition is عَلَى, for example, the Pronouns will be conjugated in this manner:

عَلَيْهِ، عَلَيْهِما، عَلَيْهِمْ، عَلَيْها، عَلَيْهِما، عَلَيْهِنَّ،

عَلَيْكَ، عَلَيْكُما، عَلَيْكُمْ، عَلَيْكِ، عَلَيْكِ، عَلَيْكُما، عَلَيْكُنَّ، عَلَيَّ، عَلَيْنا

Only in the first six *Seeghah* (the Third Person), a Noun may be used in place of the Pronoun. A pronoun must be used in the remaining Seeghah (2nd person/1st Person):

ذُهِبَ بِهِ أَوْ ذُهِبَ بِرَجُلٍ، ذُهِبَ بِهِنَّ أَوْ ذُهِبَ بِنِساءٍ

▶ THE PASSIVE VOICE VERB WITHOUT AN ACTIVE VOICE الـمَجْهُولُ بِدُونِ الـمَعْلُوم

In Arabic, there are a number of Passive Verbs whose Active Voice Verbs are not used, like: أُغْمِيَ عَلَيْهِ (to be unconscious). Or sometimes the original meaning of the Active Voice is not found in usage, like: أُولِعَ بِهِ (to have a desire or attachment to something), حُمَّ (to be feverish), غُشِيَ عَلَيْهِ (to be duped), جُنَّ (to be shielded), عُنِيَ (to be concerned).

▶ CONCLUDING NOTES

While reviewing the Passive Voice Verb (الفِعْلُ الـمَجْهُولُ), (both the Passive Voice which is Transitive in and of itself or that Verb which utilizes a Preposition) it was noted that they have only 14 Seeghah in the same manner as the Active Voice Verb. However, the Transitive Active Voice Verb (الفِعْلُ الـمَعْلُومُ الـمُتَعَدِّي) has 14 forms per Seeghah *for each its Objects or* Maf'ool (الـمَفْعُولُ بِهِ) whether it be Transitive in itself or by means of a Proposition. As a result, it has a total of 196 *Seeghah.*

The Present Tense (الفِعْلُ الـمُضَارِعُ الـمَجْهُولُ) and the Command Verb (الفِعْلُ الأَمْرُ الـمَجْهُولُ) of the Passive Voice are conjugated according to the same model as put forth above. The Passive Voice Verb is constructed from each corresponding Seeghah of the Active Voice Verb (الفِعْلُ الـماضِيُ الـمَعْلُومُ الـمُتَعَدِّي). The Pronoun of the Subject (الضَّمِيرُ الفَاعِلِي) is omitted and the Preposition along with its Noun (الجارُّ وَ الـمَجْرُورُ) is placed after the Verb in place of its Proxy Subject (نائِبُ الفاعِلِ), as in:

أَتَوَا زَيْداً *They reached Zaid,* أُتِيَ بِزَيْدٍ *Zaid was reached*

Regarding the Passive Voice Verb derived from the Intransitive Past Tense Active Voice Verb (الفِعْلُ الـماضِيُ الـمَعْلُومُ اللاَّزِمُ), the verb is constructed for the Passive Voice in each *Seeghah.* The Pronoun of the Subject (الضَّمِيرُ الفاعِلِي) is omitted and is replaced by the

Pronoun of the Object (الضَّمِيرُ المَفْعُولِي) as its Proxy Subject (نائِبُ الفاعِلِ) which is attached to the Passive Voice Verb (by means of the Preposition).

It is apparent in some Seeghah, that the Pronoun of the Proxy Subject (ضَمِيرُ نائِبِ الفاعِلِ) is a Concealed Pronoun (الضَّمِيرُ المُسْتَتِرُ), for example, the Passive Voice of: نَصَروهُنَّ becomes: نُصِرْنَ and the Passive Voice of: نَصَرْنَهُمْ becomes: نُصِروا. Given in the chart below are the equivalence between the Pronouns of the Subject (الضَّمِيرُ الفاعِلِي) and the Pronouns of the Object (الضَّمِيرُ المَفْعُولِي) are pointed out:

Table 1.13 - Equivalence Between Pronouns Of The Subject And Object (Past Tense)

علامات الضَّمير الفاعلي	الضَّمير المَفعُولي	الضَّمير الفاعلي	الصِّيغَة
Sign Pronoun/Subject	Pronoun/Object	Pronoun/Subject	Seeghah
(المُستَتِر)	هُ	هُوَ	(١)
ا	هُما	هُما	(٢)
و	هُمْ	هُمْ	(٣)
(المُستَتِر)	ها	هِيَ	(٤)
ا	هُما	هُما	(٥)
نَ	هُنَّ	هُنَّ	(٦)
تَ	كَ	أَنْتَ	(٧)
تُما	كُما	أَنْتُما	(٨)
تُمْ	كُمْ	أَنْتُمْ	(٩)
تِ	كِ	أَنْتِ	(١٠)
تُما	كُما	أَنْتُما	(١١)
تُنَّ	كُنَّ	أَنْتُنَّ	(١٢)
تُ	يْ	أَنا	(١٣)
نا	نا	نَحْنُ	(١٤)

Table 1.14 - Equivalence Between Pronouns Of The Subject And Object (Present Tense)

عَلاماتُ الضّميرِ الفاعلي	الضّميرُ المَفْعُولي	الضّميرُ الفاعلي	الصّيغَة
Sign Pronoun/Subject	Pronoun/Object	Pronoun/Subject	Seeghah
(المُسْتَتِر)	هُ	هُوَ	(١)
ا	هُما	هُما	(٢)
و	هُمْ	هُمْ	(٣)
(المُسْتَتِر)	ها	هِيَ	(٤)
ا	هُما	هُما	(٥)
نَ	هُنَّ	هُنَّ	(٦)
(المُسْتَتِر)	كَ	أَنْتَ	(٧)
ا	كُما	أَنْتُما	(٨)
و	كُمْ	أَنْتُمْ	(٩)
يْ	كِ	أَنْتِ	(١٠)
ا	كُما	أَنْتُما	(١١)
نَ	كُنَّ	أَنْتُنَّ	(١٢)
(المُسْتَتِر)	يْ	أَنا	(١٣)
(المُسْتَتِر)	نا	نَحْنُ	(١٤)

Table 1.15 - The Sound Active Voice Verb On The Pattern Of: (مَنَعَ يَمْنَعُ) فَعَلَ يَفْعَلُ

مَنَعَ، يَمْنَعُ، إِمْنَعْ، لِيَمْنَعْ، مَنعٌ، لِيَمْنَعْ، يَمْنَعُ، مَنعٌ، هُوَ مَنْعٌ و مانِعٌ و مَمْنُوعٌ

الجَمْع	المُثَنَّى	المُفْرَد	الماضِي المَعلُوم
مَنَعُوا	مَنَعا	مَنَعَ	الغائِب:
مَنَعْنَ	مَنَعَتا	مَنَعَتْ	الغائِبَة:
مَنَعْتُمْ	مَنَعْتُما	مَنَعْتَ	المُخاطَب:
مَنَعْتُنَّ	مَنَعْتُما	مَنَعْتِ	المُخاطَبة:
مَنَعْنا		مَنَعْتُ	المُتَكَلِّم:

الجَمْع	المُثَنَّى	المُفْرَد	المُضارِع المَعلُوم
يَمْنَعُونَ	يَمْنَعانِ	يَمْنَعُ	الغائِب:
يَمْنَعْنَ	تَمْنَعانِ	تَمْنَعُ	الغائِبَة:
تَمْنَعُونَ	تَمْنَعانِ	تَمْنَعُ	المُخاطَب:
تَمْنَعْنَ	تَمْنَعانِ	تَمْنَعِينَ	المُخاطَبة:
نَمْنَعُ		أَمْنَعُ	المُتَكَلِّم:

الجَمْع	المُثَنَّى	المُفْرَد	الأَمْر المَعلُوم
لِيَمْنَعُوا	لِيَمْنَعا	لِيَمْنَعْ	الغائِب:
لِيَمْنَعْنَ	لِتَمْنَعا	لِتَمْنَعْ	الغائِبَة:
إِمْنَعُوا	إِمْنَعا	إِمْنَعْ	المُخاطَب:
إِمْنَعْنَ	إِمْنَعا	إِمْنَعِي	المُخاطَبة:
لِنَمْنَعْ		لِأَمْنَعْ	المُتَكَلِّم:

Table 1.16 - The Passive Voice Sound Verb On The Pattern Of: (مُنِعَ يُمْنَعُ) فُعِلَ يُفْعَلُ

الجَمْع	المُثَنَّى	المُفْرَد	الماضِي المَجهُولُ
مُنِعوا	مُنِعا	مُنِعَ	الغائِب:
مُنِعْنَ	مُنِعَتا	مُنِعَتْ	الغائِبَة:
مُنِعْتُم	مُنِعْتُما	مُنِعْتَ	المُخاطَب:
مُنِعْتُنَّ	مُنِعْتُما	مُنِعْتِ	المُخاطَبَة:
مُنِعْنا		مُنِعْتُ	المُتَكَلِّم:

الجَمْع	المُثَنَّى	المُفْرَد	المُضارِعُ المَجهُولُ
يُمْنَعُونَ	يُمْنَعانِ	يُمْنَعُ	الغائِب:
يُمْنَعْنَ	تُمْنَعانِ	تُمْنَعُ	الغائِبَة:
تُمْنَعُونَ	تُمْنَعانِ	تُمْنَعُ	المُخاطَب:
تُمْنَعْنَ	تُمْنَعانِ	تُمْنَعينَ	المُخاطَبَة:
نُمْنَعُ		أُمْنَعُ	المُتَكَلِّم:

الجَمْع	المُثَنَّى	المُفْرَد	الأَمْر المَجهُولُ
لِيُمْنَعوا	لِيُمْنَعا	لِيُمْنَعْ	الغائِب:
لِيُمْنَعْنَ	لِتُمْنَعا	لِتُمْنَعْ	الغائِبَة:
لِتُمْنَعوا	لِتُمْنَعا	لِتُمْنَعْ	المُخاطَب:
لِتُمْنَعْنَ	لِتُمْنَعا	لِتُمْنَعي	المُخاطَبَة:
لِنُمْنَعْ		لِأُمْنَعْ	المُتَكَلِّم:

► CONCLUDING NOTES

The preceding tables give the basic conjugation of the Three Letter Transitive Primary Verb (الفِعْلُ الثُّلاثِيُّ المُجَرَّدُ المُتَعَدِّي) in the Active Voice and Passive Voice forms. When the verb is Intransitive (الفِعْلُ الثُّلاثِيُّ المُجَرَّدُاللّازِمُ), it will not possess the Passive Voice forms (as previously mentioned) unless a Particle is linked with it.

The example given in the table only represents one of the six possible patterns or *Abwaab* (فَعَلَ يَفْعَلُ). With regard to conjugation, the only difference between the example and the other *Abwaab* is the pattern of vowels. The methodology of conjugation is identical.

Table 1.14 lists an abbreviated conjugation of verbs and examples of nouns which we refer to as **Sarf Sagheer** (الصَّرْفُ الصَّغِيرُ), meaning a shortened conjugation given for demonstrative purposes. These ten patterns represent the basic verb patterns in the Active and Passive Voices, the verb's root or Masdar and two basic derivative nouns. From right to left, Sarf Sagheer is organized in the following manner:

(١) فَعَلَ (٢) يَفْعَلُ (٣) إفْعَلْ (٤) لِيَفْعَلْ (٥) فُعِلَ (٦) يُفْعَلُ (٧) لِيُفْعَلْ هُوَ

(٨) فَعْلٌ (٩) فاعِلٌ (١٠) مَفْعُولٌ

1) Active Voice Past Tense	الفِعْلُ الماضِيُّ المَعْلُومُ
2) Active Voice Present Tense	الفِعْلُ المُضارِعُ المَعْلُومُ
3) Second Person Command Verb	الأَمْرُ الحاضِرُ
4) Active Voice Command Verb	الأَمْرُ المَعْلُومُ
5) Passive Voice Past Tense	الفِعْلُ الماضِيُّ المَجْهُولُ
6) Passive Voice Present Tense	الفِعْلُ المُضارِعُ المَجْهُولُ

7) Passive Voice Command Verb	الأَمْرُ المَجْهُولُ
8) Masdar (root word)	المُصْدَرُ
9) Active Participle	إِسمُ الفَاعِلِ
10) Passive Participle	إِسمُ المَفْعُولِ

The forms comprising 1-7 have already been discussed in detail in this chapter. Forms 8-10 are all nouns. The first (No. 8), is the root word or Masdar from which Past Tense Active Voice verb is derived. Subsequently, all other forms of the verb are derived from the Past Tense Active Voice Verb, as demonstrated in this chapter. At times, more than one Masdar may be listed due to the fact that Arabic words are known to have different roots among different groups of Arabic speaking people. The Pronoun هُوَ precedes the Masdar as a means of marking the transition from verb patterns to noun patterns.

The next pattern (فَاعِلْ) is that of the Active Participle. The Active Participle is also known as the Agent Noun as it denotes the person or thing which performs an action or possesess a certain quality associated with the verb. The Active Participle is derived from the Active Voice Verb. Observe the relationship in meaning between the following verbs and their respective Active Participles: قَتَلَ *To kill* - قَاتِلْ *Killer*; عَلِمَ *To know*- عَالِمٌ *Person possessing knowledge*; فَرِحَ *To be happy*- فَارِحٌ *Happy person*.

The last pattern (مَفْعُولْ) is that of the Passive Participle. The Passive Particle is derived from the Passive Voice Verb when one exists. It embodies the meaning of the Passive Voice. Observe the relationship between the Active Voice Verb, the Passive Voice Verb and the Passive Participle in the following:

قَتَلَ *To kill* قُتِلَ *To be killed* مَقْتُولٌ *Killed*; عَلِمَ *To know* عُلِمَ *To be known*- مَعْلُومٌ *Known*

These and other nouns will be examined in detail in the second part of this book which is devoted exclusively to the noun.

CHAPTER TWO

THE NON-SOUND VERB
الفعل غير السالم

INTRODUCTION

As previously mentioned in the introduction to the book, the word that does not have doubled consonants (*Mudhaa'af*) and does not have *Hamzah* as one of its Original Letters (*Mahmooz*) is known as *Saalim*. Chapter One dealt only with the *Saalim* verb. In this chapter we will examine these two other categories of words, meaning the *Mudhaa'af* and the *Mahmooz*.

For the sake of classification, we will always refer to the *Mudhaa'af* and *Mahmooz* as **Non-Sound Verbs** (غَيْرُ السَّالِمِ). This should not, however, be confused with a Weak Verb as the Weak Verb (الْمُعْتَلُّ) contains one of the Weak Letters as an Original Letter.

SECTION ONE

THE DOUBLE CONSONANT VERB - MUDHAA'AF

المُضَاعَف

The double consonant verb or **Mudhaa'af** verb is that Kalimah whose second and third

Original Letters are the same, as in: مَدَدَ حَجَجَ. As mentioned previously, the *Mudhaa'af*

Verb may display contraction or **Idghaam** (الإِدْغامُ). *Idghaam* in some of the Seeghah is

obligatory (واجِبٌ), in some Seeghah it is permissible (جَائِزٌ) and in other Seeghah it is not

allowed (مانِعٌ).

▶ **THE RULES OF IDGHAAM IN THE MUDHAA'AF VERB** قَواعِدُ الإِدْغامِ في المُضاعَفِ

The Past Tense. In the first five Seeghah of the Past Tense, *Idghaam* or contraction is

obligatory because the third Original Letter is voweled while it is permissible to make the

second letter Saakin:

مَدَدَ – مَدَّ، مَدَدا – مَدَّا، مَدَدُوا – مَدُّوا، مَدَدَتْ – مَدَّتْ، مَدَدَتا – مَدَّتا

In the remaining Seeghah (6-14), *Idghaam* is prohibited because the third Original Letter is

Saakin as is the rule in these Seeghah.

The Present Tense. *Idghaam* is obligatory in all Seeghah of the Present Tense except two: the Feminine Plurals (Seeghah 6 and 12). In both Seeghah, the third Original Letter is Saakin as a rule. As such, *Idghaam* is not allowed: يَمْدُدْنَ، تَمْدُدْنَ. Note that in these two Seeghah, the verb reverts back to its original pattern: يَفْعَلْنَ تَفْعَلْنَ.

Table 2.1 The Mudhaa'af Verb On The Pattern Of: فَعَلَ يَفْعُلُ

مَدَّ، يَمُدُّ، مُدَّ (أُمْدُدْ)، لِيَمُدَّ، مُدَّ، يَمُدُّ، لِيَمَدَّ هُوَ مَدَّ و مادٌّ و مَمْدُودٌ

الجَمْع	المُثَنَّى	المُفْرَد	الماضِي المَعلُومُ
مَدُّوا	مَدَّا	مَدَّ	الغائِب:
مَدَدْنَ	مَدَّتا	مَدَّتْ	الغائِبَة:
مَدَدْتُمْ	مَدَدْتُما	مَدَدْتَ	المُخاطَب:
مَدَدْتُنَّ	مَدَدْتُما	مَدَدْتِ	المُخاطَبَة:
مَدَدْنا		مَدَدْتُ	المُتَكَلِّم:

الجَمْع	المُثَنَّى	المُفْرَد	المُضارِعُ المَعلُومُ
يَمُدُّونَ	يَمُدَّانِ	يَمُدُّ	الغائِب:
يَمْدُدْنَ	تَمُدَّانِ	تَمُدُّ	الغائِبَة:
تَمُدُّونَ	تَمُدَّانِ	تَمُدُّ	المُخاطَب:
تَمْدُدْنَ	تَمُدَّانِ	تَمُدِّينَ	المُخاطَبَة:
نَمُدُّ		أَمُدُّ	المُتَكَلِّم:

الجَمْع	المُثَنَّى	المُفْرَد	الأَمْرُ المَعلُوم
لِيَمُدُّوا	لِيَمُدَّا	لِيَمُدَّ	الغائِب:
لِيَمْدُدْنَ	لِتَمُدَّا	لِتَمُدَّ	الغائِبَة:
مُدُّوا	مُدَّا	مُدَّ	المُخاطَب:
أُمْدُدْنَ	مُدَّا	مُدِّي	المُخاطَبَة:
لِنَمُدَّ		لِأَمُدَّ	المُتَكَلِّم:

The first Original Letter in *Mudhaa'af* is vowelled whereas it is usually Saakin in the Present Tense Primary Verb. This is due to the fact that the second and third Original Letter are contracted. In the contraction, the Second Original Letter actually becomes *Saakin*. As a rule of 'Arabic, two *Saakin* letters are never found side by side. The Feminine Plurals, as mentioned, will undergo no contraction and, as such, the verb remains on its original pattern: يَفْعَلْنَ، تَفْعَلْنَ .

The 2nd Person Command Verb (الأَمْرُ الحَاضِرُ) can be formed in two ways. As shown above, it is formed with *Idghaam*. It can also be formed without *Idghaam*, however, and in the Feminine Plurals, the same forms are utilized. This is due to the fact that the Feminine Plural (Seeghah 6 and 12) must be formed without *Idghaam* because the letter before the Feminine Noon must always be *Saakin*.

When the *Mudhaa'af* verb is formed with *Idghaam*, the *Hamzah* of the Command is not used since the 1st Original Letter is vowelled (refer to Chapter 1, pg. 41). When *Idghaam* is used, it is impossible for the Command Verb to be *Saakin* at its end as is usually the case. In this case, *Fathah* is used in place of the *Sukoon*. Some scholars have noted that it can also be found vowelled with *Kasrah*, although infrequently.

When the Command Verb is formed without *Idghaam*, the verb reverts to its original pattern and is formed in the manner commonly used for this type of Command Verb. Note that in the last Seeghah (the feminine plural no. 12) does not allow *Idghaam* because the third Original Letter must be *Saakin*. With *Idghaam*, it is impossible for the final letter to be *Saakin*, therefore, it can only be formed without *Idghaam*.

▶ THE PASSIVE VOICE IN THE MUDHAA'AF VERB المَجهُولُ في المُضاعَف

As mentioned in the previous chapter, the Passive Voice is on the pattern of: فُعِلَ يُفْعَلُ. In the process of *Idghaam* in the Past Tense Verb, the vowel on the 2nd Original Letter is lost due to the contraction of the 2nd and 3rd Original Letters. As a result, the *Mudhaa'af* Verb will be voweled as such: مُدِدَ < مُدَّ. The vowels on the 1st and 3rd Original Letters (*Dhammah* and *Fathah*, respectively) remain after *Idghaam*.

In the Present Tense Verb, the contraction of the 2nd and 3rd Original Letters are impossible before the removal of the Sukoon on the 1st Original Letter. As a rule, the letter preceding a doubled letter (with *Shaddah*) cannot be *Saakin*. Therefore, the vowel on the 2nd Original Letter is shifted to the 1st Original Letter, then, *Idghaam* can occur:

$$يُمْدَدُ < يُمَددُ < يُمَدُّ$$

The *Dhammah* must remain on the 3rd Original Letter as it is the sign of *I'raab*. Observe the Passive Voice Mudhaa'af Verb in the following chart:

Table 2.2 - Past Tense Passive Voice Mudhaa'af Verb On The Pattern Of: فُعِلَ يُفْعَلُ

الجَمْع	المُثَنَّى	المُفْرَد	الماضِيُ المجهولُ
مُدُّوا	مُدَّا	مُدَّ	الغائِب:
مُدِدْنَ	مُدَّتا	مُدَّتْ	الغائِبَة:
مُدِدْتُمْ	مُدِدْتُما	مُدِدْتَ	المُخاطَب:
مُدِدْتُنَّ	مُدِدْتُما	مُدِدْتِ	المُخاطَبَة:
مُدِدْنا		مُدِدْتُ	المُتَكَلِّم:

الجَمْع	المُثَنَّى	المُفْرَد	المُضارِعُ المَجهولُ
يُمَدُّونَ	يُمَدَّانِ	يُمَدُّ	الغائِب:
يُمْدَدْنَ	تُمَدَّانِ	تُمَدُّ	الغائِبَة:
تُمَدُّونَ	تُمَدَّانِ	تُمَدُّ	المُخاطَب:
تُمْدَدْنَ	تُمَدَّانِ	تُمَدِّينَ	المُخاطَبَة:
نُمَدُّ		أُمَدُّ	المُتَكَلِّم:

الجَمْع	المُثَنَّى	المُفْرَد	الأَمْرُ المَجهولُ
لِيُمَدُّوا	لِيُمَدَّا	لِيُمَدَّ	الغائِب:
لِيُمْدَدْنَ	لِتُمَدَّا	لِتُمَدَّ	الغائِبَة:
لِتُمَدُّوا	لِتُمَدَّا	لِتُمَدَّ	المُخاطَب:
لِتُمْدَدْنَ	لِتُمَدَّا	لِتُمَدِّي	المُخاطَبَة:
لِنُمَدَّ		لأُمَدَّ	المُتَكَلِّم:

Here again, *Fathah* is used to indicate that the verb was originally *Saakin* at its end in those Seeghah usually having *Sukoon* (Seeghah 1, 4, 7, 13, 14).

Table - 2.3 The basic patterns (Sarf Sagheer) of the Mudhaa'af Verb:

(فَعَلَ يَفْعُلُ) مَدَّ، يَمُدُّ، مُدَّ (أُمْدُدْ)، لِيَمُدَّ، مُدَّ، يُمَدُّ، لِيُمَدَّ هُوَ مُدٌّ و مادٌّ و مَمْدُودٌ

(فَعَلَ يَفْعِلُ) شَدَّ، يَشِدُّ، شِدَّ (إِشْدِدْ)، لِيَشِدَّ، شُدَّ، يُشَدُّ، لِيُشَدَّ هُوَ شِدٌّ و شادٌّ و مَشْدُودٌ

(فَعَلَ يَفْعَلُ) لَجَّ، يَلَجُّ، لَجَّ (إِلْجَجْ)، لِيَلَجَّ، لُجَّ فِيهِ، يُلَجُّ فِيهِ، لِيُلَجَّ فِيهِ هُوَ لَجِجٌ وَ لاجٌّ

▶ CONCLUDING NOTES

The 2nd Person Command Verb and the Past Tense Passive Voice Verb are the same in appearence (مُدَّ), while each has arrived at that form by different means. The difference between them can be understood in the context of the sentence in which they are used.

SECTION TWO

THE VERB WITH HAMZAH - MAHMOOZ

المَهْمُوْز

The Kalimah that has *Hamzah* (الهَمْزَة) as one of its Original Letters, is called **Mahmooz**.
Mahmooz has three types:

› The *Hamzah* is found in the first Original Letter (مَهْمُوْزُ الفاءِ), for example: أَمَرَ.

› The *Hamzah* is found in the second Original Letter (مَهْمُوْزُ العَيْنِ), as in: سَأَلَ.

› The *Hamzah* is found in the third Original Letter (مَهْمُوْزُ اللاَّم), for example: قَرَأ.

The second and third type of *Mahmooz* (مهْمُوزُ العَيْنِ وَ اللاَّم) are conjugated in the same manner as the Verb we referred to as *Saalim*. The first type (مَهْمُوزُ الفاءِ), however, has instances where the rules of reduction of the *Hamzah* or **Takhfeef** (تَخْفِيْفُ الهَمْزَة) are applied in the following manner:

▷ There is an obligatory reduction of the *Hamzah* (تَخْفِيفُ الهَمْزَةِ وُجوباً) in Seeghah 13 of the Present Tense (Active and Passive Voice) and the Active Voice Command Verb, for example: أَعْمُرُ on the pattern of: أَفْعُلُ and أُعْمِرُ on the pattern of: أُفْعِلُ. In both verbs, the first *Hamzah* (the sign of the Present Tense) is vowelled while the second *Hamzah* is *Saakin*.

Obligatory *Takhfeef* requires that, in this situation, the *Saakin Hamzah* is elided and the vowelled *Hamzah* is elongated with **Maddah** (ـ) in the Active Voice and converted to the letter Waw in the Passive Voice, as in:

$$أَعْمُرُ < أُمُرُ،\ أُعْمَرُ < أُوْمَرُ$$

▷Also, *Takhfeef* is obligatory in Seeghah 7-12 of the Active Voice Command Verb, meaning the 2nd Person Command Verb (الأَمْرُ الحاضِرُ):

$$أُعْمُرْ < أُومُرْ،\ أُعْمُرا < أُوْمُرا،\ أُعْمُرُوا < أُوْمُرُوا،\qquad أُعْمُرِي < أُوْمُرِي،\qquad أُعْمُرا < أُوْمُرا،\ أُعْمُرْنَ < أُوْمُرْنَ$$

The rule is that whenever a *Saakin Hamzah* is preceded by a *Hamzah* with *Fathah*, the *Saakin Hamzah* will be elided and the vowelled *Hamzah* will be elogated with *Maddah*. If the letter preceding the *Saakin Hamzah* is vowelled with *Dhammah*, the *Saakin Hamzah* will be converted to the letter Waw (as shown in the above examples).

If the letter preceding the Saakin Hamzah is vowelled with Kasrah, the Hamzah is converted to the letter Yaa', as in: إِغْسِرْ on the pattern of: إِفْعِلْ becomes: إِيْسِرْ. In this manner, the Hamzah is either elided or converted to a letter which is appropriate for the vowel on the preceding letter.

▷In the remaining Seeghah, the reduction of the Hamzah is permissible (meaning a matter of choice) or **Jaa'iz** (تَخْفِيفُ الهَمْزَةِ جائِزاً), for example:

$$ \text{يَأْمُرُ} > \text{يَامُرُ، يُؤْمَرُ} > \text{يُوْمَرُ، \quad لِيُؤْمَرْ} > \text{لِيُوْمَرْ} $$

Table 2.4 - The Active Voice Mahmooz Verb On The Pattern Of: فَعَلَ يَفْعُلُ

أَمَرَ، يَأْمُرُ، أُوْمُرْ، لِيَأْمُرْ، أُومِرَ، يُؤْمَرُ، لِيُؤْمَرْ هُوَ أَمَرٌ وآمِرٌ و مَأْمُورٌ

الْمَاضِي الْمَعْلُوم	الْمُفْرَد	الْمُثَنَّى	الْجَمْع
الْغَائِب:	أَمَرَ	أَمَرا	أَمَرُوا
الْغَائِبَة:	أَمَرَتْ	أَمَرَتا	أَمَرْنَ
الْمُخَاطَب:	أَمَرْتَ	أَمَرْتُما	أَمَرْتُمْ
الْمُخَاطَبَة:	أَمَرْتِ	أَمَرْتُما	أَمَرْتُنَّ
الْمُتَكَلِّم:	أَمَرْتُ		أَمَرْنا

الْمُضَارِعُ الْمَعْلُوم	الْمُفْرَد	الْمُثَنَّى	الْجَمْع
الْغَائِب:	يَأْمُرُ	يَأْمُرانِ	يَأْمُرُونَ
الْغَائِبَة:	تَأْمُرُ	تَأْمُرانِ	يَأْمُرْنَ
الْمُخَاطَب:	تَأْمُرُ	تَأْمُرانِ	تَأْمُرُونَ
الْمُخَاطَبَة:	تَأْمُرِينَ	تَأْمُرانِ	تَأْمُرْنَ
الْمُتَكَلِّم:	آمُرُ		نَأْمُرُ

الأَمْرُ الْمَعْلُوم	الْمُفْرَد	الْمُثَنَّى	الْجَمْع
الْغَائِب:	لِيَأْمُرْ	لِيَأْمُرا	لِيَأْمُرُوا
الْغَائِبَة:	لِتَأْمُرْ	لِتَأْمُرا	لِيَأْمُرْنَ
الْمُخَاطَب:	أُوْمُرْ	أُوْمُرا	أُوْمُرُوا
الْمُخَاطَبَة:	أُوْمُرِي	أُوْمُرا	أُوْمُرْنَ
الْمُتَكَلِّم:	لِآمُرْ		لِنَأْمُرْ

Table 2.5 - The Passive Voice Mahmooz Verb On The Pattern Of: فُعِل يُفْعَل

الجَمْع	المُثَنَّى	المُفْرَد	الماضِي المَجهُولُ
أُمِرُوا	أُمِرا	أُمِرَ	الغائِب:
أُمِرْنَ	أُمِرَتا	أُمِرَت	الغائِبَة:
أُمِرْتُم	أُمِرْتُما	أُمِرْت	المُخاطَب:
أُمِرْتُنَّ	أُمِرْتُما	أُمِرْتِ	المُخاطَبَة:
أُمِرْنا		أُمِرْت	المُتَكَلِّم:

الجَمْع	المُثَنَّى	المُفْرَد	المُضارِعُ المَجهُولُ
يُؤْمَرونَ	يُؤْمَرانِ	يُؤْمَر	الغائِب:
يُؤْمَرْنَ	تُؤْمَرانِ	تُؤْمَر	الغائِبَة:
تُؤْمَرونَ	تُؤْمَرانِ	تُؤْمَر	المُخاطَب:
تُؤْمَرْنَ	تُؤْمَرانِ	تُؤْمَرينَ	المُخاطَبَة:
نُؤْمَر		أُوْمَر	المُتَكَلِّم:

الجَمْع	المُثَنَّى	المُفْرَد	الأَمْرُ المَجهُولُ
لِيُؤْمَرُوا	لِيُؤْمَرا	لِيُؤْمَر	الغائِب:
لِيُؤْمَرْنَ	لِتُؤْمَرا	لِتُؤْمَر	الغائِبَة:
لِتُؤْمَرُوا	لِتُؤْمَرا	لِتُؤْمَر	المُخاطَب:
لِتُؤْمَرْنَ	لِتُؤْمَرا	لِتُؤْمَري	المُخاطَبَة:
لِنُؤْمَر		لِأُوْمَر	المُتَكَلِّم:

There are common exceptions to the patterns set forth above, particularly in the following

verbs: أَخَذَ، أَكَلَ، أَمَرَ. Due to common usage, their Command Verbs are conjugated

employing the rule of the Elision of the *Hamzah* (التَّخْفِيفُ الحَذْفِي), as follows:

$$أُوْمُرْ-مُرْ \qquad أُوْكُلْ-كُلْ، \qquad أُوْخُذْ-خُذْ$$

In these patterns, not only is the *Hamzah* of the Command Verb eliminated, but also the

Hamzah that is the first Original Letter is eliminated as well. However, in the first two verbs

(أَخَذَ، أَكَلَ), this Elision is obligatory while in the third (أَمَرَ), it is permissible.

Another exception, is the verb سَأَلَ. In the forms the Past Tense, Present Tense and Active

Voice Command Verb, it is permitted to change the *Hamzah* of the second Original Letter to

Alif, as in:

$$سَلْ < إِسْأَلْ> إِسَالْ \qquad يَسْأَلُ > يَسَالُ، \qquad سَأَلَ > سَالَ$$

Note that the Command Verb becomes سَلْ for two reasons. One, when the *Hamzah* is

elided it becomes *Saakin*. Therefore, the letter before it must be vowelled to prevent two

Saakin letters from existing side by side (إِلْتِقَاءُ السَّاكِنَيْنِ). According to the rule of forming

the Command Verb, when the first Original Letter is vowelled, the *Hamzah* of the Command

Verb is not used.

Second, the Command Verb must be *Saakin* at the end. Since, by elision of the *Hamzah*, the vowel on the Second Original has been eliminated, it is *Saakin* as well resulting in two *Saakin* letters existing side by side. To eliminate this problem, the Second Original Letter is elided.

Also, in the Seeghah 1, 4, 6, 7, 12, 13 and 14 of the Active Voice Command Verb the Alif will be elided due to the presence of two *Saakin* letters, as in: لِيَسَلْ، لأَسَلْ – لأَسَلْ – لِيَسَالْ. In Seeghah 9 and 10, you can also find: سَلُوا and سَلِي.

Whenever the Particles (و) and (ف) precede the *Hamzah* of the Command Verb, the *Hamzah* will become silent to facilitate connection between the words. This is the characteristic of the Command Verb's *Hamzah*, also known as a **Conjunctive Hamzah** (الهَمْزَةُ الوَصلَةُ), for example:

$$ وَ + إِسأَلْ = وَ اسأَلْ، فَ + إِسأَلْ = فَاسأَلْ $$

In the verb taken from the Masdar رُؤْيَةٌ or رَأْيٌ, the Seeghah of the Present Tense (Active and Passive) and the Command Verb from these Masdar will have the *Hamzah* of the second Original Letter removed while its vowel will be placed on the preceding letter, for example: يَرْأَي يَرَى، يُرْأَى يُرَى، لِيَرْأ لِيَرَ

Some of the alterations seen in some of these patterns will be discussed in the review of the *Naaqis* Verb (الفِعْلُ النَّاقِصُ), i.e., the verb with a weak letter as its third Original Letter.

Table 2.6 - The Active Voice Mahmooz Verb On The Pattern Of: فَعَلَ يَفْعَلُ

سَأَلَ، يَسْأَلُ، إِسْأَلْ (سَلْ)، لِيَسْأَلْ، سُئِلَ، يُسْأَلُ هُوَ سُؤَالٌ (مَسْأَلَة) و سَآئِلٌ و مَسْؤُولٌ

الجَمع	المُثَنَّى	المُفرَد	الماضِي المَعلُوم
سَأَلُوا	سَأَلَا	سَأَلَ	الغائِب:
سَأَلْنَ	سَأَلَتَا	سَأَلَتْ	الغائِبَة:
سَأَلْتُم	سَأَلْتُما	سَأَلْتَ	المُخاطَب:
سَأَلْتُنَّ	سَأَلْتُما	سَأَلْتِ	المُخاطَبَة:
سَأَلْنا		سَأَلْتُ	المُتَكَلِّم:

الجَمع	المُثَنَّى	المُفرَد	المُضارعُ المَعلُوم
يَسْأَلُونَ	يَسْأَلانِ	يَسْأَلُ	الغائِب:
يَسْأَلْنَ	تَسْأَلانِ	تَسْأَلُ	الغائِبَة:
تَسْأَلُونَ	تَسْأَلانِ	تَسْأَلُ	المُخاطَب:
تَسْأَلْنَ	تَسْأَلانِ	تَسْأَلِينَ	المُخاطَبَة:
نَسْأَلُ		أَسْأَلُ	المُتَكَلِّم:

الجَمع	المُثَنَّى	المُفرَد	الأَمْرُ المَعلُوم
لِيَسْأَلُوا	لِيَسْأَلا	لِيَسْأَلْ	الغائِب:
لِيَسْأَلْنَ	لِتَسْأَلا	لِتَسْأَلْ	الغائِبَة:
إِسْأَلُوا (سَالُوا)	إِسْأَلا (سَالا)	إِسْأَلْ (سَلْ)	المُخاطَب:
إِسْأَلْنَ (سَلْنَ)	إِسْأَلا (سَالا)	إِسْأَلِي (سَالِي)	المُخاطَبَة:
لِنَسْأَلْ		لِأَسْأَلْ	المُتَكَلِّم:

Table 2.7 - The Passive Voice Mazmooz Verb On The Pattern Of: فُعِلَ يُفْعَلُ

الجَمْع	المُثَنَّى	المُفْرَد	الماضي المَجهُول
سُئِلُوا	سُئِلا	سُئِلَ	الغائِب:
سُئِلْنَ	سُئِلَتا	سُئِلَتْ	الغائِبَة:
سُئِلْتُم	سُئِلْتُما	سُئِلْتَ	المُخاطَب:
سُئِلْتُنَّ	سُئِلْتُما	سُئِلْتِ	المُخاطَبِة:
سُئِلْنا		سُئِلْتُ	المُتَكَلِّم:

الجَمْع	المُثَنَّى	المُفْرَد	المُضارِع المَجهُول
يُسْأَلُونَ	يُسْأَلانِ	يُسْأَلُ	الغائِب:
يُسْأَلْنَ	تُسْأَلانِ	تُسْأَلُ	الغائِبَة:
تُسْأَلُونَ	تُسْأَلانِ	تُسْأَلُ	المُخاطَب:
تُسْأَلْنَ	تُسْأَلانِ	تُسْأَلِينَ	المُخاطَبِة:
نُسْأَلُ		أُسْأَلُ	المُتَكَلِّم:

الجَمْع	المُثَنَّى	المُفْرَد	الأَمْر المَجهُول
لِيُسْأَلُوا	لِيُسْأَلا	لِيُسْأَلْ	الغائِب:
لِيُسْأَلْنَ	لِتُسْأَلا	لِتُسْأَلْ	الغائِبَة:
لِتُسْأَلُوا	لِتُسْأَلا	لِتُسْأَلْ	المُخاطَب:
لِتُسْأَلْنَ	لِتُسْأَلا	لِتُسْأَلي	المُخاطَبِة:
لِنُسْأَلْ		لِأُسْأَلْ	المُتَكَلِّم:

أَسَرَ، يَأْسِرُ، إِيسِرْ، لِيَأْسِرْ، أُسِرَ، يُؤْسَرُ، لِيُؤْسَرْ هُوَ أُسِرَ و آسِرٌ و مَأْسُورٌ

الجَمْع	المُثَنَّى	المُفْرَد	الماضِيُ المَعلُوم
أَسَرُوا	أَسَرا	أَسَرَ	الغائِب:
أَسَرْنَ	أَسَرَتا	أَسَرَتْ	الغائِبة:
أَسَرْتُمْ	أَسَرْتُما	أَسَرْتَ	المُخاطَب:
أَسَرْتُنَّ	أَسَرْتُما	أَسَرْتِ	المُخاطَبة:
أَسَرْنا		أَسَرْتُ	المُتَكَلِّم:

الجَمْع	المُثَنَّى	المُفْرَد	المُضارِع المَعلُوم
يَأْسِرُونَ	يَأْسِرانِ	يَأْسِرُ	الغائِب:
يَأْسِرْنَ	تَأْسِرانِ	تَأْسِرُ	الغائِبة:
تَأْسِرُونَ	تَأْسِرانِ	تَأْسِرُ	المُخاطَب:
تَأْسِرْنَ	تَأْسِرانِ	تَأْسِرينَ	المُخاطَبة:
نَأْسِرُ		آسِرُ	المُتَكَلِّم:

الجَمْع	المُثَنَّى	المُفْرَد	الأَمْر المَعلُوم
لِيَأْسِرُوا	لِيَأْسِرا	لِيَأْسِرْ	الغائِب:
لِيَأْسِرْنَ	لِتَأْسِرا	لِتَأْسِرْ	الغائِبة:
إِيسِرُوا	إِيسِرا	إِيسِرْ	المُخاطَب:
إِيسِرْنَ	إِيسِرا	إِيسِري	المُخاطَبة:
لِنَأْسِرْ		لَآسِرْ	المُتَكَلِّم:

Table 2.9 - The Passive Voice Mahmooz Verb On The Pattern Of: فُعِلَ يُفْعَلُ

الجَمع	المُثَنَّى	المُفرَد	الماضِيُ المَجهُولُ
أُسِرُوا	أُسِرا	أُسِرَ	الغائِب:
أُسِرنَ	أُسِرتا	أُسِرَت	الغائِبَة:
أُسِرتُم	أُسِرتُما	أُسِرتَ	المُخاطَب:
أُسِرتُنَّ	أُسِرتُما	أُسِرتِ	المُخاطَبَة:
أُسِرنا		أُسِرتُ	المُتَكَلِّم:
الجَمع	**المُثَنَّى**	**المُفرَد**	**المُضارِعُ المَجهُولُ**
يُؤسَرُونَ	يُؤسَرانِ	يُؤسَرُ	الغائِب:
يُؤسَرنَ	تُؤسَرانِ	تُؤسَرُ	الغائِبَة:
تُؤسَرُونَ	تُؤسَرانِ	تُؤسَرُ	المُخاطَب:
تُؤسَرنَ	تُؤسَرانِ	تُؤسَرِينَ	المُخاطَبَة:
نُؤسَرُ		أُوسَرُ	المُتَكَلِّم:
الجَمع	**المُثَنَّى**	**المُفرَد**	**الأَمرُ المَجهُولُ**
لِيُؤسَرُوا	لِيُؤسَرا	لِيُؤسَرْ	الغائِب:
لِيُؤسَرنَ	لِتُؤسَرا	لِتُؤسَرْ	الغائِبَة:
لِتُؤسَرُوا	لِتُؤسَرا	لِتُؤسَرْ	المُخاطَب:
لِتُؤسَرنَ	لِتُؤسَرا	لِتُؤسَرِي	المُخاطَبَة:
لِنُؤسَرْ		لِأُوسَرْ	المُتَكَلِّم:

Table 2.10 - The Active Voice Mazhooz Verb On The Pattern Of: فَعَلَ يَفْعَلُ

بَدَأَ، يَبْدَأُ، إِبْدَأْ، لِيَبْدَأْ، بُدِئَ، يُبْدَأُ، لِيُبْدَأُ هُوَ بَدْءٌ و بَادِئٌ و مَبْدُوءٌ

الجَمْع	المُثَنَّى	المُفْرَد	الماضِي المَعلُوم
بَدَؤُوا	بَدَأَ	بَدَأَ	الغَائِب:
بَدَأْنَ	بَدَأَتا	بَدَأَتْ	الغَائِبَة:
بَدَأْتُم	بَدَأْتُما	بَدَأْتَ	المُخاطَب:
بَدَأْتُنَّ	بَدَأْتُما	بَدَأْت	المُخاطَبَة:
بَدَأْنا		بَدَأْتُ	المُتَكَلِّم:

الجَمْع	المُثَنَّى	المُفْرَد	المُضارِع المَعلُوم
يَبْدَؤُونَ	يَبْدَآنِ	يَبْدَأُ	الغَائِب:
يَبْدَأْنَ	تَبْدَآنِ	تَبْدَأُ	الغَائِبَة:
تَبْدَؤُونَ	تَبْدَآنِ	تَبْدَأُ	المُخاطَب:
تَبْدَأْنَ	تَبْدَآنِ	تَبْدَئِينَ	المُخاطَبَة:
نَبْدَأُ		أَبْدَأُ	المُتَكَلِّم:

الجَمْع	المُثَنَّى	المُفْرَد	الأَمْرُ المَعلُوم
لِيَبْدَؤُوا	لِيَبْدَآ	لِيَبْدَأْ	الغَائِب:
لِيَبْدَأْنَ	لِتَبْدَآ	لِتَبْدَأْ	الغَائِبَة:
إِبْدَؤُوا	إِبْدَآ	إِبْدَأْ	المُخاطَب:
إِبْدَأْنَ	إِبْدَآ	إِبْدَئِي	المُخاطَبَة:
لِنَبْدَأْ		لِأَبْدَأْ	المُتَكَلِّم:

Table 2.11 - The Passive Voice Mahmooz Verb On The Pattern Of: فُعِلَ يُفْعَلُ

الجَمع	المُثَنَّى	المُفْرَد	الماضِي المَجهُولُ
بُدِئُوا	بُدِئا	بُدِئَ	الغائِب:
بُدِئْنَ	بُدِئَتا	بُدِئَتْ	الغائِبَة:
بُدِئْتُم	بُدِئْتُما	بُدِئْتَ	المُخاطَب:
بُدِئْتُنَّ	بُدِئْتُما	بُدِئْتِ	المُخاطَبَة:
بُدِئْنا		بُدِئْتُ	المُتَكَلِّم:

الجَمع	المُثَنَّى	المُفْرَد	المُضارِعُ المَجهُولُ
يُبدَئُونَ	يُبدَآن	يُبدَأُ	الغائِب:
يُبدَأْنَ	تُبدَآن	تُبدَأُ	الغائِبَة:
تُبدَئُونَ	تُبدَآن	تُبدَأُ	المُخاطَب:
تُبدَأْنَ	تُبدَآن	تُبدَئِينَ	المُخاطَبَة:
نُبدَأُ		أُبدَأُ	المُتَكَلِّم:

الجَمع	المُثَنَّى	المُفْرَد	الأَمْرُ المَجهُولُ
لِيُبدَئُوا	لِيُبدَآ	لِيُبدَأُ	الغائِب:
لِيُبدَأْنَ	لِتُبدَآ	لِتُبدَأُ	الغائِبَة:
لِتُبدَئُوا	لِتُبدَآ	لِتُبدَأُ	المُخاطَب:
لِتُبدَأْنَ	لِتُبدَآ	لِتُبدَئِي	المُخاطَبَة:
لِنُبدَأُ		لِأُبدَأُ	المُتَكَلِّم:

CHAPTER THREE

THE WEAK VERB

الفعل المعتلّ

INTRODUCTION

As previously defined, the *Weak Verb* or **Mu'tall** (المُعْتَلُّ) is that verb that has a *Weak Letter* (الحَرْفُ العِلَّةِ) as one or more of its Original Letters (الأَحْرُفُ الأَصْلِي). The Weak Letters are three: و ي ى , *Waw*, *Yaa'* and *Alif*. Often these letters will appear in words, nouns in particular, as Additional Letters (الأَحْرُفُ الزَّائِدَةُ). When this is the case, they are not considered Weak Letters. For example, the following are examples of words with weak letters: وَعَدَ، سَيِّرٌ، هُدَى. When these same letters appear in nouns or verbs as Additional Letters, they will not be considered *Mu'tall*, for example: مَعْلُومٌ، هاشِمِي، سَلْمَى.

Alif, the weak letter, is a form of the letter Alif known as the *Shortened Alif* or **Alif Maqsoorah** (الأَلِفُ المَقْصُورَةُ). This *Shortened Alif* is only found as the last letter of a word, as in: هُدَى. If another letter is added after the *Shortened Alif*, it will be converted to the normal Alif or to Yaa', as in: هَداكَ، هَدَيْتَ.

One characteristic that all the Weak Letters share is their inability to support their own vowel. As a result, the Weak Letter often undergoes a process of transformation or **I'laal** (الإِعْلالُ) that is often related to the vowel on the preceding letter.

As a result, the Weak Letter can be transformed into a totally different letter, often a long vowel connected to the preceding letter. For example, the verb: قَالَ was originally: قَوَلَ, in the process of *I'laal*, however, the letter Waw is transformed to Alif, not the Weak Letter but a long vowel that has become an extension of the preceding letter (Qaf).

This process of *I'laal* is quite extensive and exists in most types of Weak Verbs and many nouns as well. *I'laal* has specific rules which will be enumerated in their appropriate places. The Weak Verb is of four types based on the position of the Weak Letter in relation to its Original Letters:

▷ **Mithaal** (الْمِثَالُ). The *Mithaal* Verb is that verb in which the Weak Letter occurs as the first Original Letter.

▷ **Ajwaf** (الْأَجْوَفُ). The *Ajwaf* Verb is that verb in which the Weak Letter occurs as the second Original Letter.

▷ **Naaqis** (النَّاقِصُ). The *Naaqis* Verb is that verb in which the Weak Letter occurs as the third Original Letter.

▷ **Lafeef** (اللَّفِيفُ). The *Lafeef* Verb is that verb which has two Weak Letters as Original Letters.

We will examine each category in detail in its own section.

SECTION ONE

The Mithaal Verb

الفِعْلُ المِثالُ

The *Mithaal* Verb is the verb in which the Weak Letter is found as the first Original Letter
(مُعْتَلُّ الفاءِ). *Mithaal* has two types:

> ‣ If the Weak Letter is Waw, it is called *Mithaal with Waw* (المِثالُ الواوِي), as in: وَعَدَ.

> ‣ If the Weak Letter is Yaa', it is called *Mithaal with Yaa'* (المِثالُ اليائِي), as in: يَسِرَ.

▶ MITHAAL WITH WAW المِثالُ الواوِي

Due to the fact that the *Mithaal* Verb has the Weak Letter occuring in the first Original
Letter, the rules of *I'laal* are limited in this type of verb to the Command Verb. *Mithaal* with
Waw has two special rules that are particular only to the Primary Verb (الثُّلاثِيُّ المُجَرَّدُ):

▷   If the Present Tense Active Voice Verb (المُضارِعُ المَعْلُومُ) is on the pattern of: يَفْعِلُ
     (with the second Original Letter being *Maksoor*), the first Original Letter is omitted
     resulting in the pattern: يَعِلُ. For example:

وَعَدَ > يَعِدُ،   وَجَبَ > يَجِبُ،   وَجَدَ > يَجِدُ،   وَرَعَ > يَرَعُ

This rule can be found associated with a few Present Tense Verbs with the second

---

This rule can be found associated with a few Present Tense Verbs with the second Original Letter being Maftooh, on the pattern of: يَفْعَلُ, resulting in the pattern: يَعَلُ, as in:

وَسِعَ > يَسَعُ،   وَضَعَ > يَضَعُ،   وَقَعَ > يَقَعُ،   وَدَعَ > يَدَعُ،   وَطَأَ > يَطَأُ،   وَهَبَ > يَهَبُ

This rule is applied without exception when the Present Tense Pattern is: يَفْعِلُ. When the verb is on the pattern of: يَفْعَلُ, this rule is found applied according to usage (السَّماعِيُّ) and one must consult a dictionary to known whether this rule is applied or not. In some cases, both forms may be found, i.e., with the Waw removed and present, as in: وَسِعَ – يَسَعُ (يَوْسَعُ)؛ وَضَعَ – يَضَعُ (يَوْضَعُ)   .

In addition to the first Original Letter being removed in the Present Tense Active Voice Verb (المُضارِعُ المَعْلُومُ), the first Original Letter will also be removed in the Active Voice Command Verbs (الأَمْرُ المَعْلُومُ), for example: عِدُوا، عِدا، عِدْ، لِيَعِدُوا، لِيَعِدا، لِيَعِدْ.

The first Original Letter is not omitted, however, in the Present Tense Passive Voice Verb (المُضارِعُ المَجْهُولُ) nor in the Passive Voice Command Verb (الأَمْرُ المَجْهُولُ), for example:

يُوعَدُ يُوعَدانِ، يُوعَدُونَ، لِيُوعَدْ لِيُوعَدا، لِيُوعَدُوا

▷ If the Kalimah's Masdar is on the pattern of: فِعْلٌ, most often, the vowel on the Waw will be moved to the second Original Letter and the Waw itself will be elided. This would leave it on the pattern of: عِلٌ. Then, the Feminine Sign (التَّاءُ المَرْبُوطَةُ) is added to the end of the word as a substitute of the first Original Letter (Waw) that was elided resulting in the pattern: عِلَةٌ, for example: وِصْلٌ > صِلَةٌ and وُعْدٌ > عِدَةٌ.

Less frequently, when the Masdar is on the pattern of: فَعْلٌ, the above mentioned rule is also applied, as in: وَضْعٌ > ضَعَةٌ and وَسْعٌ > سَعَةٌ. In most Masdar on this pattern, however, this rule does not apply, for example: وَقْتٌ، وَزْنٌ.

▶ I'laal In The Mithaal With Waw Verb   الإِعْلالُ في المِثالِ الواوي

The only instance of *I'laal* in the *Mithaal* with Waw can be found in the 2nd Person Command Verb formed from those verbs on the pattern of: يَفْعَلُ. According to the rule of forming this Command Verb, it prefixes *Hamzah* voweled with *Kasrah* to the root letters of the verb based on the pattern: إِفْعَلْ. However, when the first Original Letter is Waw, it forms an unworkable vowel combination, meaning that the letter Waw which is *Saakin* or unvoweled cannot be preceded by a letter voweled with *Kasrah*, as in: إِوْجَعْ, based on the following sequence: إِوْجَعْ > إِفْعَلْ،   تَوْجَعُ > تَفْعَلُ

To correct this problem, the Weak Letter is changed to a letter that corresponds with the

---

vowel on the preceding letter (*Kasrah*). The letter that corresponds with *Kasrah* is Yaa'. As a result, the Waw is transformed to Yaa': إِوْجَعْ – إِيجَعْ.

The *Mithaal* verb is commonly found on only two patterns in the Present Tense: يَفْعِلُ and

يَفْعَلُ. The third pattern, يَفْعُلُ, is uncommon. (Cf.: وَثُرَ، يُوثُرُ and وَضُؤَ، يَوْضُؤُ).

The full conjugation of the *Mithaal* Verb with Waw is in the following tables:

Table 3.1 - The Active Voice Mithaal Verb With Waw On The Pattern Of: فَعَلَ يَفْعِلُ

وَعَدَ، يَعِدُ، عِدْ، لِيَعِدْ، وُعِدَ، يُوعَدُ، لِيُوعَدْ هُوَ وُعْدٌ و واعِدٌ و مَوْعُودٌ

	المُفْرَد	المُثَّنَى	الجَمْع
الماضِي المَعْلُوم			
الغائِب:	وَعَدَ	وَعَدا	وَعَدُوا
الغائِبَة:	وَعَدَتْ	وَعَدَتا	وَعَدْنَ
المُخاطَب:	وَعَدْتَ	وَعَدْتُما	وَعَدْتُمْ
المُخاطَبَة:	وَعَدْتِ	وَعَدْتُما	وَعَدْتُنَّ
المُتَكَلِّم:	وَعَدْتُ		وَعَدْنا
المُضارِعُ المَعْلُوم	المُفْرَد	المُثَّنَى	الجَمْع
الغائِب:	يَعِدُ	يَعِدانِ	يَعِدُونَ
الغائِبَة:	تَعِدُ	تَعِدانِ	يَعِدْنَ
المُخاطَب:	تَعِدُ	تَعِدانِ	تَعِدُونَ
المُخاطَبَة:	تَعِدِينَ	تَعِدانِ	تَعِدْنَ
المُتَكَلِّم:	أَعِدُ		نَعِدُ
الأَمْرُ المَعْلُوم	المُفْرَد	المُثَّنَى	الجَمْع
الغائِب:	لِيَعِدْ	لِيَعِدا	لِيَعِدُوا
الغائِبَة:	لِتَعِدْ	لِتَعِدا	لِيَعِدْنَ
المُخاطَب:	عِدْ	عِدا	عِدُوا
المُخاطَبَة:	عِدِي	عِدا	عِدْنَ
المُتَكَلِّم:	لِأَعِدْ		لِنَعِدْ

Table 3.2 - The Passive Voice Mithaal Verb With Waw On The Pattern Of: فُعِلَ يُفْعَلُ

الجَمْع	المُثَنَّى	المُفْرَد	الماضي المَجْهول
وُعِدُوا	وُعِدا	وُعِدَ	الغائب:
وُعِدْنَ	وُعِدَتا	وُعِدَتْ	الغائبة:
وُعِدْتُمْ	وُعِدْتُما	وُعِدْتَ	المُخاطَب:
وُعِدْتُنَّ	وُعِدْتُما	وُعِدْتِ	المُخاطَبة:
وُعِدْنا		وُعِدْتُ	المُتَكَلِّم:

الجَمْع	المُثَنَّى	المُفْرَد	المُضارع المَجْهول
يُوعَدونَ	يُوعَدانِ	يُوعَدُ	الغائب:
يُوعَدْنَ	تُوعَدانِ	تُوعَدُ	الغائبة:
تُوعَدونَ	تُوعَدانِ	تُوعَدُ	المُخاطَب:
تُوعَدْنَ	تُوعَدانِ	تُوعَدِينَ	المُخاطَبة:
نُوعَدُ		أُوعَدُ	المُتَكَلِّم:

الجَمْع	المُثَنَّى	المُفْرَد	الأَمْر المَجْهول
لِيُوعَدوا	لِيُوعَدا	لِيُوعَدْ	الغائب:
لِيُوعَدْنَ	لِتُوعَدا	لِتُوعَدْ	الغائبة:
لِتُوعَدونَ	لِتُوعَدا	لِتُوعَدْ	المُخاطَب:
لِتُوعَدْنَ	لِتُوعَدا	لِتُوعَدي	المُخاطَبة:
لِيُوعَدْ		لِأُوعَدْ	المُتَكَلِّم:

Table 3.3 - The Active Voice Mithaal With Waw Verb On The Pattern Of: فَعِلَ يَفْعَلُ

وَجِلَ، يَوْجَلُ، إِيجَلْ، لِيَوْجَلْ هُوَ وَجِلٌ و واجِلٌ

الجَمْع	المُثَنَّى	المُفْرَد	المَعْلُوم	الماضِي
وَجِلُوا	وَجِلا	وَجِلَ	الغائِب:	
وَجِلْنَ	وَجِلَتا	وَجِلَتْ	الغائِبَة:	
وَجِلْتُم	وَجِلْتُما	وَجِلْتَ	المُخاطَب:	
وَجِلْتُنَّ	وَجِلْتُما	وَجِلْتِ	المُخاطَبَة:	
وَجِلْنا		وَجِلْتُ	المُتَكَلِّم:	

الجَمْع	المُثَنَّى	المُفْرَد		المُضارِعُ المَعْلُوم
يَوْجَلُونَ	يَوْجَلانِ	يَوْجَلُ	الغائِب:	
يَوْجَلْنَ	تَوْجَلانِ	تَوْجَلُ	الغائِبَة:	
تَوْجَلُونَ	تَوْجَلانِ	تَوْجَلُ	المُخاطَب:	
تَوْجَلْنَ	تَوْجَلانِ	تُوْجَلِينَ	المُخاطَبَة:	
نَوْجَلُ		أُوْجَلُ	المُتَكَلِّم:	

الجَمْع	المُثَنَّى	المُفْرَد		الأَمْر المَعْلُوم
لِيَوْجَلُوا	لِيَوْجَلا	لِيَوْجَلْ	الغائِب:	
لِيَوْجَلْنَ	لِتَوْجَلا	لِتَوْجَلْ	الغائِبَة:	
إِيجَلُوا	إِيجَلا	إِيجَلْ	المُخاطَب:	
إِيجَلْنَ	إِيجَلا	إِيجَلِي	المُخاطَبَة:	
لِنَوْجَلْ		لِأَوْجَلْ	المُتَكَلِّم:	

► MITHAAL WITH YAA' المثالُ اليآئي

Mithaal with Yaa' represents the smallest group of verbs in 'Arabic. It is conjugated without any special rules. There is only one instance of *I'laal* that occurs in the Present Tense Passive Voice (المُضارِعُ المَجهُولُ). Due to the fact that the Present Tense Passive Voice is based on the pattern: يُفعَلُ, it causes the letter preceding Yaa' to be voweled with *Dhammah*. While the Yaa' is *Saakin*, it is not possible to have a letter voweled with *Dhammah* preceding it, as in: يُيسَرُ. To rectify this problem, the Yaa' is transformed to the letter that corresponds with *Dhammah*, namely the letter Waw: يُيسَرُ > يُؤسَرُ.

Here are the conjugation tables for the *Mithaal* Verb with Yaa':

Table 3.4 - Active Voice Mithaal With Yaa' Verb On The Pattern Of: فَعِلَ يَفْعَلُ

يَقِنَ، يَيْقَنُ، إِيْقَنْ، لِيَيْقَنْ، يُقِنَ، يُؤْقَنُ، لِيُؤْقَنْ هُوَ يَقِنٌ (يَقَنٌ) و ياقِنٌ و مَيْقُونٌ

الجَمع	المُثَنَّى	المُفْرَد	الماضِي المَعْلُوم
يَقِنُوا	يَقِنا	يَقِنَ	الغائِب:
يَقِنَّ	يَقِنَتا	يَقِنَتْ	الغائِبة:
يَقِنْتُم	يَقِنْتُما	يَقِنْتَ	المُخاطَب:
يَقِنْتُنَّ	يَقِنْتُما	يَقِنْتِ	المُخاطِبة:
يَقِنَّا		يَقِنْتُ	المُتَكَلِّم:

الجَمع	المُثَنَّى	المُفْرَد	المُضارِع المَعْلُوم
يَيْقَنُونَ	يَيْقَنانِ	يَيْقَنُ	الغائِب:
يَيْقَنَّ	تَيْقَنانِ	تَيْقَنُ	الغائِبة:
تَيْقَنُونَ	تَيْقَنانِ	تَيْقَنُ	المُخاطَب:
تَيْقَنَّ	تَيْقَنانِ	تَيْقَنِينَ	المُخاطِبة:
نَيْقَنُ		أَيْقَنُ	المُتَكَلِّم:

الجَمع	المُثَنَّى	المُفْرَد	الأَمْر المَعْلُوم
لِيَيْقَنُوا	لِيَيْقَنا	لِيَيْقَنْ	الغائِب:
لِيَيْقَنَّ	لَتَيْقَنا	لِتَيْقَنْ	الغائِبة:
إِيْقَنُوا	إِيْقَنا	إِيْقَنْ	المُخاطَب:
إِيْقَنَّ	إِيْقَنا	إِيْقَنِي	المُخاطِبة:
لِنَيْقَنْ		لأَيْقَنْ	المُتَكَلِّم:

Table 3.5 - Passive Voice Mithaal With Yaa' Verb On The Pattern Of: فُعِلَ يُفْعَلُ

الجَمْع	المُثَنَّى	المُفْرَد	الماضِي المَجْهُول
يُقِنُوا	يُقِنا	يُقِنَ	الغائِب:
يُقِنَّ	يُقِنَتا	يُقِنَتْ	الغائِبَة:
يُقِنْتُم	يُقِنْتُما	يُقِنْتَ	المُخاطَب:
يُقِنْتُنَّ	يُقِنْتُما	يُقِنْتِ	المُخاطَبَة:
يُقِنّا		يُقِنْتُ	المُتَكَلِّم:
الجَمْع	المُثَنَّى	المُفْرَد	المُضارِع المَجْهُول
يُوقَنُونَ	يُوقَنانِ	يُوقَنُ	الغائِب:
يُوقَنَّ	تُوقَنانِ	تُوقَنُ	الغائِبَة:
تُوقَنُونَ	تُوقَنانِ	تُوقَنُ	المُخاطَب:
تُوقَنَّ	تُوقَنانِ	تُوقَنِينَ	المُخاطَبَة:
نُوقَنُ		أُوقَنُ	المُتَكَلِّم:
الجَمْع	المُثَنَّى	المُفْرَد	الأَمْر المَجْهُول
لِيُوقَنُوا	لِيُوقَنا	لِيُوقَنْ	الغائِب:
لِيُوقَنَّ	لِتُوقَنا	لِتُوقَنْ	الغائِبَة:
لِتُوقَنُوا	لِتُوقَنا	لِتُوقَنْ	المُخاطَب:
لِتُوقَنَّ	لِتُوقَنا	لِتُوقَنِي	المُخاطَبَة:
لِنُوقَنْ		لِأُوقَنْ	المُتَكَلِّم:

SECTION TWO

The Ajwaf Verb

الفِعْلُ الأَجْوَفُ

The Kalimah that has a Weak Letter as the second Original Letter (مُعْتَلُ العَينِ) is called

Ajwaf (الأَجْوَفُ). Like *Mithaal, Ajwaf* also has two types:

- **Ajwaf with Waw** (الأَجْوَفُ الواوِي), as in: قَوْلٌ، خَوْفٌ.

- **Ajwaf with Yaa'** (الأَجْوَفُ اليَائِي), as in: بَيْعٌ، سَيْرٌ.

▶ AJWAF WITH WAW الأَجْوَفُ الواوِي

Unlike the *Mithaal* Verb, the *Ajwaf* Verb undergoes transformation or *I'laal* in most of its

forms in the Primary Verb (الثُّلاثِيُّ المُجَرَّدُ). As a result, more attention will be paid in this

section to the rules of *I'laal* in general and those which apply to the *Ajwaf* verb in particular.

▶ The Rules Of I'laal in the Ajwaf With Waw Verb قَواعِدُ الإعْلالِ في الأَجْوَفِ الواوِي

The rules of *I'laal* can be grouped into three general categories:

▷ **I'laal Sukooni** (الإِعْلالُ السُّكُونِي). This rule revolves around the principle that a Weak Letter cannot hold its own vowel and cannot be left without a vowel after the process of *I'laal* unless it forms a long vowel (in some forms of verbs).

▷ **I'laal Qalbl** (الإِعْلالُ القَلْبِي). This rule is related to the conversion of one Weak Letter to another letter.

▷ **I'laal Hazhfi** (الإِعْلالُ الحَذْفِي). An important principle of *I'laal* is that whenever two *Saakin* or voweless letters and found side by side, the Weak Letter is elided (الحَذْفُ) as a rule. These rules will be explained with more details in what follows:

▶ I'laal in the Past Tense Verb Active Voice Verb الإِعْلالُ في الفِعْلِ الماضِيِّ المَعْلُوم

The 'Arabs considered the pronunciation of a vowel on the Weak Letter in the *Ajwaf* Verb to be cumbersome (الثَّقِيلُ) and the vowel was generally elided or transferred to another letter (usually the preceding letter). In the Primary Verb, the 2nd Original Letter's vowel is always elided and the process of *I'laal Sukooni* transforms the Weak Letter into another letter more suitable for pronunciation.

Scholars differ regarding the patterns of the Past Tense Active Voice Verb. The prominent view is that there are only two patterns (فَعُلَ، فَعِلَ). They contend that the pattern: (فَعَلَ) is transferred (المَنْقُولُ) to the pattern of: (فَعُلَ).

After the vowel is removed, the letter Waw is transformed to Alif producing the pattern: فَالَ, as in: قَالَ. As a result, the pattern for the 1st Seeghah is the same irregardless of the original pattern, for example:

The pattern (فَعِلَ)   Root Letters (خَوِفَ)   Result (خَافَ)

The pattern (فَعُلَ)   Root Letters (طَوُلَ)   Result (طَالَ)

▶ Conjugation Of The Past Tense Active Voice Verb تَصْرِيفُ الماضِيِّ المَعْلُوم

To illustrate the conjugation of The Past Tense Verb, we will use two words: قَوُلٌ، خَوْفٌ. The verb derived from the Masdar (قَوُلٌ) was originally on the pattern of: (فَعَلَ يَفْعُلُ). As previously mentioned, this Past Tense pattern will be transformed into: (فَعُلَ). This will put the verb on the pattern of: قَوُلَ يَقُولُ or فَعُلَ يَفْعُلُ.

For the second word, we will derive a verb from the Masdar (خَوْفٌ) on the pattern of:

خَوِفَ يَخْوَفُ or فَعِلَ يَفْعَلُ. In both instances, the rule of *I'laal Sukooni* dictates that the Weak Letter, namely Waw, cannot support its own vowel. Therefore, the vowel is elided and the letter is transformed to Alif which is complementary to the vowel preceeding the Weak Letter (*Fathah*). Thus, we arrive at the form of the 1st Seeghah: قَالَ، خَافَ, respectively.

The 1st Seeghah through the 5th Seeghah will be conjugated in the same manner as all other Active Voice verbs: فَعَلَ، فَعَلا، فَعَلُوا، فَعَلَتْ، فَعَلَتا

قَالَ، قَالا، قَالُوا، قَالَتْ، قَالَتا – خَافَ، خَافا، خَافُوا، خَافَتْ، خَافَتا

In the sixth Seeghah (the Feminine Plural), the form would be: قَالْنَ based on the pattern: فَعَلْنَ. The rule of *I'laal Hazhfi*, dictates that two *Saakin* letters cannot exist side by side as is the case in this Seeghah (both the Alif and Lam are *Saakin*). Based on the rule, the (transformed) Weak Letter is elided resulting in: قَلْنَ and خَفْنَ. This is not, however, its final form. If we observe the formation of this verb by referring the original pattern without *I'laal,* it will be easier to arrive at its final form. The original pattern of this Seeghah is (قَوُلْنَ) and (خَوِفْنَ). The vowel of the 2nd Original Letter (*Dhammah* and *Kasrah*, respectively) is shifted to the 1st Original Letter. After becoming *Saakin*, the Weak Letter Waw is elided (due to the rule of *I'laal Hazhfi*):

خُوِفْنَ خِوُفْنَ خِفْنَ،   قُوْلْنَ قُوُلْنَ قُلْنَ

According to this, in the 6th Seeghah, the vowel on 1st Original Letter will be
Dhammah whn the original patterns were (فَعُلَ) and (فَعَلَ) and Kasrah for the pattern
(فَعِلَ). Also, as it is a condition that the 3rd Original Letter is Saakin in the remaining
Seeghah (7-14), the basic form remains the same while the Pronouns of the Subject
(الضَّمائرُ لفاعِلي) are suffixed to the end:

قُلْتَ، قُلْتُما، قُلْتُمْ قُلْتِ، قُلْتُما، قُلْتُنَّ، قُلْتُ، قُلْنا

خِفْتَ، خِفْتُما، خِفْتُمْ خِفْتِ، خِفْتُما، خِفْتُنَّ، خِفْتُ، خِفْنا

▶ I'laal in the Past Tense Verb Passive Voice Verb الإعلالُ في الماضيِ المَجهُولِ

The Past Tense Passive Tense Verb (الماضيُّ المَجهُولُ) is formed on the pattern of: (فُعِلَ), which would put the root letters on the pattern of: (قُوِلَ) and (خُوِفَ). In this pattern, the rule of I'laal Sukooni is that the vowel on the Weak Letter is transferred to the preceding letter leaving the Weak Letter Saakin. Then, the Weak Letter is transformed to Yaa' to complement the vowel on the letter before it, as in:

$$ قُوِلَ قُوْلَ قِيلَ، \quad خُوِفَ خُوْفَ خِيفَ $$

Due to the fact that the Weak Letter forms an appropriate long vowel after its transformation, it is permissible that it remains Saakin.

▶ Conjugation Of The Past Tense Passive Voice Verb تَصْرِيفُ الماضيِ المَجهُولِ

The Past Tense Passive Voice Verb is conjugated in the same manner as the Active Voice in Seeghah 1-5:

$$ قِيلَ، قِيلا، قِيلُوا، قِيلَتْ، قِيلَتا، \quad خِيفَ، خِيفا، خِيفُوا خِيفَتْ، خِيفَتا $$

Like the 6th Seeghah of the Active Voice Verb, the vowel that was originally on the Weak Letter (Kasrah) is shifted to the 1st Original Letter and the Saakin Weak Letter (Waw) is elided:

خُوِفْنَ خِوِفْنَ خِفْنَ،   قُوِلْنَ قِوِلْنَ قِلْنَ،

Thereafter, it remains in this form with the Pronouns of the subject being suffixed to

the verb: قُلْتَ، قُلْتُما، قُلْتُم، قُلْتِ، قُلْتُما، قُلْتُنَّ، قُلْتُ، قُلْنا

خِفْتَ، خِفْتُما، خِفْتُم، خِفْتِ، خِفْتُما، خِفْتُنَّ، خِفْتُ، خِفْنا

▶ I'laal in the Present Tense Verb Active Voice الإِعْلالُ في المُضارِع المَعْلُوم

The Present Tense Active Voice Verb will have two patterns in the *Ajwaf* with Waw

Verb: (يَفْعُلُ) and (يَفْعَلُ). The third pattern: (يَفْعِلُ) is only associated with the *Ajwaf* with

Yaa'.

Again, the 'Arabs considered a vowel on the Weak Letter as *Thaqeel* or troublesome.

The vowel of the Weak Letter is shifted to the letter preceding it. When it forms a long

vowel, no further change is warranted. In the pattern (يَفْعُلُ). When the vowel is shifted

forward, the Weak Letter becomes *Saakin* forming a long vowel: قُوُلُ يَقُوُلُ.

In the pattern of: (يَفْعَلُ), when the vowel is shifted from the Weak Letter to the

preceding letter a long vowel is not formed: يَخْوَفُ > يَخْوُفُ. Therefore, *I'laal* dictates

that the Weak Letter must be transformed to Alif to complement the vowel on the

preceding letter (*Fathah*): يَخَافُ > يَخْوَفُ.

▶ Conjugation Of The Present Tense Active Voice Verb تَصْرِيفُ الْمُضَارِعِ الْمَعْلُوم

After forming the 1st Seeghah يَقُولُ and يَخَافُ, the next four Seeghah are conjugated

predictably: يَقُولانِ، يَقُولُونَ، تَقُولُ، تَقُولانِ. I'laal will only occur in the 6th Seeghah due to

the meeting of two *Saakin* letters: يَقُوْلْنَ and يَخَافْنَ. As a result, the Weak Letter is

elided: يَقُوْلْنَ > يَقُلْنَ and يَخَافْنَ > يَخَفْنَ. Of course, this situation arises again in the

2nd person feminine plurals (Seeghah 12), otherwise, no other instance of I'laal

occurs:

١ تَقُولُ، تَقُولانِ، تَقُولُونَ، تَقُولِينَ، تَقُولانِ، تَقُلْنَ، أَقُولُ، نَقُولُ

تَخَافُ، تَخَافانِ، تَخَافُونَ، تَخَافِينَ، تَخَافانِ، تَخَفْنَ، أَخَافُ، نَخَافُ

▶ I'laal In The Present Tense Passive Voice Verb الْإِعْلالُ فِي الْمُضَارِعِ الْمَجْهُولِ

Applying the same principles of *I'laal*, it is necessary to convert the Weak Letter in the

Passive Voice as well. Based on the pattern: يُفْعَلُ, the verb would be: يُقْوَلُ and يُخْوَفُ.

The vowel on the Weak Letter is shifted to the preceeding letter leaving the Weak

Letter *Saakin*. As a result of becoming *Saakin*, the Weak Letter is transformed to Alif

which complements the vowel on the preceeding letter:

$$\text{يُقُوْلُ يَقُوْلُ يُقَالُ،} \qquad \text{يُخُوْفُ يُخُوْفُ يُخَافُ}$$

Thereafter, *I'laal* only occurs in the Seeghah of the Feminine Plurals (6 & 12) where two *Saakin* letters meet and the Weak Letter is elided, as in:

$$\text{يُقَالْنَ يَقُلْنَ،} \qquad \text{يُخَافْنَ يُخَفْنَ}$$

▶ I'laal In The Command Verbs الإِعْلالُ في الأَمْرِ

In the Active Voice Command Verb (الأَمْرُ المَعْلُومُ) of the third and first person, *I'laal* occurs in the 1st, 4th, 13th and 14th Seeghah due to the rule of *I'laal Hazhfi* and the Weak Letter is elided:

$$\text{لِيَقُلْ، لِتَقُلْ، لِأَقُلْ، لِنَقُلْ، } - - \text{ لِيَخَفْ، لِتَخَفْ، لِأَخَفْ، لِنَخَفْ}$$

The 2nd Person Command Verb (الأَمْرُ الحَاضِرُ) has only one instance of *I'laal* that occurs in the 7th Seeghah (the masculine singular). Because the 1st Original Letter is vowelled, the *Ajwaf* Verb does not employ the *Hamzah* when forming the Command Verb.

Rather, it only removes the Particle of the Present Tense (حَرْفُ المُضارِع) and makes the end of the verb *Saakin*. When the verb is made *Saakin* at the end, two *Saakin* letters meet. According to the rule, the Weak Letter is elided resulting in the following:

تَقُولُ قُوْلُ قُوْلْ قُلْ،   تَخَافُ خَافُ خَافْ خَفْ

The remaining Seeghah are formed by removing the Particle of the Present Tense and the *Noon Of I'raab* at the end:

خَافَا، خَافُوا، خَافِي، خَافَا، خَفْنَ   قُولا، قُولُوا، قُولِي، قُولا، قُلْنَ

I'laal has already occured in the 12th Seeghah before the Command Verb is formed, as in: تَقُلْنَ and تَخَفْنَ. Therefore, only the Particle of the Present Tense need be removed to form this Seeghah of the Command Verb.

All the forms of these two verbs will be contained in the following tables:

Table 3.6 - The Active Voice Ajwaf With Waw Verb On The Pattern Of: فَعَلَ يَفْعُلُ

قالَ، يَقُولُ، قُلْ، لِيَقُلْ، قِيلَ، يُقالُ، لِيُقَلْ هُوَ قَوْلٌ و قائِلٌ و مَقُولٌ

الجَمع	المُثَنَّى	المُفْرَد	الماضِيُ المَعْلُوم
قالُوا	قالا	قالَ	الغائِب:
قُلْنَ	قالَتا	قالَتْ	الغائِبة:
قُلْتُمْ	قُلْتُما	قُلْتَ	المُخاطَب:
قُلْتُنَّ	قُلْتُما	قُلْتِ	المُخاطَبة:
قُلْنا		قُلْتُ	المُتَكَلِّم:

الجَمع	المُثَنَّى	المُفْرَد	المُضارِعُ المَعْلُوم
يَقُولُونَ	يَقُولانِ	يَقُولُ	الغائِب:
يَقُلْنَ	تَقُولانِ	تَقُولُ	الغائِبة:
تَقُولُونَ	تَقُولانِ	تَقُولُ	المُخاطَب:
تَقُلْنَ	تَقُولانِ	تَقُولِينَ	المُخاطَبة:
نَقُولُ		أَقُولُ	المُتَكَلِّم:

الجَمع	المُثَنَّى	المُفْرَد	الأَمْرُ المَعْلُوم
لِيَقُولُوا	لِيَقُولا	لِيَقُلْ	الغائِب:
لِيَقُلْنَ	لِتَقُولا	لِتَقُلْ	الغائِبة:
قُولُوا	قُولا	قُلْ	المُخاطَب:
قُلْنَ	قُولا	قُولِي	المُخاطَبة:
لِنَقُلْ		لأَقُلْ	المُتَكَلِّم:

Table 3.7 - The Passive Voice Verb On The Pattern Of: فُعِلَ يُفْعَلُ

الماضِي المَجْهُول	المُفْرَد	المُثَنَّى	الجَمْع
الغائِب:	قِيلَ	قِيلا	قِيلُوا
الغائِبَة:	قِيلَتْ	قِيلَتا	قِلْنَ
المُخاطَب:	قِلْتَ	قِلْتُما	قِلْتُمْ
المُخاطَبَة:	قِلْتِ	قِلْتُما	قِلْتُنَّ
المُتَكَلِّم:	قِلْتُ		قِلْنا

المُضارِعُ المَجْهُول	المُفْرَد	المُثَنَّى	الجَمْع
الغائِب:	يُقالُ	يُقالانِ	يُقالُونَ
الغائِبَة:	تُقالُ	تُقالانِ	يُقَلْنَ
المُخاطَب:	تُقالُ	تُقالانِ	تُقالُونَ
المُخاطَبَة:	تُقالِينَ	تُقالانِ	تُقَلْنَ
المُتَكَلِّم:	أُقالُ		نُقالُ

الأَمْرُ المَجْهُول	المُفْرَد	المُثَنَّى	الجَمْع
الغائِب:	لِيُقَلْ	لِيُقالا	لِيُقالُوا
الغائِبَة:	لِتُقَلْ	لِتُقالا	لِيُقَلْنَ
المُخاطَب:	لِتُقَلْ	لِتُقالا	لِتُقالُوا
المُخاطَبَة:	لِتُقالي	لِتُقالا	لِتُقَلْنَ
المُتَكَلِّم:	لِأُقَلْ		لِنُقَلْ

Table 3.8 - Active Voice Ajwaf With Waw Verb On The Pattern Of: فَعِلَ يَفْعَلُ

خَافَ، يَخَافُ، خَفْ، لِيَخَفْ، خِيفَ، يُخَافُ، لِيُخَفْ هُوَ خَوْفٌ و خَائِفٌ و مَخُوفٌ

الجَمْع	المُثَنَّى	المُفْرَد	الماضِي المَعْلُوم
خَافُوا	خَافَا	خَافَ	الغائِب:
خِفْنَ	خَافَتَا	خَافَتْ	الغائِبَة:
خِفْتُم	خِفْتُما	خِفْتَ	المُخاطَب:
خِفْتُنَّ	خِفْتُما	خِفْتِ	المُخاطَبَة:
خِفْنا		خِفْتُ	المُتَكَلِّم:

الجَمْع	المُثَنَّى	المُفْرَد	المُضارِعُ المَعْلُوم
يَخافُونَ	يَخافانِ	يَخافُ	الغائِب:
يَخَفْنَ	تَخافانِ	تَخافُ	الغائِبَة:
تَخافُونَ	تَخافانِ	تَخافُ	المُخاطَب:
تَخَفْنَ	تَخافانِ	تَخافِينَ	المُخاطَبَة:
نَخافُ		أخافُ	المُتَكَلِّم:

الجَمْع	المُثَنَّى	المُفْرَد	الأَمْرُ المَعْلُوم
لِيَخافُوا	لِيَخافا	لِيَخَفْ	الغائِب:
لِيَخَفْنَ	لِتَخافا	لِتَخَفْ	الغائِبَة:
خافُوا	خافا	خَفْ	المُخاطَب:
خَفْنَ	خافَ	خافِي	المُخاطَبَة:
لِنَخَفْ		لِأَخَفْ	المُتَكَلِّم:

Table 3.9 - The Passive Voice Verb On The Pattern Of: فُعِلَ يُفعَلُ

الجَمع	المُثَنَّى	المُفرَد	الماضِيُ المَجهُول
خِيفُوا	خِيفا	خِيفَ	الغائب:
خِفْنَ	خُيِفَتا	خِيفَتْ	الغائبة:
خِفْتُمْ	خِفْتُما	خِفْتَ	المُخاطَب:
خِفْتُنَّ	خِفْتُما	خِفْتِ	المُخاطَبَة:
خِفْنا		خِفْتُ	المُتَكَلِّم:

الجَمع	المُثَنَّى	المُفرَد	المُضارِعُ المَجهُول
يُخافُونَ	يُخافانِ	يُخافُ	الغائب:
يُخَفْنَ	تُخافانِ	تُخافُ	الغائبة:
تُخافُونَ	تُخافانِ	تُخافُ	المُخاطَب:
تُخَفْنَ	تُخافانِ	تُخافِينَ	المُخاطَبَة:
نُخافُ		أُخافُ	المُتَكَلِّم:

الجَمع	المُثَنَّى	المُفرَد	الأَمرُ المَجهُول
لِيُخافُوا	لِيُخافا	لِيُخَفْ	الغائب:
لِيُخَفْنَ	لِتُخافا	لِتُخَفْ	الغائبة:
لِتُخافُوا	لِتُخافا	لِتُخَفْ	المُخاطَب:
لِتُخَفْنَ	لِتُخافا	لِتُخافِي	المُخاطَبَة:
لِنُخَفْ		لِأُخَفْ	المُتَكَلِّم:

▶ **AJWAF WITH YAA'** الأَجوَفُ اليَائي

For the most part, the *Ajwaf* with Yaa' verb follows the same general rules of *I'laal* that are associated with the *Ajwaf* with Waw with a few exceptions that will be mentioned in their appropriate places.

▷ **I'laal in the Ajwaf With Yaa" Verb** الإِعلالُ في الأَجوَفِ اليَائي

Naturally, the *Ajwaf* with Yaa' Verb is found on only two patterns: فَعَلَ and فَعِلَ. The third pattern (فَعُلَ) is not found in the verb with Yaa' since its pronunciation is cumbersome (الثَّقيل). A number of scholars are also of the opinion that the pattern (فَعَلَ) is transformed to the pattern (فَعِلَ) meaning in reality, that this is the only pattern to be found. The rules of *I'laal* mentioned in the *Ajwaf* with Waw Verb apply to the *Ajwaf* with Yaa' verb, without exception. Refer below to a summary of the patterns:

Verb Pattern	(فَعَلَ يَفْعِلُ)	(فَعِلَ يَفْعَلُ)
Past Tense Active Voice Verb	باعَ	هابَ
Pres. Tense Active Voice Verb	يَبيعُ	يَهابُ
2nd Pers. Command Verb	بِعْ	هَبْ
Active Voice Command Verb	لِيَبِعْ	لِيَهَبْ

Past Tense Passive Voice Verb	بِيعَ	هِيبَ
Present Tense Passive Voice Verb	يُباعُ	يُهابُ
Passive Voice Command Verb	لِيُبَعْ	لِيُهَبْ

▶ CONCLUDING NOTES

It should be noted that the defective verb (لَيسَ) also employs the rule I'laal Hazhfi. Unlike other verbs, its 2nd Original Letter remains Saakin without undergoing I'laal. It is defective from the point of view that it only is found in the form of the Past Tense, it has no Present Tense, no Command Verbs and No Passive Voice. Also, from the point of view of its meaning, it is a verb of negation that is used to negate noun sentences, such as:

لَيس مُضطَفَى مُدَرِّساً (Mustafa is not a teacher) مُضطَفَى مُدَرِّسٌ (Mustafa is a teacher)

Table 3.10 - Conjugation Of The Defective Verb لَيسَ

الجَمْع	المُثَنَّى	المُفْرَد		الماضي
لَيسُوا	لَيسا	لَيسَ	الغائب:	
لَسنَ	لَيسَتا	لَيسَتْ	الغائبة:	
لَستُمْ	لَستُما	لَستَ	المُخاطَب:	
لَستُنَّ	لَستُما	لَستِ	المُخاطَبة:	
لَسنا		لَستُ	المُتَكَلِّم:	

Full conjugation of the Ajwaf with Yaa' verb is given in the tables below:

Table 3.11 - Active Voice Ajwaf Verb With Yaa' On The Pattern Of: فَعَلَ يَفْعِلُ

باعَ، يَبِيعُ، بِعْ، لِيَبِيعْ، بِيعَ، يُباعُ، لِيُبَعْ هُوَ بَيْعٌ و بائِعٌ و مَبِيعٌ

الجَمْع	المُثَنَّى	المُفْرَد	الماضِي المَعلُوم
باعُوا	باعا	باعَ	الغائِب:
بِعْنَ	باعَتا	باعَتْ	الغائِبَة:
بِعْتُمْ	بِعْتُما	بِعْتَ	المُخاطَب:
بِعْتُنَّ	بِعْتُما	بِعْتِ	المُخاطَبَة:
بِعْنا		بِعْتُ	المُتَكَلِّم:

الجَمْع	المُثَنَّى	المُفْرَد	المُضارِعُ المَعلُوم
يَبِيعُونَ	يَبِيعانِ	يَبِيعُ	الغائِب:
يَبِعْنَ	تَبِيعانِ	تَبِيعُ	الغائِبَة:
تَبِيعُونَ	تَبِيعانِ	تَبِيعُ	المُخاطَب:
تَبِعْنَ	تَبِيعانِ	تَبِيعِينَ	المُخاطَبَة:
نَبِيعُ		أَبِيعُ	المُتَكَلِّم:

الجَمْع	المُثَنَّى	المُفْرَد	الأَمْرُ المَعلُوم
لِيَبِيعُوا	لِيَبِيعا	لِيَبِيعْ	الغائِب:
لِيَبِعْنَ	لِتَبِيعا	لِتَبِعْ	الغائِبَة:
بِيعُوا	بِيعا	بِعْ	المُخاطَب:
بِعْنَ	بِيعا	بِيعِي	المُخاطَبَة:
لِنَبِعْ		لِأَبِعْ	المُتَكَلِّم:

Table 3.12 - Passive Voice Ajwaf With Yaa' Verb On The Pattern Of: فُعِلَ يُفْعَ

الجَمْع	المُثَنَّى	المُفْرَد	الماضِي المَجْهُول
بِيعُوا	بِيعا	بِيعَ	الغائِب:
بِعْنَ	بِيعَتا	بِيعَتْ	الغائِبَة:
بِعْتُمْ	بِعْتُما	بِعْتَ	المُخاطَب:
بِعْتُنَّ	بِعْتُما	بِعْتِ	المُخاطَبَة:
بِعْنا		بِعْتُ	المُتَكَلِّم:

الجَمْع	المُثَنَّى	المُفْرَد	المُضارِعُ المَجْهُول
يُباعُونَ	يُباعانِ	يُباعُ	الغائِب:
يُبَعْنَ	تُباعانِ	تُباعُ	الغائِبَة:
تُباعُونَ	تُباعانِ	تُباعُ	المُخاطَب:
تُبَعْنَ	تُباعانِ	تُباعِينَ	المُخاطَبَة:
نُباعُ		أُباعُ	المُتَكَلِّم:

الجَمْع	المُثَنَّى	المُفْرَد	الأَمْرُ المَجْهُول
لِيُباعُوا	لِيُباعا	لِيُباعْ	الغائِب:
لِيُبَعْنَ	لِتُباعا	لِتُباعْ	الغائِبَة:
لِتُباعُوا	لِتُباعا	لِتُباعْ	المُخاطَب:
لِتُبَعْنَ	لِتُباعا	لِتُباعِي	المُخاطَبَة:
لِنُبَعْ		لِأُبَعْ	المُتَكَلِّم:

Table 3.13 - Active Voice Ajwaf With Yaa' Verb On The Pattern Of: فَعَلَ يَفْعَلُ

هابَ، يَهابُ، هَبْ، لِيَهَبْ، هِيبَ، يُهابُ، هِيبَ (مَهابَةً) هائِبٌ هُوَ هَيِّنَةً (مَهابَةً) هائِبٌ و مَهِيبٌ

الجَمْع	المُثَنَّى	المُفْرَد	الماضِي المَعْلُوم
هابُوا	هابا	هابَ	الغائِب:
هِبْنَ	هابَتا	هابَتْ	الغائِبَة:
هِبْتُمْ	هِبْتُما	هِبْتَ	المُخاطَب:
هِبْتُنَّ	هِبْتُما	هِبْتِ	المُخاطَبَة:
هِبْنا		هِبْتُ	المُتَكَلِّم:

الجَمْع	المُثَنَّى	المُفْرَد	المُضارِع المَعْلُوم
يَهابُونَ	يَهابانِ	يَهابُ	الغائِب:
يَهَبْنَ	تَهابانِ	تَهابُ	الغائِبَة:
تَهابُونَ	تَهابانِ	تَهابُ	المُخاطَب:
تَهَبْنَ	تَهابانِ	تَهابِينَ	المُخاطَبَة:
نَهابُ		أهابُ	المُتَكَلِّم:

الجَمْع	المُثَنَّى	المُفْرَد	الأمْر المَعْلُوم
لِيَهابُوا	لِيَهابا	لِيَهَبْ	الغائِب:
لِيَهَبْنَ	لِتَهابا	لِتَهَبْ	الغائِبَة:
هابُوا	هابا	هَبْ	المُخاطَب:
هَبْنَ	هابا	هابِي	المُخاطَبَة:
لِنَهَبْ		لأَهَبْ	المُتَكَلِّم:

Table 3.14 - Passive Voice Ajwaf With Yaa' Verb On The Pattern Of: فُعِلَ يُفْعَلُ

الجَمْع	المُثَنَّى	المُفْرَد	الماضِيُ المَجْهُول
هِيبوا	هِيبا	هِيبَ	الغائِب:
هِبْنَ	هِيبَتا	هِيبَتْ	الغائِبَة:
هِبْتُمْ	هِبْتُما	هِبْتَ	المُخاطَب:
هِبْتُنَّ	هِبْتُما	هِبْتِ	المُخاطَبَة:
هِبْنا		هِبْتُ	المُتَكَلِّم:

الجَمْع	المُثَنَّى	المُفْرَد	المُضارِعُ المَجْهُول
يُهابونَ	يُهابانِ	يُهابُ	الغائِب:
يُهَبْنَ	تُهابانِ	تُهابُ	الغائِبَة:
تُهابونَ	تُهابانِ	تُهابُ	المُخاطَب:
تُهَبْنَ	تُهابانِ	تُهابِينَ	المُخاطَبَة:
نُهابُ		أُهابُ	المُتَكَلِّم:

الجَمْع	المُثَنَّى	المُفْرَد	الأَمْرُ المَجْهُول
لِيُهابوا	لِيُهابا	لِيُهَبْ	الغائِب:
لِيُهَبْنَ	لِتُهابا	لِتُهَبْ	الغائِبَة:
لِتُهابوا	لِتُهابا	لِتُهَبْ	المُخاطَب:
لِتُهَبْنَ	لِتُهابا	لِتُهابي	المُخاطَبَة:
لِنُهَبْ		لِأُهَبْ	المُتَكَلِّم:

SECTION THREE

The Naaqis Verb

الفِعْلُ النَّاقِصُ

The *Naaqis* Kalimah is that word whose third Original Letter is a Weak Letter (مُعْتَلُّ اللَّامِ).
The *Naaqis* Kalimah is also of two types:

> • **Naaqis with Waw** (النَّاقِصُ الواوِي), as in: دَعْوَةٌ.

> • **Naaqis with Yaa'** (النَّاقِصُ اليآئِي), as in رَمِيٌّ.

▶ **NAAQIS WITH WAW** النَّاقِصُ الواوِي

The *Naaqis* Verb, whether with Waw or Yaa', undergoes a great deal of transformation in its various forms and great attention should be paid to the various rules of *I'laal* which govern the formation of *Naaqis* words, both nouns and verbs. There are a number of rules of *I'laal* related specifically to the *Naaqis* Verb with Waw Verb. These rules will be mentioned in the appropriate places.

▷ **I'LAAL IN THE PAST TENSE ACTIVE VOICE VERB** الإِعْلالُ في الماضِيِّ المَعْلُومِ

To illustrate the methodology of *I'laal*, we will use the Masdar دَعْوَةٌ or دُعَاءٌ (both are considered to be root words). The pattern of the first Seeghah of the verb will be on the pattern of: فَعَلَ. The verb, then, according to the pattern should be: دَعَوَ. However, according to the rules of *I'laal*, the verb cannot remain on this pattern since the Weak Letter cannot carry its own vowel.

The rule governing the *Naaqis* verb dictates that the Weak Letter does not support its own vowel, in most instances. The vowel on the Weak Letter is elided leaving it *Saakin*. The *Saakin* Weak Letter will be transformed to Alif to complement the vowel on the preceding letter. Based on this, the verb will be changed from: دَعَوَ to: دَعَا.

The second Seeghah, the Masculine Dual, is on the pattern of: فَعَلَا or دَعَوَا. It is not possible to simply add on the Alif of the Dual to the end of the first Seeghah as ususal since the first Seeghah has an Alif at its end (دَعَا) resultant from the conversion of the Weak Letter. As a result, the rule of *I'laal* is not applied here since it would cause two *Saakin* letters to exist side by side. Therefore, it remains on its original pattern دَعَوَا.

The third Seeghah, the Masculine Plural, is on the pattern of: فَعَلُوا and the verb is on the pattern of: دَعَوُوا. According to the rule of *I'laal*, the vowel on the Weak Letter will be elided. Then, the Weak Letter will be transformed to Alif to complement the preceding letter: دَعَاوُوا. However, the creation of this Alif also creates a situation where two *Saakin* letters are existing side by side. To remedy the conflict between the two *Saakin* letters, the Alif (transformed from the Weak Letter) will be elided: دَعَوُوا.

The same rule is applied in the next Seeghah, the Feminine Singular, and the same conflict arises and the solution is the same. The fourth Seeghah is on the pattern of: فَعَلَتْ or دَعَوَتْ. According to the same rule, the Weak Letter will be changed to Alif after eliding its vowel دَعَاتْ. The conflict of two *Saakin* letters being joined together dictates that the Weak Letter (Alif) is elided دَعَتْ. The Fifth Seeghah simply adds the Alif of the Dual to the end of the fourth Seeghah: دَعَتَا.

Beginning with the sixth Seeghah, the third Original Letter must be *Saakin* as a rule, therefore, the Weak Letter will become Saakin beginning in this Seeghah: دَعَوْنَ on the pattern of: فَعَلْنَ.

Since the Weak Letter is not originally vowelled according to the pattern, there is no need to apply any rule of *I'laal*. The Weak Letter will remain *Saakin* in this manner until the last Seeghah. All together, the Past Tense Active Voice Verb is conjugated as follows:

دَعَا، دَعَوْا، دَعَتْ، دَعَتَا، دَعَوْنَ، دَعَوْتَ، دَعَوْتُمَا، دَعَوْتُمْ،

دَعَوْتِ، دَعَوْتُمَا، دَعَوْتُنَّ، دَعَوْتُ، دَعَوْنَا.

▷ **I'LAAL IN THE PRESENT TENSE ACTIVE VOICE VERB** الإعلالُ في المُضارِعِ المَعْلُوم

The first Seeghah of the Present Tense Active Voice Verb is based on the pattern of: يَدْعُوُ or يَفْعُلُ. According to the rule of *I'laal*, the vowel on the Weak Letter is elided leaving the Weak Letter *Saakin*. Due to the fact the Weak Letter (Waw) also complements the Dhammah on the preceding letter, it is possible to remain *Saakin* as any other vowel would be inappropriate: يَدْعُو.

The next Seeghah, the Masculine Dual will add the Alif-Noon suffix to the first Seeghah. In order to add this Dual suffix, the Weak Letter is made Maftooh since leaving it *Saakin* results in the meeting of two *Saakin* letters: يَدْعُوَانِ on the pattern of: يَفْعُلانِ. Forming the third Seeghah according to the pattern يَفْعُلُونَ results in the meeting of two *Saakin* letters يَدْعُوُونَ, therefore, the Weak Letter (the first Waw) is elided: يَدْعُونَ. The fourth and fifth Seeghah are similar to the first and second Seeghah: تَدْعُو and: تَدْعُوَانِ.

The sixth Seeghah will find the third Original Letter Saakin, as usual: يَدْعُوْنَ. Note that this Seeghah is the same as the Masculine Plural. Due to the fact that the Weak Letter is Saakin according to the pattern يَفْعُلْنَ, no I'laal occurs. The remaining Seeghah are formed in a manner similar to what has been mentioned.

In the tenth Seeghah, the 2nd Person Feminine Singular, the Weak Letter will be elided due to the conflict between two Saakin letters being side by side, as in: تَدْعُوْيْنَ. Then, the letter preceding the Yaa' (the sign of the Pronoun of the Subject) will be changed to Kasrah for agreement: تَدْعِيْنَ. All together, the Present Tense Active Voice Verb will conjugated as follows:

يَدْعُوْ، يَدْعُوَانِ، يَدْعُوْنَ، تَدْعُوْ، تَدْعُوَانِ، تَدْعُوْنَ، يَدْعُوْ، تَدْعُوَانِ، تَدْعُوْنَ،

تَدْعِيْنَ، تَدْعُوَانِ، تَدْعُوْنَ، أَدْعُوْ، نَدْعُوْ

▷ **I'LAAL IN THE ACTIVE VOICE COMMAND VERBS** الإعلالُ في الأَمرِ المَعلُوم

One important rule to be noted in the Command Verbs is that both types of Command Verbs will be Saakin at the end due to different reasons. The 2nd Person Command Verb, it is Saakin due to the verb being Mabniy while in the Active Voice Command Verb it is due to the verb being in the state of Jazm. In the Naaqis Verb, the Weak Letter is generally Saakin whenever it occurs at the end of the verb, as in the first Seeghah يَدْعُوْ. Therefore, to indicated that the verb is Saakin the Weak Letter will be elided all together. As mentioned, this only occurrs when the Weak Letter is found as the last letter in a verb. According to this, the Command Verbs of the third person (1st Seeghah) will be based on the 1st Seeghah of the Active Voice Present Tense يَدْعُوْ, the Weak Letter will be elided when the Command Verb is formed, as in: لِيَدْعُ.

In the 2nd person Command Verb, the pattern is: اُفْعُلْ, based on this pattern, the verb would be اُدْعُوْ being derived from تَدْعُوْ. Since both forms are Saakin, the Weak Letter is elided in the Command Verb to indicate that the verb is Mabniy or fixed at its end اُدْعُ. A complete conjugation of the Command Verb will be given shortly.

▷ **I'LAAL IN THE PAST TENSE PASSIVE VOICE VERB** الإعلالُ في الماضيِّ المَجْهُول

The Passive Voice, being based on the pattern فُعِلَ also dictates that *I'laal* should occur to rectify the vowelization of the Weak Letter. According to the pattern, the verb should be: دُعِوَ. When the vowel is elided, leaving the Weak Letter *Saakin*, the Weak Letter must be transformed to a letter which complements the preceding letter which is Maksoor. Yaa' is the letter which complements Kasrah and the Waw is transformed to Yaa': دُعِي. It will be mentioned in the section dealing with *Naaqis* with Yaa', that whenever the letter Yaa' is the final consonant in a word and it is preceded by Kasrah, the Yaa' can accept a vowel, provided that it is Fathah. Therefore, the final form of the Passive Voice Verb is: دُعِيَ.

The 2nd Seeghah, the Masculine Dual, simply adds the Alif of the Dual to the first Seeghah, as in: دُعِيَا. In the Masculine Plural, the pattern is: فُعِلُوا, meaning that the verb should be دُعِوُوْا. When the vowel on the Weak Letter is elided, two *Saakin* letters are left existing side by side دُعُوْوْا. As is the rule, the Weak Letter is elided دُعُوْا. The Feminine Singular is formed in a similar manner as the Masculine singular with the Feminine Taa' being suffixed to its end: دُعِيَتْ. The next Seeghah, the Feminine Dual simply suffixs the Alif of the Dual to Feminine Singular: دُعِيَتا.

From the 6th Seeghah to the 14th, the pattern dictates that the third Original Letter (Waw) must be Saakin. If we apply the rule without *I'laal*, the verb would be: دُعِوْنَ. Of course, this vowelization pattern is impossible, therefore *I'laal* is required to transform it to a form that can be pronounced: دُعِينَ. The Waw is transformed to Yaa' to complement the Kasrah on the preceding letter. The remaining Seeghah will keep this same form while suffixing the Pronouns of the Subject to the verb.

▷ **I'LAAL IN THE PRESENT TENSE PASSIVE VOICE VERB** الإِعْلالُ في المُضارِعِ المَجْهُولِ

The Present Tense Passive Voice Verb is on the pattern of: يُفْعَلُ, meaning that the original pattern of the verb would be: يُدْعَوُ. When the vowel on the Weak Letter (Waw) is elided, the Weak Letter will be changed to Alif: يُدْعَى to complement the Fathah on the preceding letter. Then, the Dhammah on the Weak Letter will be elided because the Alif Maqsoorah never accepts its own vowel يُدْعَى. The next Seeghah, the Masculine Dual, adds the Alif-Noon suffix to the verb. Whenever something is suffixed to Alif Maqsoorah, the Alif is converted to Yaa', as in: يُدْعَيانِ. In the third Seeghah, according to the original pattern يُفْعَلُونَ, the verb should be: يُدْعَوُونَ. Again, because the letter preceding the Weak Letter Waw is Maftooh, the Waw is converted to Alif يُدْعَاوْنَ. This leaves two Saakin letters side by side and the Alif is elided resulting in the form: يُدْعَوْنَ.

▷ **I'LAAL IN THE PASSIVE VOICE COMMAND VERB** الإِعْلالُ في الأَمْرِ المَجْهُولِ

The Passive Voice Command Verb is formed in a similar manner to what has been mentioned in the Active Voice Command Verb. In those Seeghah in which the Weak Letter is the last consonant of the verb (Seeghah 1,4,7,13,14), the Weak Letter will be elided to indicate the state of Jazm, as in: يُدْعَى > لِيُدْعَ.

► CONCLUDING NOTES

As previously mentioned, the Weak Letter, as the third Original Letter and the last
consonant of the verb, will always become *Saakin* as a result of *I'laal*. One exception to this
rule can be found. This is when the *Naaqis* with Waw is Mansoob or in the state of Nasb.
The state of Nasb, like the state of Jazm, is caused by the presence of a Particle, like: أَنْ or
لَنْ. In this state, the verb will accept Fathah as the sign of Nasb, as in: يَدْعُو > أَنْ يَدْعُوَ.

If the Weak Letter Waw has been converted to another letter, like Alif Maqsoorah, It will not
accept Fathah (or any other vowel), as in: يُدْعَى > أَنْ يُدْعَى.

▷ CONJUGATION OF THE NAAQIS WITH WAW VERB تَصْرِيفُ النَّاقِصِ الوَاوِي

In pratical terms, the *Naaqis* Verb with Waw is only found on one pattern: فَعَلَ يَفْعُلُ.
Some scholars maintain that another pattern, namely: فَعِلَ يَفْعَلُ also can be found.
They cite that the Kalimah (رضو) is found on this pattern, as in: رَضِوَ. However, the
rules of *I'laal* dictates that the Weak Letter is to be *Saakin* رَضْوَ. As this vowelization
pattern is improper, the Weak Letter is transformed to Yaa' to agree with the
preceding letter رَضِي. In reality, the verb appears the same as the *Naaqis* with Yaa'
verb (to mentioned shortly). In such a verb, the Yaa' which is preceded by Kasrah can
accept the vowel Fathah. As a result, the verb becomes: رَضِيَ. Therefore, even if the
root word is *Naaqis* with Waw, its final form puts it in the category of *Naaqis* with Yaa'.

A full conjugation of the verb دَعَا يَدْعُو is listed in the following tables:

Table 3.15 - The Active Voice Naaqis With Waw Verb On The Pattern Of: فَعَلَ يَفْعُلُ

دَعا، يَدْعُو، أُدْعُ، لِيَدْعُ، دُعِي، يُدْعَى، لِيُدْعَ هُوَ دَعْوَةٌ (دُعَاءٌ) داعٍ و مَدْعُوٌّ

الجَمْع	المُثَنَّى	المُفْرَد	الماضِي المَعْلُوم
دَعَوْا	دَعَوا	دَعا	الغائِب:
دَعَوْنَ	دَعَتا	دَعَتْ	الغائِبة:
دَعَوْتُم	دَعَوْتُما	دَعَوْتَ	المُخاطَب:
دَعَوْتُنَّ	دَعَوْتُما	دَعَوْتِ	المُخاطَبة:
دَعَوْنا		دَعَوْتُ	المُتَكَلِّم:

الجَمْع	المُثَنَّى	المُفْرَد	المُضارِع المَعْلُوم
يَدْعُونَ	يَدْعُوانِ	يَدْعُو	الغائِب:
يَدْعُونَ	تَدْعُوانِ	تَدْعُو	الغائِبة:
تَدْعُونَ	تَدْعُوانِ	تَدْعُو	المُخاطَب:
تَدْعُونَ	تَدْعُوانِ	تَدْعِينَ	المُخاطَبة:
نَدْعُو		أَدْعُو	المُتَكَلِّم:

الجَمْع	المُثَنَّى	المُفْرَد	الأَمْر المَعْلُوم
لِيَدْعُوا	لِيَدْعُوا	لِيَدْعُ	الغائِب:
لِيَدْعُونَ	لِتَدْعُوا	لِتَدْعُ	الغائِبة:
أُدْعُوا	أُدْعُوا	أُدْعُ	المُخاطَب:
أُدْعُونَ	أُدْعُوا	أُدْعِي	المُخاطَبة:
لِنَدْعُ		لِأَدْعُ	المُتَكَلِّم:

Table 3.16 - The Passive Voice Naaqis With Waw Verb On The Pattern Of: فُعِلَ يُفْعَلُ

الجَمْع	المُثَنَّى	المُفْرَد	الماضِي المَجْهُول
دُعُوا	دُعِيا	دُعِيَ	الغائِب:
دُعِينَ	دُعِيَتا	دُعِيَتْ	الغائِبَة:
دُعِيتُم	دُعِيتُما	دُعِيتَ	المُخاطَب:
دُعِيتُنَّ	دُعِيتُما	دُعِيتِ	المُخاطَبَة:
دُعِينا		دُعِيتُ	المُتَكَلِّم:

الجَمْع	المُثَنَّى	المُفْرَد	المُضارِعُ المَجْهُول
يُدْعَونَ	يُدْعَيانِ	يُدْعَى	الغائِب:
يُدْعَونَ	تُدْعَيانِ	تُدْعَى	الغائِبَة:
تُدْعَونَ	تُدْعَيانِ	تُدْعَى	المُخاطَب:
تُدْعَونَ	تُدْعَيانِ	تُدْعَيْنَ	المُخاطَبَة:
نُدْعَى		أُدْعَى	المُتَكَلِّم:

الجَمْع	المُثَنَّى	المُفْرَد	الأَمْر المَجْهُول
لِيُدْعَوا	لِيُدْعَيا	لِيُدْعَ	الغائِب:
لِيُدْعَونَ	لِيُدْعَيا	لِتُدْعَ	الغائِبَة:
لِتُدْعَوا	لِتُدْعَيا	لِتُدْعَ	المُخاطَب:
لِتُدْعَونَ	لِتُدْعَيا	لِتُدْعَيْ	المُخاطَبَة:
لِنُدْعَ		لِأُدْعَ	المُتَكَلِّم:

▶ **NAAQIS WITH YAA'** النَّاقِصُ اليَائِي

One important distinction of the *Naaqis* with Yaa' is that it is sometimes terminated with Yaa' and sometimes terminated with Alif Maqsoorah. What determines which letter the verb is terminated with is the vowel on the letter preceding the Weak Letter. When the Weak Letter is preceded by a letter vowelled with Fathah, the Weak Letter must be Alif Maqsoorah, as in: رَمَى. When the Weak Letter is preceded by a letter with Kasrah, the Weak Letter must be Yaa', as in: رَضِيَ. It is impossible for the Yaa' or Alif Maqsoorah to be preceded by Dhammah.

▷ **I'LAAL IN THE PAST TENSE ACTIVE VOICE VERB** الإِعلالُ في الماضِيِ المَعْلُوم

According to what has been mentioned in the previous paragraph, the *Naaqis* with Yaa' verb can be found on two patterns in the Past Tense, namely: فَعَلَ and فَعِلَ , as in: رَمَى and رَضِيَ. Also, the Alif and Yaa' are determined by the vowel preceding it, thus the pattern of the first Seeghah is relatively self-evident.

The 2nd Seeghah, however, based on the pattern: فَعَلا or فَعِلا, will find the Alif changed to Yaa'. This is due to the fact that Alif Maqsoorah can only exist as the final letter of a word. As it is necessary to suffix Alif (of the Dual) to the 1st Seeghah, it is necessary to convert the Alif to Yaa', as in: رَمَيا. With Yaa', the Alif of the Dual is simply suffixed, as in: رَضِيا. The 3rd Seeghah, on the pattern of: فَعَلُوا or فَعِلُوا, the verbs would be on the pattern of: رَمَيُوا and رَضِيُوا, respectively. However, it is not possible to vowelize the Weak Letter in this manner.

As mentioned previously, Alif never supports any vowel and Yaa' only supports Fathah with the condition that the preceding vowel is Kasrah. Therefore, the Dhammah on the Weak Letter is impossible.

In both instances, the vowel on the Weak Letter must be elided leaving the letter Saakin. This elision also allows two *Saakin* letters to exist side by side. Therefore, the Weak Letter must also be elided according to the rule of *I'laal*, as in: رَمَوْا > رَمَيُوْا and رَضِيُوْا > رَضُوْا. While the first verb is proper, the second has an unworkable vowel pattern as a *Saakin* Waw cannot be preceded by Kasrah. To correct the problem, the Kasrah is changed to Dhammah which complements the *Saakin* Waw: رَضُوْا.

The 4th Seeghah, on the pattern of: فَعَلَتْ and فَعِلَتْ, will have the verbs on the patterns of: رَمَيَتْ and رَضِيَتْ. Again, since the Alif cannot support a vowel, its vowel must be elided. The elision brings two *Saakin* letters together necessitating the elision of the Weak Letter producing: رَمَتْ. The 5th Seeghah simply suffixes the Alif of the Dual to the 4th Seeghah. The other verb is proper as the Yaa' may support Fathah when preceded by Kasrah.

As always, the 6th Seeghah dictates that the 3rd Original Letter (here the Weak Letter) is *Saakin*, based on the pattern: فَعَلْنَ and فَعِلْنَ, producing the verbs: رَمَيْنَ and رَضِينَ. From this point onward, the form of the verb remains constant

▷ **I'LAAL IN THE PRESENT TENSE ACTIVE VOICE VERB** الإِعْلالُ في المُضارِعِ المَعْلُوم

The pattern of the Present Tense for each of these verbs are: يَفْعَلُ and يَفْعِلُ respectively. The verbs will be: يَرْمِي and يَرْضَى. According to rule explained previously, neither Weak Letter can support a vowel with this vowelization pattern. Predictably, the 2nd Seeghah is يَرْمِيانِ and يَرْضَيانِ. The 3rd Seeghah, based on the patterns: يَفْعِلُونَ and يَفْعَلُونَ, produces the verbs: يَرْضَيُونَ and يَرْمِيُونَ. In both instances, the vowel on the Weak Letter must be elided producing two *Saakin* letters side by side. Therefore, the Weak Letter must also be elided producing the following: يَرْمِوْنَ and يَرْضَوْنَ.

The first has an improper vowel combination with the Kasrah preceding the *Saakin* Waw. The Kasrah must be changed to Dhammah: يَرْمُونَ. The 4th and 5th are made in a similar manner to the 1st and 2nd. The 6th Seeghah, based on the patterns: يَفْعِلْنَ and يَفْعَلْنَ, produces the verbs: يَرْمِينَ and يَرْضَيْنَ. The 10th Seeghah (تَفْعِلِينَ) and (تَفْعَلِينَ) produces: تَرْمِيِينَ and تَرْضَيِينَ. Again, both Weak Letters must have their vowels elided, then, the Weak Letter itself must be elided since it creates two *Saakin* letters side by side. The result is: تَرْضَيْنَ and تَرْمِينَ. Note that both of these forms are identical to the 12th Seeghah, the Feminine Plurals, although the Yaa' in the 12th Seeghah is the Weak letter and the sign of the pronoun of the subject in the 10th.

▷ **I'LAAL IN THE ACTIVE VOICE COMMAND VERBS** الإِعْلالُ في الأَمْرِ المَعْلُوم

Keeping in mind that the *Naaqis* Verb will elide the Weak Letter to indicate that it is *Saakin* at its end, you will form the Active Voice Command Verbs in a similar manner. For example, the Command Verb of the 1st Seeghah is: لِيَرْمِ and لِيَرْضَ.

In the 2nd person Command Verbs, the 7th Seeghah is إِرْمِ and إِرْضَ. Refer to the Tables below for a complete conjugation of the Command Verbs.

▷ **I'LAAL IN THE PAST TENSE PASSIVE VOICE VERB** الإِعلالُ في الماضِي المَجهُول

Based on the Passive Voice Pattern فُعِلَ, the two verbs will be: رُمِيَ and رُضِيَ respectively in the 1st Seeghah. The 2nd Seeghah is predictable: رُمِيَا and رُضِيَا. The 3rd Seeghah, based on the pattern: فُعِلُوا produces: رُمِيُوا and رُضِيُوا. As before, the vowel on the Weak Letter is elided, then, the Weak Letter itself must be elided due to two *Saakin* letters: رُمْوُا and رُضْوُا. The vowel combination dictates that the vowel on the 2nd Original Letter must be changed to Dhammah to complement the *Saakin* Waw at the end: رُمُوا and رُضُوا.

The remaining Seeghah have no I'laal and are formed according to the Passive Voice pattern.

▷ **I'LAAL IN THE PRESENT TENSE PASSIVE VOICE** الإِعلالُ في المُضارِع المَجهُول

Based on the pattern for the Present Tense Active Voice, يُفْعَلُ, the two verbs will be: يُرْمَى and يُرْضَى respectively. Both verbs will be conjugated in the same manner as the verb: يَرْضَى in the Active Voice. The only difference being that in the Passive Voice the Particle of the Present Tense (حَرْفُ المُضارِع) will be vowelled with Dhammah instead of Fathah يُرْضَى.

▶ CONCLUDING NOTES

The two important rules governing the formation of the Naaqis with Yaa' verb are:

▷ The verb will be terminated with Yaa' whenever the letter preceding the Weak Letter (i.e. the 2nd Original Letter) is vowelled with Kasrah. The verb will be terminated with Alif Maqsoorah whenever the letter preceding the Weak Letter is vowelled with Fathah.

▷ The nature of Alif Maqsoorah is that it is *Saakin* and cannot accept a vowel under any circumstances. If anything is suffixed to Alif Maqsoorah, it must be converted to Yaa' as Alif must always be the final letter of a word. Yaa', on the other hand, is also *Saakin* naturally, however, it can accept the vowel Fathah with the condition that the preceding letter is Kasrah.

A full conjugation of the *Naaqis* Verb is given in the following Tables:

Table 3.17 - The Naaqis With Yaa' Active Voice Verb On The Pattern Of: فَعَلَ يَفْعِلُ

رَمَى، يَرْمِي، إِرْمِ، لِيَرْمِ، رَمَى، يُرْمَى، لِيُرْمَ هُوَ رَمِيٌّ (رِمايَةً) و رامٍ و مَرْمِيٌّ

الجَمْع	المُثَنَّى	المُفْرَد	الماضِيُّ المَعْلُوم
رَمَوا	رَمَيا	رَمَى	الغائِب:
رَمَيْنَ	رَمَتا	رَمَتْ	الغائِبَة:
رَمَيْتُمْ	رَمَيْتُما	رَمَيْتَ	المُخاطَب:
رَمَيْتُنَّ	رَمَيْتُما	رَمَيْتِ	المُخاطَبَة:
رَمَيْنا		رَمَيْتُ	المُتَكَلِّم:

الجَمْع	المُثَنَّى	المُفْرَد	المُضارِعُ المَعْلُوم
يَرْمُونَ	يَرْمِيانِ	يَرْمِي	الغائِب:
يَرْمِينَ	تَرْمِيانِ	تَرْمِي	الغائِبَة:
تَرْمُونَ	تَرْمِيانِ	تَرْمِي	المُخاطَب:
تَرْمِينَ	تَرْمِيانِ	تَرْمِينَ	المُخاطَبَة:
نَرْمِي		أَرْمِي	المُتَكَلِّم:

الجَمْع	المُثَنَّى	المُفْرَد	الأَمْرُ المَعْلُوم
لِيَرْمُوا	لِيَرْمِيا	لِيَرْمِ	الغائِب:
لِيَرْمِينَ	لِتَرْمِيا	لِتَرْمِ	الغائِبَة:
إِرْمُوا	إِرْمِيا	إِرْمِ	المُخاطَب:
إِرْمِينَ	إِرْمِيا	إِرْمِي	المُخاطَبَة:
لِنَرْمِ		لأَرْمِ	المُتَكَلِّم:

Table 3.18 - The Naaqis With Yaa' Passive Voice Verb On The Pattern Of: فُعِلَ يُفْعَلُ

الجَمْع	المُثَنَّى	المُفْرَد	الماضِي المَجْهُول
رُموا	رُمِيا	رُمِيَ	الغائِب:
رُمِينَ	رُمِتا	رُمَتْ	الغائِبَة:
رُمِيتُم	رُمِيتُما	رُمِيتَ	المُخاطَب:
رُمِيتُنَّ	رُمِيتُما	رُمِيتِ	المُخاطَبَة:
رُمِينا		رُمِيتُ	المُتَكَلِّم:

الجَمْع	المُثَنَّى	المُفْرَد	المُضارِع المَجْهُول
يُرمَونَ	يُرمَيانِ	يُرمَى	الغائِب:
يُرمَينَ	تُرمَيانِ	تُرمَى	الغائِبَة:
تُرمَونَ	تُرمَيانِ	تُرمَى	المُخاطَب:
تُرمَينَ	تُرمَيانِ	تُرمَينَ	المُخاطَبَة:
نُرمَى		أُرمَى	المُتَكَلِّم:

الجَمْع	المُثَنَّى	المُفْرَد	الأمْر المَجْهُول
لِيُرمَوا	لِيُرمَيا	لِيُرمَ	الغائِب:
لِيُرمَينَ	لِتُرمَيا	لِتُرمَ	الغائِبَة:
لِتُرمَوا	لِتُرمَيا	لِتُرمَ	المُخاطَب:
لِتُرمَينَ	لِتُرمَيا	لِتُرمَيْ	المُخاطَبَة:
لِنُرمَ		لِأُرمَ	المُتَكَلِّم:

Table 3.19 - The Naaqis With Yaa' Active Voice Verb On The Pattern Of: فَعِلَ يَفْعَلُ

رَضِيَ، يَرْضَى، إرْضَ، لِيَرْضَ، رُضِيَ، يُرْضَى، رِضِيَ، لِيُرْضَى هُوَ رِضِيَ (رِضْوانٌ، مَرْضَاةٌ) و راضٍ و مَرْضِيٌّ

الجَمع	المُثَنَّى	المُفْرَد	الماضِيُ المَعْلُوم
رَضُوا	رَضِيَا	رَضِيَ	الغائب:
رَضِينَ	رَضِيَتَا	رَضِيَتْ	الغائبة:
رَضِيتُمْ	رَضِيتُما	رَضِيتَ	المُخاطَب:
رَضِيتُنَّ	رَضِيتُما	رَضِيتِ	المُخاطِبَة:
رَضِينا		رَضِيتُ	المُتَكَلِّم:

الجَمع	المُثَنَّى	المُفْرَد	المُضارِعُ المَعْلُوم
يَرْضَوْنَ	يَرْضَيانِ	يَرْضَى	الغائب:
يَرْضَيْنَ	تَرْضَيانِ	تَرْضَى	الغائبة:
تَرْضَوْنَ	تَرْضَيانِ	تَرْضَى	المُخاطَب:
تَرْضَيْنَ	تَرْضَيانِ	تَرْضَيْنَ	المُخاطِبَة:
نَرْضَى		أَرْضَى	المُتَكَلِّم:

الجَمع	المُثَنَّى	المُفْرَد	الأَمْرُ المَعْلُوم
لِيَرْضَوْا	لِيَرْضَيا	لِيَرْضَ	الغائب:
لِيَرْضَيْنَ	لِتَرْضَيا	لِتَرْضَ	الغائبة:
إرْضَوْا	إرْضَيا	إرْضَ	المُخاطَب:
إرْضَيْنَ	إرْضَيا	إرْضَيْ	المُخاطِبَة:
لِنَرْضَ		لِأَرْضَ	المُتَكَلِّم:

Table 3.20 - The Naaqis With Yaa' Passive Voice Verb On The Pattern Of: فُعِلَ يُفْعَ

الجَمع	المُثَنَّى	المُفْرَد	الماضِي المَجْهُول
رُضُوا	رُضِيا	رُضِيَ	الغائِب:
رُضِينَ	رُضِيَتا	رُضِيَتْ	الغائِبَة:
رُضِيتُم	رُضِيتُما	رُضِيتَ	المُخاطَب:
رُضِيتُنَّ	رُضِيتُما	رُضِيتِ	المُخاطَبَة:
رُضِينا		رُضِيتُ	المُتَكَلِّم:

الجَمع	المُثَنَّى	المُفْرَد	المُضارِع المَجْهُول
يُرْضَونَ	يُرْضَيانِ	يُرْضَى	الغائِب:
يُرْضَينَ	تُرْضَيانِ	تُرْضَى	الغائِبَة:
تُرْضَونَ	تُرْضَيانِ	تُرْضَى	المُخاطَب:
تُرْضَينَ	تُرْضَيانِ	تُرْضَينَ	المُخاطَبَة:
نُرْضَى		أُرْضَى	المُتَكَلِّم:

الجَمع	المُثَنَّى	المُفْرَد	الأَمْر المَجْهُول
لِيُرْضَوا	لِيُرْضَيا	لِيُرْضَ	الغائِب:
لِيُرْضَينَ	لِتُرْضَيا	لِتُرْضَ	الغائِبَة:
لِتُرْضَوا	لِتُرْضَيا	لِتُرْضَ	المُخاطَب:
لِتُرْضَينَ	لِتُرْضَيا	لِتُرْضَي	المُخاطَبَة:
لِنُرْضَ		لِأُرْضَ	المُتَكَلِّم:

SECTION FOUR

The Lafeef Verb

الفِعْلُ اللَّفِيفُ

The Kalimah in which two of its Original Letters are Weak Letters is termed **Lafeef**. *Lafeef* has two types:

- › **Lafeef Mafrooq** (اللَّفِيفُ المَفْرُوقُ). *Lafeef Mafrooq* is the word in which the two Weak Letters are separated by a Sound Letter, like: وَقَى .

- › **Lafeef Maqroon** (اللَّفِيفُ المَقْرُونُ). *Lafeef Maqroon* is the word in which the two Weak letters exist side by side, as in: لَوَى.

▶ LAFEEF MAFROOQ اللَّفِيفُ المَفْرُوقُ

Lafeef Mafrooq is the *Lafeef* Verb in which the 1st and 3rd Original Letters are Weak Letters (مُعْتَلُّ الفَاءِ وَ اللَّامِ). From the point of view of the 1st Original Letter, *Lafeef Mafrooq* employs the sames rules of *I'laal* and conjugation as the *Mithaal* Verb. Meaning that when *Lafeef Mafrooq* is found on the pattern of: يَفْعِلُ, the 1st Original Letter will be elided as is the case in the *Mithaal* with Waaw Verb, for example: وَقَى يَقِي.

From the point of view of the 3rd Original Letter, Lafeef Mafrooq is similar to the *Naaqis* Verb. Therefore, keeping the rules associated with *Mithaal* and *Naaqis* in mind, the *Lafeef* Verb will be formed in the same manner. Since *Mithaal* and *Naaqis* have already been discussed in detail, we will present *Lafeef Mafrooq* in a summarized manner.

For the purpose of presenting an model verb, we will use the verb derived from the Masdar وِقَايَةٌ or وَقْيٌ.

Table 3.21 - The Active Voice Lafeef Mafrooq Verb On The Pattern Of: فَعَلَ يَفْعِلُ

وَقَى، يَقِي، قِ، لِيَقِ، وُقِيَ، يُوقَى، لِيُوقَ هُوَ وَقِيٌّ (وِقَايَةٌ) و واقٍ و مَوقِيٌّ

الجَمع	المُثَنَّى	المُفْرد	الماضِي المَعلُوم
وَقَوا	وَقَيا	وَقَى	الغائِب:
وَقَينَ	وَقَتا	وَقَتْ	الغائِبَة:
وَقَيتُم	وَقَيتُما	وَقَيتَ	المُخاطَب:
وَقَيتُنَّ	وَقَيتُما	وَقَيتِ	المُخاطَبَة:
وَقَينا		وَقَيتُ	المُتَكَلِّم:

الجَمع	المُثَنَّى	المُفْرد	المُضارِع المَعلُوم
يَقُونَ	يَقِيانِ	يَقِي	الغائِب:
يَقِينَ	تَقِيانِ	تَقِي	الغائِبَة:
تَقُونَ	تَقِيانِ	تَقِي	المُخاطَب:
تَقِينَ	تَقِيانِ	تَقِينَ	المُخاطَبَة:
نَقِي		أَقِي	المُتَكَلِّم:

الجَمع	المُثَنَّى	المُفْرد	الأَمْر المَعلُوم
لِيَقُوا	لِيَقِيا	لِيَقِ	الغائِب:
لِيَقِينَ	لِتَقِيا	لِتَقِ	الغائِبَة:
قُوا	قِيا	قِ	المُخاطَب:
قِينَ	قِيا	قِيْ	المُخاطَبَة:
لِنَقِ		لِأَقِ	المُتَكَلِّم:

Table 3.22 - The Passive Voice Lafeef Mafrooq Verb On The Pattern Of: فُعِلَ يُفْعَلُ

الجَمع	المُثَنَّى	المُفْرَد	الماضِي المَجْهُول
وُقُوا	وُقِيَا	وُقِيَ	الغائِب:
وُقِينَ	وُقِيَتا	وُقِيَتْ	الغائِبَة:
وُقِيتُم	وُقِيتُما	وُقِيتَ	المُخاطَب:
وُقِيتُنَّ	وُقِيتُما	وُقِيتِ	المُخاطَبَة:
وُقِينا		وُقِيتُ	المُتَكَلِّم:

الجَمع	المُثَنَّى	المُفْرَد	المُضارِعُ المَجْهُول
يُوقَونَ	يُوقَيانِ	يُوقَى	الغائِب:
يُوقَينَ	تُوقَيانِ	تُوقَى	الغائِبَة:
تُوقَونَ	تُوقَيانِ	تُوقَى	المُخاطَب:
تُوقَينَ	تُوقَيانِ	تُوقَينَ	المُخاطَبَة:
نُوقَى		أُوقَى	المُتَكَلِّم:

الجَمع	المُثَنَّى	المُفْرَد	الأَمْرُ المَجْهُول
لِيُوقَوا	لِيُوقَيَا	لِيُوقَ	الغائِب:
لِيُوقَينَ	لِيُوقَيَا	لِتُوقَ	الغائِبَة:
لِتُوقَوا	لِتُوقَيَا	لِتُوقَ	المُخاطَب:
لِتُوقَينَ	لِتُوقَيَا	لِتُوقَيْ	المُخاطَبَة:
لِنُوقَ		لِأُوقَ	المُتَكَلِّم:

▶ LAFEEF MAQROON اللَّفِيفُ المَقْرُونُ

Lafeef Maqroon has two types:

› Wherein the Weak Letters are the 1st and 2nd Original Letters (مُعْتَلُّ الفَآءِ وَ العَيْنِ), as in: يَوْمٌ and وَيْلٌ. This type is only found in nouns.

› Wherein the Weak Letters are the 2nd and 3rd Original Letters (مُعْتَلُّ العَيْنِ وَ اللاَّم), as in: لَوَى.

In the archaic Arabic, there are said to be words in which all three letters are Weak Letters. It said, for example, that the names of the letters Yaa' and Waw were originally: يَائِيٌّ and وَاوَوٌّ respectively.

From the point of view of the 2nd Original Letter, *Lafeef Maqroon* is similar to *Ajwaf*. From the point of view of the 3rd Original Letter, *Lafeef Maqroon* is similar to *Naaqis*. However, *Lafeef Maqroon* only accepts the rules that can be applied to *Naaqis*. Those rules associated with *Ajwaf* are not applicable to *Lafeef Maqroon*.

We will examine the verbs derived from the Masdar رِوَايَةٌ and سَوَىٌ in a summarized manner:

Table 3.23 - The Active Voice Lafeef Maqroon Verb On The Pattern Of: فَعَلَ يَفْعِلُ

رَوَى، يَرْوِي، إِرْوِ، لِيَرْوِ، رُوِيَ، يُرْوَى، لِيُرْوَ هُوَ رِوَايَةٌ و رَاوٍ و مَرْوِيٌّ

الجَمْع	المُثَنَّى	المُفْرَد	الماضِي المَعْلُوم
رَوَوْا	رَوَيَا	رَوَى	الغائِب:
رَوَيْنَ	رَوَتَا	رَوَتْ	الغائِبَة:
رَوَيْتُمْ	رَوَيْتُما	رَوَيْتَ	المُخاطَب:
رَوَيْتُنَّ	رَوَيْتُما	رَوَيْتِ	المُخاطَبَة:
رَوَيْنا		رَوَيْتُ	المُتَكَلِّم:

الجَمْع	المُثَنَّى	المُفْرَد	المُضارِعُ المَعْلُوم
يَرْوُونَ	يَرْوِيَانِ	يَرْوِي	الغائِب:
يَرْوِينَ	تَرْوِيَانِ	تَرْوِي	الغائِبَة:
تَرْوُونَ	تَرْوِيَانِ	تَرْوِي	المُخاطَب:
تَرْوِينَ	تَرْوِيَانِ	تَرْوِينَ	المُخاطَبَة:
نَرْوِي		أَرْوِي	المُتَكَلِّم:

الجَمْع	المُثَنَّى	المُفْرَد	الأَمْر المَعْلُوم
لِيَرْوُوا	لِيَرْوِيَا	لِيَرْوِ	الغائِب:
لِيَرْوِينَ	لِتَرْوِيَا	لِتَرْوِ	الغائِبَة:
إِرْوُوا	إِرْوِيَا	إِرْوِ	المُخاطَب:
إِرْوِينَ	إِرْوِيَا	إِرْوِي	المُخاطَبَة:
لِنَرْوِ		لِأَرْوِ	المُتَكَلِّم:

Table 3.24 - The Passive Voice Lafeef Maqroon Verb On The Pattern Of: فُعِلَ يُفْعَلُ

الجَمْع	المُثَنَّى	المُفْرَد	المَاضِي المَجْهُول
رُوُوا	رُوِيَا	رُوِيَ	الغَائِب:
رُوِينَ	رُوِيَتا	رُوِيَتْ	الغَائِبَة:
رُوِيتُمْ	رُوِيتُما	رُوِيتَ	المُخاطَب:
رُوِيتُنَّ	رُوِيتُما	رُوِيتِ	المُخاطَبَة:
رُوِينا		رُوِيتُ	المُتَكَلِّم:

الجَمْع	المُثَنَّى	المُفْرَد	المُضارِعُ المَجْهُول
يُرْوَوْنَ	يُرْوَيَانِ	يُرْوَى	الغَائِب:
يُرْوَيْنَ	تُرْوَيَانِ	تُرْوَى	الغَائِبَة:
تُرْوَوْنَ	تُرْوَيَانِ	تُرْوَى	المُخاطَب:
تُرْوَيْنَ	تُرْوَيَانِ	تُرْوَيْنَ	المُخاطَبَة:
نُرْوَى		أُرْوَى	المُتَكَلِّم:

الجَمْع	المُثَنَّى	المُفْرَد	الأَمْرُ المَجْهُول
لِيُرْوَوْا	لِيُرْوَيَا	لِيُرْوَ	الغَائِب:
لِيُرْوَيْنَ	لِتُرْوَيَا	لِتُرْوَ	الغَائِبَة:
لِتُرْوَوْا	لِتُرْوَيَا	لِتُرْوَ	المُخاطَب:
لِتُرْوَيْنَ	لِتُرْوَيَا	لِتُرْوَيْ	المُخاطَبَة:
لِنُرْوَ		لِأُرْوَ	المُتَكَلِّم:

Table 3.25 - The Active Voice Lafeef Maqroon Verb On The Pattern of: فَعِلَ يَفعَلُ

سَوِيَ، يَشوَى، إِسوَ، لِيَشوَ، سُوِيَ، يُشوَى، لِيُشوَ هُوَ سَوَىً و ساوٍ و مَشوِيٌّ

الجَمع	المُثَنَّى	المُفرَد	الماضِيُ المَعلُوم
سَوُوا	سَوِيَا	سَوِيَ	الغائِب:
سَوِينَ	سَوِيَتا	سَوِيَتْ	الغائِبَة:
سَوِيتُم	سَوِيتُما	سَوِيتَ	المُخاطَب:
سَوِيتُنَّ	سَوِيتُما	سَوِيتِ	المُخاطَبَة:
سَوِينا		سَوِيتُ	المُتَكَلِّم:

الجَمع	المُثَنَّى	المُفرَد	المُضارِعُ المَعلُوم
يَشوَونَ	يَشوَيانِ	يَشوَى	الغائِب:
يَشوَينَ	تَشوَيانِ	تَشوَى	الغائِبَة:
تَشوَونَ	تَشوَيانِ	تَشوَى	المُخاطَب:
تَشوَينَ	تَشوَيانِ	تَشوَينَ	المُخاطَبَة:
نَشوَى		أَشوَى	المُتَكَلِّم:

الجَمع	المُثَنَّى	المُفرَد	الأَمرُ المَعلُوم
لِيَشوَوا	لِيَشوَيا	لِيَشوَ	الغائِب:
لِيَشوَونَ	لِتَشوَيا	لِتَشوَ	الغائِبَة:
إِشوَوا	إِشوَيا	إِشوَ	المُخاطَب:
إِشوَينَ	إِشوَيا	إِشوَيْ	المُخاطَبَة:
لِنَشوَ		لِأَشوَ	المُتَكَلِّم:

Table 3.26 - The Passive Voice Lafeef Maqroon Verb On The Pattern Of: فُعِلَ يُفْعَلُ

الجَمع	المُثَنَّى	المُفْرَد	الماضي المَجهُول
سُوُّوا	سُوِيا	سُوِيَ	الغائِب:
سُوِينَ	سُوِيَتا	سُوِيَتْ	الغائِبة:
سُوِيتُمْ	سُوِيتُما	سُوِيتَ	المُخاطَب:
سُوِيتُنَّ	سُوِيتُما	سُوِيتِ	المُخاطَبة:
سُوِينا		سُوِيتُ	المُتَكَلِّم:

الجَمع	المُثَنَّى	المُفْرَد	المُضارِع المَجهُول
يُسوَونَ	يُسوَيانِ	يُسوَى	الغائِب:
يُسوَينَ	تُسوَيانِ	تُسوَى	الغائِبة:
تُسوَونَ	تُسوَيانِ	تُسوَى	المُخاطَب:
تُسوَينَ	تُسوَيانِ	تُسوَينَ	المُخاطَبة:
نُسوَى		أُسوَى	المُتَكَلِّم:

الجَمع	المُثَنَّى	المُفْرَد	الأمْر المَجهُول
لِيُسوَوا	لِيُسوَيا	لِيُسوَ	الغائِب:
لِيُسوَينَ	لِيُسوَيا	لِتُسوَ	الغائِبة:
لِتُسوَوا	لِتُسوَيا	لِتُسوَ	المُخاطَب:
لِتُسوَينَ	لِتُسوَيا	لِتُسوَيْ	المُخاطَبة:
لِنُسوَ		لِأُسوَ	المُتَكَلِّم:

CHAPTER FOUR

THE THREE LETTER
DERIVATIVE VERB

الفعل الثلاثي المزيد فيه

INTRODUCTION

Until this point, our study of the verb has focused exclusively on the Three Letter Primary Verb (الثُّلَاثِيُّ المُجَرَّدُ), meaning the three letter verb that is comprised of only its Original Letters (الأَحْرُفُ الأَصْلِيُّ). *Derivative Verbs* are derived from these Primary Verbs by including Additional Letters (الأَحْرُفُ الزَّائِدَةُ) in their construction. Like the Primary Verb, the *Derivative Verb* has its own Masdar from which it is derived.

It is in the study of the *Derivative Verb* that we can clearly see the benefit of the verb pattern or *Wazn* (الوَزْنُ). The verb pattern is based on the three Original Letters represented by the letters: فعل. The Additional Letters appear in the pattern in the same manner that they appear in the word, for example, the following word: إكْرَام, is on the pattern of: إفْعَال. The Original Letters, then, are: كرم and the Additional Letters are Hamzah (in the beginning of the word) and Alif (following the second Original Letter).

These Additional Letters form the *Special Letters* (الأَحْرُفُ الخُصُوصِيُّ) that generally appear in all or most of the related forms of the derivative Kalimah. The *Derivative Verbs* have their exclusive patterns and own particularities which distinguish them from the Primary Verb.

The method of derivation in the *Derivative Verb* is identical to that of the Primary Verb, meaning that the Past Tense Verb is derived from the Masdar, the Present Tense Verb is derived from the Past Tense Verb, the Command Verb is derived from the Present Tense Verb and so forth.

The Masdar itself, however, is somewhat different in the derivative Kalimah. The patterns of the Masdar of the Primary Kalimah were all known according to usage (السَّمَاعِيُّ) and not constructed according to set patterns or rules. In total, grammarians have listed more than fifty patterns of the Masdar of the Primary Kalimah, many of which are still in common usage (refer to chapter eight). The Masdar of the derivative Kalimah are all constructed according to specific rules (القِيَاسِيُّ) as opposed to being known according to usage.

Like the Primary Verb, the *Derivative Verb* is also organized into *Abwaab* or primary patterns. As previously mentioned, the Primary Verb has six *Abwaab*, meaning each combination of the Past Tense Verb and its Present Tense is considered one *Baab* (Table 1.4). The *Derivative Verb* is organized in the same manner. The primary difference is that each *Baab* is named according to the Masdar from which its verbs are derived. For example, the first *Baab* is named إِفْعَال or the *Baab of If'aal*, the second is تَفْعِيل the *Baab of Taf'eel*. This is possible since the Derivative Masdar is *Qiyaasi* or known by its pattern.

Therefore, the *Abwaab* of the *Derivative Verbs* gives us three pieces of information: the pattern of the Masdar; the pattern of the Past Tense and the pattern of the Present Tense. The Three Letter Derivative Verb has twenty five (25) *Abwaab*. Of these twenty five *Abwaab*, only ten are in common usage today. These ten *Abwaab* are listed in the following table:

Table 4.1 - The Abwaab Of The Three Letter Derivative Verb أبوابُ الثُّلاثيِّ المَزيدِ فيه

المُضارِعُ	الماضيُ	المَصدَرُ		المُضارِعُ	الماضيُ	المَصدَرُ	
يَتَفَعَّلُ	تَفَعَّلَ	تَفَعُّلٌ	(٦)	يُفْعِلُ	أَفْعَلَ	إفْعالٌ	(١)
يَتَفاعَلُ	تَفاعَلَ	تَفاعُلٌ	(٧)	يُفَعِّلُ	فَعَّلَ	تَفْعيلٌ	(٢)
يَفْعَلُّ	إفْعَلَّ	إفْعِلالٌ	(٨)	يُفاعِلُ	فاعَلَ	مُفاعَلَةٌ	(٣)
يَسْتَفْعِلُ	إسْتَفْعَلَ	إسْتِفْعالٌ	(٩)	يَفْتَعِلُ	إفْتَعَلَ	إفْتِعالٌ	(٤)
يَفْعالُّ	إفْعالَّ	إفْعيلالٌ	(١٠)	يَنْفَعِلُ	إنْفَعَلَ	إنْفِعالٌ	(٥)

The Three Letter Derivative Verb (الثُّلاثِيُّ المَزِيدُ فِيهِ) is constructed based on the Three Letter Primary Verb (الثُّلاثِيُّ المَجَرَّدُ). The manner in which the *Derivative Verb* is conjugated is the same as that of the Primary Verb in regards to the Past/Present Tense and the Active/Passive Voice. Similarly, the system of the Pronouns are the same as those of the Primary Verb. The rules of Contraction or *Idghaam*, the Reduction or *Takhfeef* of the Hamzah, the general and particular rules of *I'laal* and the particular rules of *Naaqis* are also applied in the *Abwaab* of the *Derivative Verb*.

There are two last points to be mindful of regarding the Three Letter *Derivative Verb*. Although there are ten common *Abwaab*, it does not mean, in reality, that a verb will actually have a derivative from each *Baab*. The *Abwaab* from which any particular word might be derived is established completely according to usage (السَّماعِيُّ). Some words might have derivatives in only one *Baab* while others might have derivatives in three, four or more *Abwaab*. There is no way to estimate or predict which Primary Kalimah will have which derivatives. The dictionary is the most useful tool in obtaining such information.

The last point is that *Abwaab* of the Three Letter *Derivative Verb* has certain meanings associated with them by common usage. The meanings associated with these *Abwaab* will be mentioned in their appropriate places.

SECTION ONE

The Baab Of If'aal

بابُ إِفْعالٍ

أَفْعَلَ، يُفْعِلُ، أَفْعِلْ، لِيُفْعِلْ، أُفْعِلَ، يُفْعَلُ، لِيُفْعَلْ هُوَ إِفْعالٌ و مُفْعِلٌ و مُفْعَلٌ

As previously mentioned, each *Abwaab* of the Derivative Verb has special letters (Additional Letters) which form the pattern for that particular *Baab*. In *Baab of If'aal*, Hamzah is the special letter that is added to the Masdar (إِفْعال), the Seeghah of the Past Tense Verb (أَفْعَلَ) and the Seeghah of the Command Verb (أَفْعِلْ). This Hamzah in this particular pattern happens to be the **Disjunctive Hamzah** (الهَمْزَةُ القَطْعَةُ), meaning that its vowel is never elided to facilitate pronunciation. Compare the two types of Hamzah, the **Conjunctive Hamzah** (الهَمْزَةُ الوَصْلَةُ) of the Primary Command Verb with the *Disjunctive Hamzah* of this *Baab*:

(المُجَرَّدُ): وَ + إِضْرِبْ = وَ اضْرِبْ   (المَزِيدُ فِيهِ): وَ + أَكْرَمَ = وَ أَكْرَمَ

In this *Baab*, the Hamzah of the Past Tense Verb and the 2nd Person Command Verb are both disjunctive. This Hamzah is not found in the Present Tense Verb, although it is said to have been written originally.

Another characteristic of this *Baab* is that the Particle of the Present Tense (حَرْفُ المُضارِعِ) is vowelled with Dhammah in the Active Voice. In the Primary Verb it is always vowelled with Fathah in the Active Voice.

Based on this, the patterns for *Baab If'aal* in the Active Voice and Passive Voice are as follows:

Table 4.2 - Patterns Of Baab Of If'aal Active Voice Verb On The Pattern Of: أَفْعَلَ يُفْعِلُ

أَفْعَلَ، يُفْعِلُ، أَفْعِلْ، أَفْعَلَ، لِيُفْعِلْ، يُفْعَلَ، أُفْعِلَ هُوَ إِفْعالٌ و مُفْعَلٌ و مُفْعِلٌ

الجَمْع	المُثَنَّى	المُفْرَد	الماضِي المَعْلُوم
أَفْعَلوا	أَفْعَلا	أَفْعَلَ	الغائِب:
أَفْعَلْنَ	أَفْعَلَتا	أَفْعَلَتْ	الغائِبة:
أَفْعَلْتُمْ	أَفْعَلْتُما	أَفْعَلْتَ	المُخاطَب:
أَفْعَلْتُنَّ	أَفْعَلْتُما	أَفْعَلْتِ	المُخاطَبة:
أَفْعَلْنا		أَفْعَلْتُ	المُتَكَلِّم:

الجَمْع	المُثَنَّى	المُفْرَد	المُضارِع المَعْلُوم
يُفْعِلُونَ	يُفْعِلانِ	يُفْعِلُ	الغائِب:
يُفْعِلْنَ	تُفْعِلانِ	تُفْعِلُ	الغائِبة:
تُفْعِلُونَ	تُفْعِلانِ	تُفْعِلُ	المُخاطَب:
تُفْعِلْنَ	تُفْعِلانِ	تُفْعِلِينَ	المُخاطَبة:
نُفْعِلُ		أُفْعِلُ	المُتَكَلِّم:

الجَمْع	المُثَنَّى	المُفْرَد	الأَمْرُ المَعْلُوم
لِيُفْعِلوا	لِيُفْعِلا	لِيُفْعِلْ	الغائِب:
لِيُفْعِلْنَ	لِتُفْعِلا	لِتُفْعِلْ	الغائِبة:
أَفْعِلوا	أَفْعِلا	أَفْعِلْ	المُخاطَب:
أَفْعِلْنَ	أَفْعِلا	أَفْعِلي	المُخاطَبة:
لِنُفْعِلْ		لأُفْعِلْ	المُتَكَلِّم:

Table 4.3 - Patterns Of Baab Of If'aal Passive Voice Verb On The Pattern Of: أُفْعِلَ يُفْعَلُ

الجَمْع	المُثَنَّى	المُفْرَد	الماضِي المَجْهُول
أُفْعِلُوا	أُفْعِلا	أُفْعِلَ	الغائِب:
أُفْعِلْنَ	أُفْعِلَتا	أُفْعِلَتْ	الغائِبَة:
أُفْعِلْتُمْ	أُفْعِلْتُما	أُفْعِلْتَ	المُخاطَب:
أُفْعِلْتُنَّ	أُفْعِلْتُما	أُفْعِلْتِ	المُخاطَبَة:
أُفْعِلْنا		أُفْعِلْتُ	المُتَكَلِّم:

الجَمْع	المُثَنَّى	المُفْرَد	المُضارِعُ المَجْهُول
يُفْعَلُونَ	يُفْعَلانِ	يُفْعَلُ	الغائِب:
يُفْعَلْنَ	تُفْعَلانِ	تُفْعَلُ	الغائِبَة:
تُفْعَلُونَ	تُفْعَلانِ	تُفْعَلُ	المُخاطَب:
تُفْعَلْنَ	تُفْعَلانِ	تُفْعَلِينَ	المُخاطَبَة:
نُفْعَلُ		أُفْعَلُ	المُتَكَلِّم:

الجَمْع	المُثَنَّى	المُفْرَد	الأَمْرُ المَجْهُول
لِيُفْعَلُوا	لِيُفْعَلا	لِيُفْعَلْ	الغائِب:
لِيُفْعَلْنَ	لِتُفْعَلا	لِتُفْعَلْ	الغائِبَة:
لِتُفْعَلُوا	لِتُفْعَلا	لِتُفْعَلْ	المُخاطَب:
لِتُفْعَلْنَ	لِتُفْعَلا	لِتُفْعَلِي	المُخاطَبَة:
لِنُفْعَلْ		لأُفْعَلْ	المُتَكَلِّم:

► THE MEANINGS OF THE BAAB OF IF'AAL مَعاني بابِ إِفْعالٍ

The Baab of If'aal has ten meanings associated with it:

▷ **Transitivity** (التَّعْدِيَةُ). Meaning that the verb which is Instransitive as a Primary Verb will become Transitive when found in this *Baab*. The Intransitive Verb (الفِعْلُ اللَّازِمُ) is that verb which does not require an Object (المَفْعُولُ بِهِ) to complete its meaning while the Transitive Verb (الفِعْلُ المُتَعَدِّيُ) requires an Object or its meaning will be deficient. Most often, the meaning associated with this Baab is Transitivity. Observe the transition from Instransitive to Transitive in the following Primary and Derivative Verbs:

ذَهَبَ زَيدٌ *Zaid Left* أَذْهَبَ زَيدٌ بَكْراً *Zaid sent Bakr*

ضَحِكَتْ سَلْمَى *Salma laughed* أَضْحَكَتْ سَلْمَى فاطِمَةَ *Salma made Fatimah laugh*

▷ **The Subject Enters Into A Particular Time** (دَخَلَ الفاعِلُ في الوَقْتِ). This meaning occurs in verbs whose meaning is associated with time, for example: أَصْبَحَ زَيدٌ بُكاءً *Zaid entered the morning in tears;* أَمْسَى بَكْرٌ نائِماً *Bakr entered the evening sleeping.* Refer to the following verse:

﴿فَسُبْحانَ اللَّهِ حِينَ تُمْسُونَ وَ حِينَ تُصْبِحُونَ...وَ حِينَ تُظْهِرُونَ﴾

"Therefore, Glory be to Allah when you enter upon the time of the evening and when you enter upon the time of the morning...and when you are at midday..." (Ar-Rum 30:17-18)

▷ **Arrival Of A Particular Time** (وُصُولُ وَقْتٍ). Meaning that the verb conveys the meaning of the arrival of a particular time for its subject, for example: أَحْصَدَ الزَّرْعُ *The harvest time of the crops arrived*; أَقْطَفَ الثَّمَرَةَ *The cutting time of dates arrived*.

▷ **Finding The Object To Possess A Particular Attribute** (وُجُود صِفَةٍ في المَفْعُولِ). Meaning that the verb signifies an Attribute (الصِّفَة) for the Object (المَفْعُولُ) in such a manner that it can be said that the particular attribute is possessed by the Object, for example: أَعْظَمْتُ اللَّه *I deem Allah to be Magnificent*, meaning that the quality of being Magnificent (العَظِيمُ) is found to be possessed by Allah, which is the Object and أَبْخَلْتُ خالِداً *I found Khalid to be a miser* (miserliness being a quality found in Khalid). Most often, the Intransitive Verb associates a particular attribute with the subject, as in: حَسُنَ زَيْدٌ *Zaid was handsome*.

▷ **Finding The Subject Or Object To Have Accepted An Attribute** (الواجِديَّةُ) or as we say: to become something (صيرُورَةُ), as in: أَقْفَرَ البَلَدُ *The city became desolate*; أَرْكَبْتُ أَبِي *I mounted my father* (i.e., he became a mount); ﴿ثُمَّ أَمَاتَهُ فَأَقْبَرَهُ﴾ *Then, He causes him to die, then, assigns to him a grave* (Abasa 80:21).

▷ **Negation** (السَّلْبُ). The action is negated in either the Subject or Object, for example: أَشْفَى المَرِيضُ *The patient became incurable*; أَعْجَمَ الكِتَابَ *He rendered the book illegible*.

▷ **To Offer, Exhibit** (التَّعْرِيضُ), for example: أَبَاعَ زَيْدٌ كِتَابُهُ *Zaid offered his book for sale*.

▷ **Meaning Of The Passive Voice** (المُطَاوَعَةُ). Meaning that the verb conveys a meaning that accepts the effect of an action. This is opposite of the meaning of the Transitivity (التَّعْدِيَةُ) which is to cause the affect in something else (the Object), for example: كَبَّ زَيدٌ الإِنَاءَ *Zaid overturned the vase*, أَكَبَّ الإِنَاءُ *The vase overturned*. In the first sentence, the verb is Transitive and the effect of the action is found in the Object. The second sentence, however, has the effect (being overturned) already implied in the meaning of the verb. This meaning is also known as a reflexive meaning.

▷ **Opposite The Meaning Of The Primary Verb**(ضِدُّ مَعْنَى الثُّلاثِيِّ المَجَرَّدِ) for example: نَشَطْتُ الحَبلَ *I tied a knot in the rope*, أَنْشَطْتُ الحَبلَ *I unknotted the rope.*

▷ **The Meaning Of The Primary Verb** (مَعْنَى الثُّلاثِيِّ المُجَرَّدِ), as in: قَالَ أَو أَقَالَ زَيدٌ البَيعَ *Zaid rescinded the sale.*

It is possible for a verb in any *Baab* to convey more than one of the meanings associated with it, for example: أَعْظَمْتُ اللَّهَ *I found Allah to be Almighty*, has both the meaning of Transitivity and Finding an attribute in the Object.

Sample Conjugation Of The Non-Sound And Weak Verb In The Baab Of If'aal

Table 4.4 - The Active Voice Non-Sound Verb (Mahmooz): أثر

آثَرَ، يُؤثِرُ، آثِرْ، لِيُؤثِرْ، أُوثِرْ، يُؤثَرُ، لِيُؤثَرْ هُوَ إِيثَارٌ وَ مُؤثِرٌ و مُؤثَرٌ

الجَمْع	المُثَنَّى	المُفْرَد	الماضِي المَعْلُوم
آثَرُوا	آثَرا	آثَرَ	الغائِب:
آثَرْنَ	آثَرَتا	آثَرَتْ	الغائِبة:
آثَرْتُمْ	آثَرْتُما	آثَرْتَ	المُخاطَب:
آثَرْتُنَّ	آثَرْتُما	آثَرْتِ	المُخاطَبة:
آثَرْنا		آثَرْتُ	المُتَكَلِّم:

الجَمْع	المُثَنَّى	المُفْرَد	المُضارِع المَعْلُوم
يُؤثِرُونَ	يُؤثِرانِ	يُؤثِرُ	الغائِب:
يُؤثِرْنَ	تُؤثِرانِ	تُؤثِرُ	الغائِبة:
تُؤثِرُونَ	تُؤثِرانِ	تُؤثِرُ	المُخاطَب:
تُؤثِرْنَ	تُؤثِرانِ	تُؤثِرِينَ	المُخاطَبة:
نُؤثِرُ		أُوثِرُ	المُتَكَلِّم:

الجَمْع	المُثَنَّى	المُفْرَد	الأَمْر المَعْلُوم
لِيُؤثِرُوا	لِيُؤثِرا	لِيُؤثِرْ	الغائِب:
لِتُؤثِرْنَ	لِتُؤثِرا	لِتُؤثِرْ	الغائِبة:
آثِرُوا	آثِرا	آثِرْ	المُخاطَب:
آثِرْنَ	آثِرا	آثِرِي	المُخاطَبة:
لِنُؤثِرْ		لِأُوثِرْ	المُتَكَلِّم:

Table 4.5 - The Passive Voice Non-Sound Verb (Mahmooz): أَثَرَ (أُوثِرَ، يُؤْثَرُ)

الجَمْع	المُثَنَّى	المُفْرَد		الماضِي المَجْهُول
أُوثِرُوا	أُوثِرَا	أُوثِرَ	الغائِب:	
أُوثِرْنَ	أُوثِرَتَا	أُوثِرَتْ	الغائِبَة:	
أُوثِرْتُم	أُوثِرْتُما	أُوثِرْتَ	المُخاطَب:	
أُوثِرْتُنَّ	أُوثِرْتُما	أُوثِرْتِ	المُخاطِبَة:	
أُوثِرْنا		أُوثِرْتُ	المُتَكَلِّم:	

الجَمْع	المُثَنَّى	المُفْرَد		المُضارِع المَجْهُول
يُؤْثَرُونَ	يُؤْثَرانِ	يُؤْثَرُ	الغائِب:	
يُؤْثَرْنَ	تُؤْثَرانِ	تُؤْثَرُ	الغائِبَة:	
تُؤْثَرُونَ	تُؤْثَرانِ	تُؤْثَرُ	المُخاطَب:	
تُؤْثَرْنَ	تُؤْثَرانِ	تُؤْثَرِينَ	المُخاطِبَة:	
نُؤْثَرُ		أُوثَرُ	المُتَكَلِّم:	

الجَمْع	المُثَنَّى	المُفْرَد		الأَمْر المَجْهُول
لِيُؤْثَرُوا	لِيُؤْثَرا	لِيُؤْثَرْ	الغائِب:	
لِيُؤْثَرْنَ	لِتُؤْثَرا	لِتُؤْثَرْ	الغائِبَة:	
لِتُؤْثَرُوا	لِتُؤْثَرا	لِتُؤْثَرْ	المُخاطَب:	
لِتُؤْثَرْنَ	لِتُؤْثَرا	لِتُؤْثَرِي	المُخاطِبَة:	
لِنُؤْثَرْ		لِأُوثَرْ	المُتَكَلِّم:	

Table 4.6 - The Active Voice Non-Sound Verb (Mudhaa'af): تَمَّ

أَتَمَّ، يُتِمُّ، أَتِمَّ (أَتْمِمْ)، لِيُتِمَّ (لِيُتْمِمْ)، لِيَتِمَّ، يَتَمُّ، لِيَتَمَّ (لِيَتْمِمْ) أَتَمَّ، هُوَ إِتْمامٌ و مُتَمٌّ و مُتَمٌّ

الجَمْع	المُثَنَّى	المُفْرَد	الماضِي المَعلُوم
أَتَمُّوا	أَتَمَّا	أَتَمَّ	الغائِب:
أَتْمَمْنَ	أَتَمَّتا	أَتَمَّتْ	الغائِبَة:
أَتْمَمْتُم	أَتْمَمْتُما	أَتْمَمْتَ	المُخاطَب:
أَتْمَمْتُنَّ	أَتْمَمْتُما	أَتْمَمْتِ	المُخاطَبَة:
أَتْمَمْنا		أَتْمَمْتُ	المُتَكَلِّم:

الجَمْع	المُثَنَّى	المُفْرَد	المُضارِعُ المَعلُوم
يُتِّمُّونَ	يُتِمَّانِ	يُتِمُّ	الغائِب:
يُتْمِمْنَ	تُتِمَّانِ	تُتِمُّ	الغائِبَة:
تُتِمُّونَ	تُتِمَّانِ	تُتِمُّ	المُخاطَب:
تُتْمِمْنَ	تُتِمَّانِ	تُتِمِّينَ	المُخاطَبَة:
نُتِمُّ		أُتِمُّ	المُتَكَلِّم:

الجَمْع	المُثَنَّى	المُفْرَد	الأَمْرُ المَعلُوم
لِيُتِمُّوا	لِيُتِمَّا	لِيُتِمَّ (لِيُتْمِمْ)	الغائِب:
لِيُتْمِمْنَ	لِتُتِمَّا	لِتُتِمَّ	الغائِبَة:
تِمُّوا	تِمَّا	تِمَّ (أَتْمِمْ)	المُخاطَب:
أَتْمِمْنَ	تِمَّا	تِمِّي	المُخاطَبَة:
لِنُتِمَّ		لِأُتِمَّ	المُتَكَلِّم:

Table 4.7 - Passive Voice Non-Sound Verb (Mudhaa'af): (تَمَّ (أُتِمَّ، يُتَمُّ

الجَمْع	المُثَنَّى	المُفْرَد	الماضِي المَجْهُول
أُتِمُّوا	أُتِمَّا	أُتِمَّ	الغائِب:
أُتِمِمْنَ	أُتِمَّتا	أُتِمَّتْ	الغائِبَة:
أُتِمِمْتُم	أُتِمِمْتُما	أُتِمِمْتَ	المُخاطَب:
أُتِمِمْتُنَّ	أُتِمِمْتُما	أُتِمِمْتِ	المُخاطَبَة:
أُتِمِمْنا		أُتِمِمْتُ	المُتَكَلِّم:

الجَمْع	المُثَنَّى	المُفْرَد	المُضارِعُ المَجْهُول
يُتَمُّونَ	يُتَمَّانِ	يُتَمُّ	الغائِب:
يُتْمَمْنَ	تُتَمَّانِ	تُتَمُّ	الغائِبَة:
تُتَمُّونَ	تُتَمَّانِ	تُتَمُّ	المُخاطَب:
تُتْمَمْنَ	تُتَمَّانِ	تُتَمِّينَ	المُخاطَبَة:
نُتَمُّ		أُتَمُّ	المُتَكَلِّم:

الجَمْع	المُثَنَّى	المُفْرَد	الأَمْرُ المَجْهُول
لِيُتَمُّوا	لِيُتَمَّا	لِيُتَمَّ (لِيُتْمَم)	الغائِب:
لِيُتْمَمْنَ	لِتُتَمَّا	لِتُتَمَّ	الغائِبَة:
لِتُتَمُّوا	لِتُتَمَّا	لِتُتَمَّ	المُخاطَب:
لِتُتْمَمْنَ	لِتُتَمَّا	لِتُتَمِّي	المُخاطَبَة:
لِنُتَمَّ		لِأُتَمَّ	المُتَكَلِّم:

Table 4.8 - The Active Voice Weak Verb (Mithaal): وجب

أَوْجَبَ، يُوجِبُ، أَوْجِبْ، لِيُوجِبْ، أَوْجِبْ، يُوجَبَ، لِيُوجَبْ هُوَ إِيجَابٌ و مُوجِبٌ و مُوجَبٌ

الجَمْع	المُثَنَّى	المُفْرَد	الماضِي المَعلُوم
أَوْجَبوا	أَوْجَبا	أَوْجَبَ	الغائِب:
أَوْجَبْنَ	أَوْجَبَتا	أَوْجَبَتْ	الغائِبة:
أَوْجَبْتُم	أَوْجَبْتُما	أَوْجَبْتَ	المُخاطَب:
أَوْجَبْتُنَّ	أَوْجَبْتُما	أَوْجَبْتِ	المُخاطَبة:
أَوْجَبْنا		أَوْجَبْتُ	المُتَكَلِّم:

الجَمْع	المُثَنَّى	المُفْرَد	المُضارِع المَعلُوم
يُوجِبونَ	يُوجِبانِ	يُوجِبُ	الغائِب:
يُوجِبْنَ	تُوجِبانِ	تُوجِبُ	الغائِبة:
تُوجِبونَ	تُوجِبانِ	تُوجِبُ	المُخاطَب:
تُوجِبْنَ	تُوجِبانِ	تُوجِبينَ	المُخاطَبة:
نُوجِبُ		أُوجِبُ	المُتَكَلِّم:

الجَمْع	المُثَنَّى	المُفْرَد	الأَمْر المَعلُوم
لِيُوجِبوا	لِيُوجِبا	لِيُوجِبْ	الغائِب:
لِيُوجِبْنَ	لِتُوجِبا	لِتُوجِبْ	الغائِبة:
أَوْجِبوا	أَوْجِبا	أَوْجِبْ	المُخاطَب:
أَوْجِبْنَ	أَوْجِبا	أَوْجِبي	المُخاطَبة:
لِنُوجِبْ		لِأُوجِبْ	المُتَكَلِّم:

Table 4.9 - The Passive Voice Weak Verb (Mithaal): (وَجَبَ (أُوجِبَ، يُوجَبُ

الجَمع	المُثَنَّى	المُفرَد	المَاضِي المَجهُول
أُوجِبوا	أُوجِبا	أُوجِبَ	الغَائِب:
أُوجِبنَ	أُوجِبتا	أُوجِبَت	الغَائِبَة:
أُوجِبتُم	أُوجِبتُما	أُوجِبتَ	المُخاطَب:
أُوجِبتُنَّ	أُوجِبتُما	أُوجِبتِ	المُخاطَبة:
أُوجِبنا		أُوجِبتُ	المُتَكَلِّم:

الجَمع	المُثَنَّى	المُفرَد	المُضارِع المَجهُول
يُوجَبونَ	يُوجَبانِ	يُوجَبُ	الغَائِب:
يُوجَبنَ	يُوجَبانِ	تُوجَبُ	الغَائِبَة:
تُوجَبونَ	تُوجَبانِ	تُوجَبُ	المُخاطَب:
تُوجَبنَ	تُوجَبانِ	تُوجَبِينَ	المُخاطَبة:
نُوجَبُ		أُوجَبُ	المُتَكَلِّم:

الجَمع	المُثَنَّى	المُفرَد	الأَمر المَجهُول
لِيُوجَبوا	لِيُوجَبا	لِيُوجَبْ	الغَائِب:
لِيُوجَبنَ	لِتُوجَبا	لِتُوجَبْ	الغَائِبَة:
لِتُوجَبوا	لِتُوجَبا	لِتُوجَبْ	المُخاطَب:
لِتُوجَبنَ	لِتُوجَبا	لِتُوجَبِي	المُخاطَبة:
لِنُوجَبْ		لِأُوجَبْ	المُتَكَلِّم:

Table 4.10 - The Active Voice Weak Verb (Ajwaf): رود

أراكَ يُريكُ، أَرِدْ، لِيُرِدْ، أُرِيدَ، يُراكُ، يُراكَ لِيُرَدْ هُوَ إرائةٌ و مُرِيدٌ و مُرادٌ

الجَمع	المُثَنَّى	المُفرَد	الماضِي المَعلُوم
أرادُوا	أرادَا	أرادَ	الغائِب:
أرَدنَ	أرادَتا	أرادَتْ	الغائِبة:
أرَدتُمْ	أرَدتُما	أرَدتَ	المُخاطَب:
أرَدتُنَّ	أرَدتُما	أرَدتِ	المُخاطَبة:
أرَدنا		أرَدتُ	المُتَكَلِّم:

الجَمع	المُثَنَّى	المُفرَد	المُضارِع المَعلُوم
يُريدُونَ	يُريدانِ	يُريدُ	الغائِب:
يُرِدنَ	تُريدانِ	تُريدُ	الغائِبة:
تُريدُونَ	تُريدانِ	تُريدُ	المُخاطَب:
تُرِدنَ	تُريدانِ	تُريدينَ	المُخاطَبة:
نُريدُ		أُريدُ	المُتَكَلِّم:

الجَمع	المُثَنَّى	المُفرَد	الأَمْر المَعلُوم
لِيُريدُوا	لِيُريدا	لِيُرِدْ	الغائِب:
لِيُرِدنَ	لِتُريدا	لِتُرِدْ	الغائِبة:
أرِيدُوا	أرِيدا	أرِدْ	المُخاطَب:
أرِدنَ	أرِيدا	أرِيدِي	المُخاطَبة:
لِنُرِدْ		لأُرِدْ	المُتَكَلِّم:

Table 4.11 - Passive Voice Weak Verb (Ajwaf): (رود (أُرِيدَ، يُرادُ

الجَمْع	المُثَنَّى	المُفْرد	الماضِي المَجْهُول
أُرِيدُوا	أُرِيدا	أُرِيدَ	الغائِب:
أُرِدْنَ	أُرِيدا	أُرِيدَتْ	الغائِبَة:
أُرِدْتُم	أُرِدْتُما	أُرِدْتَ	المُخاطَب:
أُرِدْتُنَّ	أُرِدْتُما	أُرِدْتِ	المُخاطَبَة:
أُرِدْنا		أُرِدْتُ	المُتَكَلِّم:

الجَمْع	المُثَنَّى	المُفْرد	المُضارِعُ المَجْهُول
يُرادُونَ	يُرادانِ	يُرادُ	الغائِب:
يُرَدْنَ	تُرادانِ	تُرادُ	الغائِبَة:
تُرادُونَ	تُرادانِ	تُرادُ	المُخاطَب:
تُرَدْنَ	تُرادانِ	تُرادِينَ	المُخاطَبَة:
نُرادُ		أُرادُ	المُتَكَلِّم:

الجَمْع	المُثَنَّى	المُفْرد	الأَمْرُ المَجْهُول
لِيُرادُوا	لِيُرادا	لِيُرَدْ	الغائِب:
لِيُرَدْنَ	لِتُرادا	لِتُرَدْ	الغائِبَة:
لِتُرادُوا	لِتُرادا	لِتُرَدْ	المُخاطَب:
لِتُرَدْنَ	لِتُرادا	لِتُرادِي	المُخاطَبَة:
لِنُرَدْ		لِأُرَدْ	المُتَكَلِّم:

Table 4.12 - The Active Voice Weak Verb (Naaqis): لقِي

ألْقَى، يُلْقِي، ألْقِ، ليُلْقِ، ليُلْقَى، يُلْقَى، أُلْقِيَ، أُلْقِي هُوَ إلْقَاءً و مُلْقٍ و مُلْقىً

الجَمْع	المُثَنَّى	المُفْرَد		الماضِي المَعلُوم
ألْقَوا	ألْقَيا	ألْقَى	الغائِب:	
ألْقَيْنَ	ألْقَتا	ألْقَتْ	الغائِبَة:	
ألْقَيْتُمْ	ألْقَيْتُما	ألْقَيْتَ	المُخاطَب:	
ألْقَيْتُنَّ	ألْقَيْتُما	ألْقَيْتِ	المُخاطَبَة:	
ألْقَيْنا		ألْقَيْتُ	المُتَكَلِّم:	

الجَمْع	المُثَنَّى	المُفْرَد		المُضارِعُ المَعلُوم
يُلْقُونَ	يُلْقِيانِ	يُلْقِي	الغائِب:	
يُلْقِينَ	تُلْقِيانِ	تُلْقِي	الغائِبَة:	
تُلْقُونَ	تُلْقِيانِ	تُلْقِي	المُخاطَب:	
تُلْقِينَ	تُلْقِيانِ	تُلْقِينَ	المُخاطَبَة:	
نُلْقِي		أُلْقِي	المُتَكَلِّم:	

الجَمْع	المُثَنَّى	المُفْرَد		الأَمْرُ المَعلُوم
ليُلْقُوا	ليُلْقِيا	ليُلْقِ	الغائِب:	
ليُلْقِينَ	لتُلْقِيا	لتُلْقِ	الغائِبَة:	
ألْقُوا	ألْقِيا	ألْقِ	المُخاطَب:	
ألْقِينَ	ألْقِيا	ألْقِي	المُخاطَبَة:	
لنُلْقِ		لأُلْقِ	المُتَكَلِّم:	

Table 4.13 - The Passive Voice Weak Verb (Naaqis): (لَقِيَ أُلْقِيَ، يُلْقَى)

الجَمْع	المُثَنَّى	المُفْرَد	الماضِي المَجْهول
أُلْقُوا	أُلْقِيا	أُلْقِيَ	الغائِب:
أُلْقِينَ	أُلْقِيتا	أُلْقِيَتْ	الغائِبَة:
أُلْقِيتُمْ	أُلْقِيتُما	أُلْقِيتَ	المُخاطَب:
أُلْقِيتُنَّ	أُلْقِيتُما	أُلْقِيتِ	المُخاطَبَة:
أُلْقِينا		أُلْقِيتُ	المُتَكَلِّم:

الجَمْع	المُثَنَّى	المُفْرَد	المُضارِعُ المَجْهول
يُلْقَوْنَ	يُلْقَيانِ	يُلْقَى	الغائِب:
يُلْقَيْنَ	تُلْقَيانِ	تُلْقَى	الغائِبَة:
تُلْقَوْنَ	تُلْقَيانِ	تُلْقَى	المُخاطَب:
تُلْقَيْنَ	تُلْقَيانِ	تُلْقَيْنَ	المُخاطَبَة:
نُلْقَى		أُلْقَى	المُتَكَلِّم:

الجَمْع	المُثَنَّى	المُفْرَد	الأَمْرُ المَجْهول
لِيُلْقَوْا	لِيُلْقَيا	لِيُلْقَ	الغائِب:
لِيُلْقَيْنَ	لِتُلْقَيا	لِتُلْقَ	الغائِبَة:
لِتُلْقَوْا	لِتُلْقَيا	لِتُلْقَ	المُخاطَب:
لِتُلْقَيْنَ	لِتُلْقَيا	لِتُلْقَيْ	المُخاطَبَة:
لِنُلْقَ		لِأُلْقَ	المُتَكَلِّم:

Table 4.14 - The Active Voice Weak Verb (Lafeef): وصي

أُوصى، يُوصي، أُوصِ، لِيُوصِ، أُوصِ، أُوصي، يُوصى، لِيُوصَ هُوَ إِيصاءً و مُوصٍ و مُوصىً

الجَمْع	المُثَنَّى	المُفْرَد	الماضيُ المَعلُوم
أُوصوا	أُوصيا	أُوصى	الغائِب:
أُوصينَ	أُوصتا	أُوصتْ	الغائِبة:
أُوصيتُمْ	أُوصيتُما	أُوصيتَ	المُخاطَب:
أُوصيتُنَّ	أُوصيتُما	أُوصيتِ	المُخاطَبة:
أُوصينا		أُوصيتُ	المُتَكَلِّم:

الجَمْع	المُثَنَّى	المُفْرَد	المُضارِعُ المَعلُوم
يُوصُونَ	يُوصيانِ	يُوصي	الغائِب:
يُوصينَ	تُوصيانِ	تُوصي	الغائِبة:
تُوصُونَ	تُوصيانِ	تُوصي	المُخاطَب:
تُوصينَ	تُوصيانِ	تُوصينَ	المُخاطَبة:
نُوصي		أُوصي	المُتَكَلِّم:

الجَمْع	المُثَنَّى	المُفْرَد	الأَمْرُ المَعلُوم
لِيُوصوا	لِيُوصيا	لِيُوصِ	الغائِب:
لِيُصينَ	لِتُوصيا	لِتُوصِ	الغائِبة:
أُوصوا	أُوصيا	أُوصِ	المُخاطَب:
أُوصينَ	أُوصيا	أُوصي	المُخاطَبة:
لِنُوصِ		لأُوصِ	المُتَكَلِّم:

Table 4.15 - The Passive Voice Weak Verb (Lafeef): (أُوصِي، يُوصَى) وصي

الجَمع	المُثَنَّى	المُفْرَد	الماضِي المَجْهُول
أُوصُوا	أُوصِيا	أُوصِيَ	الغائِب:
أُوصِينَ	أُوصِيَتا	أُوصِيَتْ	الغائِبَة:
أُوصِيتُنَّ	أُوصِيتُما	أُوصِيتَ	المُخاطَب:
أُوصِيتُنَّ	أُوصِيتُما	أُوصِيتِ	المُخاطَبَة:
أُوصِينا		أُوصِيتُ	المُتَكَلِّم:

الجَمع	المُثَنَّى	المُفْرَد	المُضارِع المَجْهُول
يُوصَونَ	يُوصَيانِ	يُوصَى	الغائِب:
يُوصَينَ	تُوصَيانِ	تُوصَى	الغائِبَة:
تُوصَونَ	تُوصَيانِ	تُوصَى	المُخاطَب:
تُوصَينَ	تُوصَيانِ	تُوصَينَ	المُخاطَبَة:
نُوصَى		أُوصَى	المُتَكَلِّم:

الجَمع	المُثَنَّى	المُفْرَد	الأَمْرُ المَجْهُول
لِيُوصَوا	لِيُوصَيا	لِيُوصَ	الغائِب:
لِيُوصَينَ	لِتُوصَيا	لِتُوصَ	الغائِبَة:
لِتُوصَوا	لِتُوصَيا	لِتُوصَ	المُخاطَب:
لِتُوصَينَ	لِتُوصَيا	لِتُوصَيْ	المُخاطَبَة:
لِنُوصَ		لِأُوصَ	المُتَكَلِّم:

▶ CONCLUDING NOTES

The Masdar of the *Ajwaf* Kalimah will have its second Original Letter (عَينُ الكَلِمَةِ), meaning the Weak Letter, omitted due to the application of the rules of *I'laal* and the **Feminine Taa'** (التَّاءُ المَرْبُوطَةُ) at the end of the word is substituted for the omitted letter, as in: إِرَاكةٌ on the pattern of: إِفَالَةٌ. It was originally: إِزوَاكٌ on the pattern of: إِفْعَالٌ, however, after *I'laal* two *Saakin* letters were created (إِراوُدٌ), therefore, the Weak Letter is omitted. Observe this formation in a few other *Ajwaf* Masdar:

(عيش) إِعْياش إِعاشَةٌ؛ (قوم) إِقْوام إِقامَةٌ

The verb رَأى , when found in the *Baab of If'aal*, the second Original Letter is removed after its vowel is transferred to the preceding letter (أَرَى). In the Masdar of the same word, the *Feminine Taa'* is added in place of the second Original Letter which was omitted and the Alif at its end is converted to Hamzah, as in: أَرَى إِرايَة إِرآءَةٌ.

The *Lafeef* Kalimah, like حَيَّ and عَيَّ, when put in the *Baab of If'aal*, the rules of *Mu'tall* will be applied upon them not the rules of *Mudhaa'af*. For example:

حَيَّ أَحْيَيَ أَحايَ يُحْيِي إِحْياءٌ

SECTION TWO

The Baab Of Taf'eel

بابُ تَفْعِيلٍ

فَعَّلَ، يُفَعِّلُ، فَعِّلْ، لِيُفَعِّلْ، فَعِّلْ، يُفَعِّلُ، لِيُفَعِّلْ هُوَ تَفْعِيلٌ و مُفَعِّلٌ و مُفَعَّلٌ

The Masdar of this Baab is: *Taf'eel* (تَفْعِيلٌ), and most verbs are derived from this Masdar. However, there are additional Masdar associated with this *Baab*:

(١) فَعَالٌ:	سَلَّمَ، يُسَلِّمُ	تَسْلِيمٌ وَ سَلامٌ
(٢) فِعَالٌ و فَعَّالٌ:	كَذَّبَ، يُكَذِّبُ	تَكْذِيبٌ و كِذَابٌ و كِذَّابٌ
(٣) تَفْعَالٌ:	كَرَّرَ، يُكَرِّرُ	تَكْرِيرٌ و تَكْرَارٌ
(٤) تَفْعِلَةٌ:	كَرَّمَ، يُكَرِّمُ	تَكْرِيمٌ و تَكْرِمَةٌ

The Masdar of the *Mahmooz* Kalimah which has the Hamzah as its third Original Letter (مَهْمُوزُ اللّام) and the *Naaqis* and *Lafeef* Kalimah are predominately on one pattern in this *Baab*: تَفْعِلَةٌ , as in:

(هنا) هَنَّأَ، يُهَنِّئُ، تَهْنِئَةٌ؛ (ربو) رَبَّى، يُرَبِّي، تَرْبِيَةٌ؛ (وصى) وَصَّى، يُوَصِّي، تَوْصِيَةٌ

The Special Letter characterizing this *Baab* is the Additional Letter produced when the second Original Letter bocomes doubled or *Mushaddad*. The first of these doubled letters is considered to be the Original Letter and the second, the Additional Letter. These doubled letters are the most obvious characteristic of verbs and nouns that are derived from the Masdar *Taf'eel*. In addition, the *Particle of the Present Tense* (حَرْفُ الْمُضَارِعِ) is again vowelled with Dhammah.

The second person Command Verb does not use Hamzah as is usually the case. This is due to the fact that the 1st Original Letter is vowelled whereas the verbs which have been reviewed to this point have mostly been *Saakin*. As a rule, when the 1st Original Letter is *Saakin* (in the Present Tense), Hamzah is not employed in the Command Verb. Here are the basic patterns of the verbs in this *Baab*:

Table 4.16 - Patterns Of Baab Of Taf'eel Active Voice Verb On The Pattern Of: فَعَّلَ يُفَعِّلُ

فَعَّلَ، يُفَعِّلُ، فَعِّلْ، لِيُفَعِّلْ، فَعِّلَ، يُفَعِّلُ هُوَ تَفْعِيلٌ و مُفَعِّلٌ و مُفَعَّلٌ

الجَمع	المُثَنَّى	المُفْرَد	الماضِي المَعلُوم
فَعَّلُوا	فَعَّلا	فَعَّلَ	الغائِب:
فَعَّلْنَ	فَعَّلَتا	فَعَّلَتْ	الغائِبة:
فَعَّلْتُم	فَعَّلْتُما	فَعَّلْتَ	المُخاطَب:
فَعَّلْتُنَّ	فَعَّلْتُما	فَعَّلْتِ	المُخاطِبة:
فَعَّلْنا		فَعَّلْتُ	المُتَكَلِّم:

الجَمع	المُثَنَّى	المُفْرَد	المُضارِعُ المَعلُوم
يُفَعِّلُونَ	يُفَعِّلانِ	يُفَعِّلُ	الغائِب:
يُفَعِّلْنَ	تُفَعِّلانِ	تُفَعِّلُ	الغائِبة:
تُفَعِّلُونَ	تُفَعِّلانِ	تُفَعِّلُ	المُخاطَب:
تُفَعِّلْنَ	تُفَعِّلانِ	تُفَعِّلِينَ	المُخاطِبة:
نُفَعِّلُ		أُفَعِّلُ	المُتَكَلِّم:

الجَمع	المُثَنَّى	المُفْرَد	الأَمرُ المَعلُوم
لِيُفَعِّلُوا	لِيُفَعِّلا	لِيُفَعِّلْ	الغائِب:
لِيُفَعِّلْنَ	لِتُفَعِّلا	لِتُفَعِّلْ	الغائِبة:
فَعِّلُوا	فَعِّلا	فَعِّلْ	المُخاطَب:
فَعِّلْنَ	فَعِّلا	فَعِّلي	المُخاطِبة:
لِنُفَعِّلْ		لِأُفَعِّلْ	المُتَكَلِّم:

Table 4.17 - Patterns Of Baab Of Taf'eel Passive Voice Verb On The Pattern Of: فُعِّلَ يُفَعَّلُ

الجَمع	المُثَنَّى	المُفرَد	الماضِي المَجهُول
فُعِّلُوا	فُعِّلا	فُعِّلَ	الغائِب:
فُعِّلنَ	فُعِّلَتا	فُعِّلَتْ	الغائِبة:
فُعِّلتُم	فُعِّلتُما	فُعِّلتَ	المُخاطَب:
فُعِّلتُنَّ	فُعِّلتُما	فُعِّلتِ	المُخاطَبة:
فُعِّلنا		فُعِّلتُ	المُتَكَلِّم:

الجَمع	المُثَنَّى	المُفرَد	المُضارِع المَجهُول
يُفَعَّلُونَ	يُفَعَّلانِ	يُفَعَّلُ	الغائِب:
يُفَعَّلنَ	تُفَعَّلانِ	تُفَعَّلُ	الغائِبة:
تُفَعَّلُونَ	تُفَعَّلانِ	تُفَعَّلُ	المُخاطَب:
تُفَعَّلنَ	تُفَعَّلانِ	تُفَعَّلِينَ	المُخاطَبة:
نُفَعَّلُ		أُفَعَّلُ	المُتَكَلِّم:

الجَمع	المُثَنَّى	المُفرَد	الأمر المَجهُول
لِيُفَعَّلُوا	لِيُفَعَّلا	لِيُفَعَّلْ	الغائِب:
لِتُفَعَّلنَ	لِتُفَعَّلا	لِتُفَعَّلْ	الغائِبة:
لِتُفَعَّلُوا	لِتُفَعَّلا	لِتُفَعَّلْ	المُخاطَب:
لِتُفَعَّلنَ	لِتُفَعَّلا	لِتُفَعَّلِي	المُخاطَبة:
لِنُفَعَّلْ		لِأُفَعَّلْ	المُتَكَلِّم:

▶ THE MEANINGS OF THE BAAB OF TAF'EEL مَعاني باب تَفْعيلٍ

The *Baab of Taf'eel* has seven meanings associated with it:

▷ **Transitivity** (التَّعْدِيَةُ), for example: فَرِحَ زَيدٌ *Zaid was happy* فَرَّحَ بَكْرٌ زَيداً *Bakr made Zaid happy*. The first verb is Instransitive while the second became Transitive and, thus, requires an Object (Zaid) to complete its meaning.

﴿وَ لَكِنَّ اللَّهَ حَبَّبَ إِلَيْكُمُ الإِيمانَ وَ زَيَّنَهُ في قُلُوبِكُمْ وَ كَرَّهَ إِلَيْكُمُ الكُفْرَ وَ الفُسُوقَ وَ العِصْيانَ...﴾

"...*But Allah has endeared the faith to you and has made it seemly in your hearts, and He has made hateful to you unbelief and transgression and disobedience...*" [Al-Hujaraat 49:7]

In this verse, the verbs: حَبَّبَ، زَيَّنَ، كَرَّهَ are all either intransitive (اللّازِمُ) as Primary Verbs or transitive by means of a Particle (المُتَعَدِّي بِحَرْفِ الجَرِّ). When entered into the *Baab of Taf'eel* they become either transitive or doubly transitive, meaning those verbs which were intransitive will become transitive. The verbs which were transitive by means of a Particle will require an Object, although the use of a Particle may still be needed. Verbs that were already transitive may become doubly transitive, meaning that two objects may be required, as in: ﴿عَلَّمَهُ البَيانَ﴾ "*He (Allah) taught him the mode of expression*" [55:4]. The Objects being the attached pronoun and *al-Bayaan*. The verbs from this *Baab* are most often found in this meaning.

▷ **Abundance** (التَّكْثِيرُ), meaning that the verb itself indicates upon abundance, excess and increase (الزِّيادَةُ), as in: طَوَّفَ زَيدٌ *Zaid made numerous Tawaaf*, or abundance in the Subject, as in the following: مَوَّتَ المالُ *A lot of property was made to perish*, or abundance in the Object, for example: غَلَّقْتُ الأَبْوابَ *I locked all the doors*. Observe the following verse:

﴿وَ إِذْ أَنْجَيْناكُمْ مِنْ آلِ فِرْعَوْنَ يَسُومُونَكُمْ سُوءَ العَذابِ، يُقَتِّلُونَ أَبْناءَكُمْ وَ يَسْتَحْيُونَ نِساءَكُمْ...﴾

"And when We delivered you from Pharoah's people who subjected you to severe torment, slaughtering your sons and sparing your women..." [Al-A'raaf 7:141]

The word signifying *slaughtering* (يُقَتِّلُونَ) means only *to kill* as a Primary Verb.

▷ **Negation** (السَّلْبُ), Meaning that the foundation of the action is negated in the Object, as in: قَشَرْتُ البَيْضَةَ *I gave the egg a shell*; جَلَّدْتُ الجُزُورَ *I put the hide on the slaughtered camel.* As a Primary Verb, these same verbs meant to shell and skin (an animal), respectively.

▷ **Attributive** (النِّسْبَةُ), meaning the derivative verb makes an attribution to the Object, as in: وَحَّدَ اللَّهَ *Allah is declared to be One* and: عَدَّلْتُ زَيْداً *I deem Zaid to be just*; كَفَّرْتُ بَكْراً *I deem Bakr to be a disbeliever.*

▷ **Gradation** (التَّدْرِيجُ), meaning that the action occurs progressively in stages, as in:

﴿وَ قُرْآناً فَرَقْناهُ لِتَقْرَأَهُ عَلَى النَّاسِ عَلَى مُكْثٍ وَ نَزَّلْناهُ تَنْزِيلاً﴾

"And it is a Quran which We revealed in portions so that you may read it to the people by slow degrees and We have revealed it, revealing in portions." [Al-Israa' 17:106]

▷ *Opposite The Meaning Of The Baab Of If'aal* (ضِدُّ مَعْنَى بابِ إِفْعالٍ), for example the verb فَرَّطَ can have the meaning of renouncing something while its meaning in the *Baab of If'aal* أَفْرَطَ is to go the extreme or exceed the limits.

▷ **The Meaning Of The Primary Verb** (مَعْنَى الثُّلاثِيِّ المُجَرَّدِ), as in: زالَ زَيْدٌ بَيْنَ القَومِ *Zaid disappeared among the people* or زَيَّلَ زَيْدٌ بَيْنَهُم.

SAMPLE CONJUGATION OF NON-SOUND AND MU'TALL VERBS IN THE BAAB OF TAF'EEL

Table 4.18 - Active Voice Non-Sound Verb (Mudhaa'af): قَرَّ

قَرَّرَ، يُقَرِّرُ، قَرِّرْ، لِيُقَرِّرْ، قُرِّرَ، يُقَرَّرُ، لِيُقَرَّرْ هُوَ تَقْرِيرٌ و مُقَرِّرٌ و مُقَرَّرٌ

المَاضِي المَعلُوم	المُفرَد	المُثَنَّى	الجَمع
الغَائِب:	قَرَّرَ	قَرَّرا	قَرَّروا
الغَائِبَة:	قَرَّرَث	قَرَّرَتا	قَرَّرنَ
المُخاطَب:	قَرَّرتَ	قَرَّرتُما	قَرَّرتُم
المُخاطَبَة:	قَرَّرتِ	قَرَّرتُما	قَرَّرتُنَّ
المُتَكَلِّم:	قَرَّرتُ		قَرَّرنا

المُضارِع المَعلُوم	المُفرَد	المُثَنَّى	الجَمع
الغَائِب:	يُقَرِّرُ	يُقَرِّرانِ	يُقَرِّرونَ
الغَائِبَة:	تُقَرِّرُ	تُقَرِّرانِ	يُقَرِّرنَ
المُخاطَب:	تُقَرِّرُ	تُقَرِّرانِ	تُقَرِّرونَ
المُخاطَبَة:	تُقَرِّرينَ	تُقَرِّرانِ	تُقَرِّرنَ
المُتَكَلِّم:	أُقَرِّرُ		نُقَرِّرُ

الأَمْر المَعلُوم	المُفرَد	المُثَنَّى	الجَمع
الغَائِب:	لِيُقَرِّرْ	لِيُقَرِّرا	لِيُقَرِّروا
الغَائِبَة:	لِتُقَرِّرْ	لِتُقَرِّرا	لِيُقَرِّرنَ
المُخاطَب:	قَرِّرْ	قَرِّرا	قَرِّروا
المُخاطَبَة:	قَرِّري	قَرِّرا	قَرِّرنَ
المُتَكَلِّم:	لِأُقَرِّرْ		لِنُقَرِّرْ

Table 4.19 - The Passive Voice Non-Sound Verb (Mudhaa'af): ‏(قَرَّ (قُرَّ، يُقَرَّ

الماضِي المَجْهُول	المُفْرَد	المُثَنَّى	الجَمْع
الغائب:	قُرَّ	قُرَّرا	قُرَّروا
الغائبة:	قُرَّتْ	قُرَّرَتا	قُرَّرْنَ
المُخاطَب:	قُرِّرْتَ	قُرِّرْتُما	قُرِّرْتُم
المُخاطَبة:	قُرِّرْتِ	قُرِّرْتُما	قُرِّرْتُنَّ
المُتَكَلِّم:	قُرِّرْتُ		قُرِّرْنا

المُضارِعُ المَجْهُول	المُفْرَد	المُثَنَّى	الجَمْع
الغائب:	يُقَرَّر	يُقَرَّرانِ	يُقَرَّرونَ
الغائبة:	تُقَرَّر	تُقَرَّرانِ	يُقَرَّرنَ
المُخاطَب:	تُقَرَّر	تُقَرَّرانِ	تُقَرَّرونَ
المُخاطَبة:	تُقَرَّرينَ	تُقَرَّرانِ	تُقَرَّرنَ
المُتَكَلِّم:	أُقَرَّر		نُقَرَّر

الأَمْرُ المَجْهُول	المُفْرَد	المُثَنَّى	الجَمْع
الغائب:	لِيُقَرَّر	لِيُقَرَّرا	لِيُقَرَّروا
الغائبة:	لِتُقَرَّر	لِتُقَرَّرا	لِيُقَرَّرنَ
المُخاطَب:	لِتُقَرَّر	لِتُقَرَّرا	لِتُقَرَّروا
المُخاطَبة:	لِتُقَرَّري	لِتُقَرَّرا	لِتُقَرَّرنَ
المُتَكَلِّم:	لِأُقَرَّر		لِنُقَرَّر

Table 4.20 - Active Voice Weak Verb (Mithaal): وكل

وَكَّلَ، يُوَكِّلُ، وَكِّلْ، وَكِّلْ، لِيُوَكَّلَ، يُوَكَّلُ، وَكِّلَ، لِيُوَكَّلُ هُوَ تَوْكِيلٌ و مُوَكِّلٌ و مُوَكَّلٌ

الجَمْع	المُثَنَّى	المُفْرَد		الماضِيُ المَعْلُوم
وَكَّلُوا	وَكَّلا	وَكَّلَ	الغائِب:	
وَكَّلْنَ	وَكَّلَتا	وَكَّلَتْ	الغائِبَة:	
وَكَّلْتُمْ	وَكَّلْتُما	وَكَّلْتَ	المُخاطَب:	
وَكَّلْتُنَّ	وَكَّلْتُما	وَكَّلْتِ	المُخاطَبَة:	
وَكَّلْنا		وَكَّلْتُ	المُتَكَلِّم:	

الجَمْع	المُثَنَّى	المُفْرَد		المُضارِعُ المَعْلُوم
يُوَكِّلُونَ	يُوَكِّلانِ	يُوَكِّلُ	الغائِب:	
يُوَكِّلْنَ	تُوَكِّلانِ	تُوَكِّلُ	الغائِبَة:	
تُوَكِّلُونَ	تُوَكِّلانِ	تُوَكِّلُ	المُخاطَب:	
تُوَكِّلْنَ	تُوَكِّلانِ	تُوَكِّلِينَ	المُخاطَبَة:	
نُوَكِّلُ		أُوَكِّلُ	المُتَكَلِّم:	

الجَمْع	المُثَنَّى	المُفْرَد		الأَمْرُ المَعْلُوم
لِيُوَكِّلُوا	لِيُوَكِّلا	لِيُوَكِّلْ	الغائِب:	
لِيُوَكِّلْنَ	لِيُوَكِّلا	لِتُوَكِّلْ	الغائِبَة:	
وَكِّلُوا	وَكِّلا	وَكِّلْ	المُخاطَب:	
وَكِّلْنَ	وَكِّلا	وَكِّلِي	المُخاطَبَة:	
لِنُوَكِّلْ		لِأُوَكِّلْ	المُتَكَلِّم:	

Table 4.21 - The Passive Voice Weak Verb (Mithaal): (وَكَّلَ، يُوَكَّلُ) وكل

الجَمع	المُثَنَّى	المُفرَد	الماضي المَجهُول
وُكِّلُوا	وُكِّلا	وُكِّلَ	الغائِب:
وُكِّلنَ	وُكِّلتا	وُكِّلتْ	الغائِبة:
وُكِّلتُم	وُكِّلتُما	وُكِّلتَ	المُخاطَب:
وُكِّلتُنَّ	وُكِّلتُما	وُكِّلتِ	المُخاطَبة:
وُكِّلنا		وُكِّلتُ	المُتَكَلِّم:

الجَمع	المُثَنَّى	المُفرَد	المُضارِع المَجهُول
يُوَكَّلُونَ	يُوَكَّلانِ	يُوَكَّلُ	الغائِب:
يُوَكَّلنَ	تُوَكَّلانِ	تُوَكَّلُ	الغائِبة:
تُوَكَّلُونَ	تُوَكَّلانِ	تُوَكَّلُ	المُخاطَب:
تُوَكَّلنَ	تُوَكَّلانِ	تُوَكَّلِينَ	المُخاطَبة:
نُوَكَّلُ		أُوَكَّلُ	المُتَكَلِّم:

الجَمع	المُثَنَّى	المُفرَد	الأمُر المَجهُول
لِيُوَكَّلُوا	لِيُوَكَّلا	لِيُوَكَّلْ	الغائِب:
لِيُوَكَّلنَ	لِتُوَكَّلا	لِتُوَكَّلْ	الغائِبة:
لِتُوَكَّلُوا	لِتُوَكَّلا	لِتُوَكَّلْ	المُخاطَب:
لِتُوَكَّلنَ	لِتُوَكَّلا	لِتُوَكَّلِي	المُخاطَبة:
لِنُوَكَّلْ		لِأُوَكَّلْ	المُتَكَلِّم:

Table 4.22 - The Active Voice Weak Verb (Ajwaf): عين

عَيَّنَ، يُعَيِّنُ، عَيِّنْ، لِيُعَيِّنْ، عُيِّنَ، يُعَيَّنُ، عَيِّنَ، لِيُعَيَّنْ هُوَ تَعْيِينٌ و مُعَيِّنٌ و مُعَيَّنٌ

الجَمْع	المُثَنَّى	المُفْرَد	الماضِي المَعلُوم
عَيَّنُوا	عَيَّنا	عَيَّنَ	الغائب:
عَيَّنَّ	عَيَّنَتا	عَيَّنَتْ	الغائبة:
عَيَّنْتُمْ	عَيَّنْتُما	عَيَّنْتَ	المُخاطَب:
عَيَّنْتُنَّ	عَيَّنْتُما	عَيَّنْتِ	المُخاطَبة:
عَيَّنّا		عَيَّنْتُ	المُتَكَلِّم:

الجَمْع	المُثَنَّى	المُفْرَد	المُضارِع المَعلُوم
يُعَيِّنُونَ	يُعَيِّنانِ	يُعَيِّنُ	الغائب:
يُعَيِّنَّ	تُعَيِّنانِ	تُعَيِّنُ	الغائبة:
تُعَيِّنُونَ	تُعَيِّنانِ	تُعَيِّنُ	المُخاطَب:
تُعَيِّنَّ	تُعَيِّنانِ	تُعَيِّنينَ	المُخاطَبة:
نُعَيِّنُ		أُعَيِّنُ	المُتَكَلِّم:

الجَمْع	المُثَنَّى	المُفْرَد	الأَمْرُ المَعلُوم
لِيُعَيِّنُوا	لِيُعَيِّنا	لِيُعَيِّنْ	الغائب:
لِيُعَيِّنَّ	لِتُعَيِّنا	لِتُعَيِّنْ	الغائبة:
عَيِّنُوا	عَيِّنا	عَيِّنْ	المُخاطَب:
عَيِّنَّ	عَيِّنا	عَيِّني	المُخاطَبة:
لِنُعَيِّنْ		لأُعَيِّنْ	المُتَكَلِّم:

Table 4.23 - The Passive Voice Weak Verb (Ajwaf): (عين (عُيِّنَ، يُعَيَّنُ

الجَمْع	المُثَنَّى	المُفْرَد	الماضِيُّ المَجْهُول
عُيِّنُوا	عُيِّنا	عُيِّنَ	الغائِب:
عُيِّنَّ	عُيِّنَتا	عُيِّنَتْ	الغائِبَة:
عُيِّنْتُمْ	عُيِّنْتُما	عُيِّنْتَ	المُخاطَب:
عُيِّنْتُنَّ	عُيِّنْتُما	عُيِّنْتِ	المُخاطَبَة:
عُيِّنَّا		عُيِّنْتُ	المُتَكَلِّم:

الجَمْع	المُثَنَّى	المُفْرَد	المُضارِعُ المَجْهُول
يُعَيَّنُونَ	يُعَيَّنانِ	يُعَيَّنُ	الغائِب:
يُعَيَّنَّ	تُعَيَّنانِ	تُعَيَّنُ	الغائِبَة:
تُعَيَّنُونَ	تُعَيَّنانِ	تُعَيَّنُ	المُخاطَب:
تُعَيَّنَّ	تُعَيَّنانِ	تُعَيَّنِينَ	المُخاطَبَة:
نُعَيَّنُ		أُعَيَّنُ	المُتَكَلِّم:

الجَمْع	المُثَنَّى	المُفْرَد	الأَمْرُ المَجْهُول
لِيُعَيَّنُوا	لِيُعَيَّنا	لِيُعَيَّنْ	الغائِب:
لِيُعَيَّنَّ	لِتُعَيَّنا	لِتُعَيَّنْ	الغائِبَة:
لِتُعَيَّنُوا	لِتُعَيَّنا	لِتُعَيَّنْ	المُخاطَب:
لِتُعَيَّنَّ	لِتُعَيَّنا	لِتُعَيَّنِي	المُخاطَبَة:
لِنُعَيَّنْ		لِأُعَيَّنْ	المُتَكَلِّم:

Table 4.24 - The Active Voice Weak Verb (Naaqis): سمو

سَمَّى، يُسَمِّي، سَمِّ، لِيُسَمِّ، سُمِّيَ، لِيُسَمَّ، يُسَمَّى، سُمِّيَ هُوَ تَسْمِية و مُسَمِّ و مُسَمَّى

الجَمْع	المُثَنَّى	المُفْرَد		الماضِي المَعْلُوم
سَمَّوا	سَمَّيَا	سَمَّى	الغائِب:	
سَمَّيْنَ	سَمَّتَا	سَمَّتْ	الغائِبَة:	
سَمَّيْتُمْ	سَمَّيْتُما	سَمَّيْتَ	المُخاطَب:	
سَمَّيْتُنَّ	سَمَّيْتُما	سَمَّيْتِ	المُخاطَبَة:	
سَمَّيْنا		سَمَّيْتُ	المُتَكَلِّم:	

الجَمْع	المُثَنَّى	المُفْرَد		المُضارِع المَعْلُوم
يُسَمُّونَ	يُسَمِّيانِ	يُسَمِّي	الغائِب:	
يُسَمِّينَ	تُسَمِّيانِ	تُسَمِّي	الغائِبَة:	
تُسَمُّونَ	تُسَمِّيانِ	تُسَمِّي	المُخاطَب:	
تُسَمِّينَ	تُسَمِّيانِ	تُسَمِّينَ	المُخاطَبَة:	
نُسَمِّي		أُسَمِّي	المُتَكَلِّم:	

الجَمْع	المُثَنَّى	المُفْرَد		الأَمْر المَعْلُوم
لِيُسَمُّوا	لِيُسَمِّيَا	لِيُسَمِّ	الغائِب:	
لِيُسَمِّينَ	لِتُسَمِّيَا	لِتُسَمِّ	الغائِبَة:	
سَمُّوا	سَمِّيَا	سَمِّ	المُخاطَب:	
سَمِّينَ	سَمِّيَا	سَمِّي	المُخاطَبَة:	
لِنُسَمِّ		لِأُسَمِّ	المُتَكَلِّم:	

Table 4.25 - The Passive Voice Weak Verb (Naaqis): (سمو (سُمِّيَ، يُسَمَّى))

الجَمْع	المُثَنَّى	المُفْرَد	الماضي المَجْهُول
سُمُّوا	سُمِّيَا	سُمِّيَ	الغَائِب:
سُمِّينَ	سُمِّيَتا	سُمِّيَتْ	الغَائِبَة:
سُمِّيتُمْ	سُمِّيتُما	سُمِّيتَ	المُخَاطَب:
سُمِّيتُنَّ	سُمِّيتُما	سُمِّيتِ	المُخَاطَبَة:
سُمِّينا		سُمِّيتُ	المُتَكَلِّم:

الجَمْع	المُثَنَّى	المُفْرَد	المُضَارِعُ المَجْهُول
يُسَمَّونَ	يُسَمَّيانِ	يُسَمَّى	الغَائِب:
يُسَمَّينَ	تُسَمَّيانِ	تُسَمَّى	الغَائِبَة:
تُسَمَّونَ	تُسَمَّيانِ	تُسَمَّى	المُخَاطَب:
تُسَمَّينَ	تُسَمَّيانِ	تُسَمَّينَ	المُخَاطَبَة:
نُسَمَّى		أُسَمَّى	المُتَكَلِّم:

الجَمْع	المُثَنَّى	المُفْرَد	الأَمْرُ المَجْهُول
لِيُسَمَّوا	لِيُسَمَّيا	لِيُسَمَّ	الغَائِب:
لِيُسَمَّينَ	لِتُسَمَّيا	لِتُسَمَّ	الغَائِبَة:
لِتُسَمَّوا	لِتُسَمَّيا	لِتُسَمَّ	المُخَاطَب:
لِتُسَمَّينَ	لِتُسَمَّيا	لِتُسَمَّي	المُخَاطَبَة:
لِيُسَمَّ		لِأُسَمَّ	المُتَكَلِّم:

Table 4.26 - The Active Voice Weak Verb (Lafeef): سوي

سَوَّى، يُسَوِّي، سَوِّ، لِيُسَوِّ، سُوِّيَ، يُسَوَّى، لِيُسَوَّ هُوَ تَسْوِيَةً و مُسَوٍّ و مُسَوَّىً

الجَمْع	المُثَنَّى	المُفْرَد	الماضي المَعْلُوم
سَوَّوا	سَوَّيَا	سَوَّى	الغائِب:
سَوَّيْنَ	سَوَّتا	سَوَّتْ	الغائِبة:
سَوَّيْتُمْ	سَوَّيْتُما	سَوَّيْتَ	المُخاطَب:
سَوَّيْتُنَّ	سَوَّيْتُما	سَوَّيْتِ	المُخاطَبة:
سَوَّيْنا		سَوَّيْتُ	المُتَكَلِّم:

الجَمْع	المُثَنَّى	المُفْرَد	المُضارِع المَعْلُوم
يُسَوُّونَ	يُسَوِّيانِ	يُسَوِّي	الغائِب:
يُسَوِّينَ	تُسَوِّيانِ	تُسَوِّي	الغائِبة:
تُسَوُّونَ	تُسَوِّيانِ	تُسَوِّي	المُخاطَب:
تُسَوِّينَ	تُسَوِّيانِ	تُسَوِّينَ	المُخاطَبة:
نُسَوِّي		أُسَوِّي	المُتَكَلِّم:

الجَمْع	المُثَنَّى	المُفْرَد	الأَمْر المَعْلُوم
لِيُسَوُّوا	لِيُسَوِّيَا	لِيُسَوِّ	الغائِب:
لِيُسَوِّينَ	لِتُسَوِّيَا	لِتُسَوِّ	الغائِبة:
سَوُّوا	سَوِّيَا	سَوِّ	المُخاطَب:
سَوِّينَ	سَوِّيَا	سَوِّي	المُخاطَبة:
لِنُسَوِّ		لِأُسَوِّ	المُتَكَلِّم:

Table 4.27 - The Passive Voice Weak Verb (Lafeef): (سُوِّيَ، يُسَوَّى) سوي

الجَمع	المُثَنَّى	المُفرَد	الماضي المَجهُول
سُوُّوا	سُوِّيَا	سُوِّيَ	الغَائِب:
سُوِّينَ	سُوِّيَتا	سُوِّيَتْ	الغَائِبَة:
سُوِّيتُم	سُوِّيتُما	سُوِّيتَ	المُخَاطَب:
سُوِّيتُنَّ	سُوِّيتُما	سُوِّيتِ	المُخَاطَبَة:
سُوِّينا		سُوِّيتُ	المُتَكَلِّم:
الجَمع	المُثَنَّى	المُفرَد	المُضارع المَجهُول
يُسَوَّونَ	يُسَوَّيَانِ	يُسَوَّى	الغَائِب:
يُسَوَّينَ	تُسَوَّيَانِ	تُسَوَّى	الغَائِبَة:
تُسَوَّونَ	تُسَوَّيَانِ	تُسَوَّى	المُخَاطَب:
تُسَوَّينَ	تُسَوَّيَانِ	تُسَوَّينَ	المُخَاطَبَة:
نُسَوَّى		أُسَوَّى	المُتَكَلِّم:
الجَمع	المُثَنَّى	المُفرَد	الأَمرُ المَجهُول
لِيُسَوَّوا	لِيُسَوَّيَا	لِيُسَوَّ	الغَائِب:
لِيُسَوَّينَ	لِتُسَوَّيَا	لِتُسَوَّ	الغَائِبَة:
لِتُسَوَّوا	لِتُسَوَّيَا	لِتُسَوَّ	المُخَاطَب:
لِتُسَوَّينَ	لِتُسَوَّيَا	لِتُسَوَّيْ	المُخَاطَبَة:
لِنُسَوَّ		لِأُسَوَّ	المُتَكَلِّم:

SECTION THREE

The Baab Of Mufaa'alah

بابُ مُفَاعَلَةٍ

فَاعَلَ، يُفَاعِلُ، فَاعِلْ، لِيُفَاعِلْ، فُوعِلَ، يُفَاعَلُ، لِيُفَاعَلْ هُوَ مُفَاعَلَةٌ و مُفَاعِلٌ و مُفَاعَلٌ

The Masdar of this *Baab* can be found on the patterns of مُفَاعَلَةٌ and فِعَالٌ. The Masdar of the *Mithaal* Kalimah with Yaa' (المِثَالُ اليَائِيُّ) only comes on the pattern of مُفَاعَلَةٌ, while most other Masdar also have the pattern فِعَالٌ. The Special Letter in this *Baab* is the Alif which is found following the first Original Letter. This Additional Letter is found in most of the derivatives associated with this *Baab*.

It should be noted that in the Past Tense Passive Voice Verb this same Alif is converted to Waw as the pattern of the Passive Voice is: (فُعِلَ) and the first Original Letter is vowelled with Dhammah. This vowelization is unworkable (فُاعِلَ) and the Alif is changed to the letter appropriate for Dhammah, meaning Waw: (فُوعِلَ).

The *Particle of the Present Tense* (حَرْفُ المُضَارِعِ) is also vowelled with Dhammah as were the previous Derivative Verbs. Here are the patterns of its major divisions:

Table 4.28 - Patterns Of Baab Of Mufaa'alah Active Voice Verb - Pattern Of: فَاعَلَ يُفَاعِلُ

فَاعَلَ، يُفَاعِلُ، فَاعِلْ، لِيُفَاعِلْ، يُفاعَلَ، فُوعِلَ، لِيُفَاعِلُ هُوَ مُفَاعَلَةً و مُفاعِلٌ و مُفاعَلٌ

الجَمع	المُثَنَّى	المُفرَد		الماضِيُ المَعلُوم
فَاعَلُوا	فَاعَلا	فَاعَلَ	الغَائِب:	
فَاعَلنَ	فَاعَلَتا	فَاعَلَتْ	الغَائِبَة:	
فَاعَلتُم	فَاعَلتُما	فَاعَلتَ	المُخاطَب:	
فَاعَلتُنَّ	فَاعَلتُما	فَاعَلتِ	المُخاطَبة:	
فَاعَلنا		فَاعَلتُ	المُتَكَلِّم:	

الجَمع	المُثَنَّى	المُفرَد		المُضارِعُ المَعلُوم
يُفاعِلُونَ	يُفاعِلانِ	يُفاعِلُ	الغَائِب:	
يُفاعِلنَ	تُفاعِلانِ	تُفاعِلُ	الغَائِبَة:	
تُفاعِلُونَ	تُفاعِلانِ	تُفاعِلُ	المُخاطَب:	
تُفاعِلنَ	تُفاعِلانِ	تُفاعِلِينَ	المُخاطَبة:	
نُفاعِلُ		أُفاعِلُ	المُتَكَلِّم:	

الجَمع	المُثَنَّى	المُفرَد		الأَمرُ المَعلُوم
لِيُفاعِلُوا	لِيُفاعِلا	لِيُفاعِلْ	الغَائِب:	
لِيُفاعِلنَ	لِتُفاعِلا	لِتُفاعِلْ	الغَائِبَة:	
فَاعِلُوا	فَاعِلا	فَاعِلْ	المُخاطَب:	
فَاعِلنَ	فَاعِلا	فَاعِلي	المُخاطَبة:	
لِنُفاعِلْ		لِأُفاعِلْ	المُتَكَلِّم:	

Table 4.29 - Patterns Of Baab Of Mufaa'alah Passive Voice Verb - Pattern Of: فُوعِلَ يُفاعَلُ

الجَمع	المُثَنَّى	المُفرَد	الماضِي المَجهُول
فُوعِلُوا	فُوعِلا	فُوعِلَ	الغائِب:
فُوعِلْنَ	فُوعِلَتا	فُوعِلَتْ	الغائِبَة:
فُوعِلْتُم	فُوعِلْتُما	فُوعِلْتَ	المُخاطَب:
فُوعِلْتُنَّ	فُوعِلْتُما	فُوعِلْتِ	المُخاطَبَة:
فُوعِلْنا		فُوعِلْتُ	المُتَكَلِّم:
الجَمع	المُثَنَّى	المُفرَد	المُضارِعُ المَجهُول
يُفاعَلُونَ	يُفاعَلانِ	يُفاعَلُ	الغائِب:
يُفاعَلْنَ	تُفاعَلانِ	تُفاعَلُ	الغائِبَة:
تُفاعَلُونَ	تُفاعَلانِ	تُفاعَلُ	المُخاطَب:
تُفاعَلْنَ	تُفاعَلانِ	تُفاعَلِينَ	المُخاطَبَة:
نُفاعَلُ		أُفاعَلُ	المُتَكَلِّم:
الجَمع	المُثَنَّى	المُفرَد	الأَمْرُ المَجهُول
لِيُفاعَلُوا	لِيُفاعَلا	لِيُفاعَلْ	الغائِب:
لِيُفاعَلْنَ	لِتُفاعَلا	لِتُفاعَلْ	الغائِبَة:
لِتُفاعَلُوا	لِتُفاعَلا	لِتُفاعَلْ	المُخاطَب:
لِتُفاعَلْنَ	لِتُفاعَلا	لِتُفاعَلي	المُخاطَبَة:
لِنُفاعَلْ		لأُفاعَلْ	المُتَكَلِّم:

▶ **THE MEANINGS OF THE BAAB OF MUFAA'ALAH** مَعَانِي بَابِ مُفَاعَلَةٍ

▷ **Partnership** (الْمُشَارَكَةُ). Most often, the verbs from this *Baab* will signify the meaning of partnership, meaning that the action is being shared by two parties, the Subject and the Object, for example:

ضَارَبَ زَيدٌ بَكُراً *Zaid and Bakr struck one another*

جَادَلْتُ زَيداً *I debated with Zaid.*

﴿إِنْ جَادَلُوكَ فَقُلِ اللَّهُ أَعْلَمُ بِما تَعْمَلُونَ﴾

"*And when they contend with you, say: Allah best knows what you do.*"

[Al-Hajj 22:68]

▷ **Transitivity** (التَّعْدِيَةُ) , as in: بَعُدَ زَيدٌ *Zaid was far;* بَاعَدَ بَكُرٌ زَيداً *Bakr sent Zaid far away.*

▷ **Abundance** (التَّكْثِيرُ), as in: نَاعَمَهُ اللَّهُ *Allah was Most Gracious upon him.*

▷ **The Meaning of the Primary Verb**(مَعْنَى الثُّلَاثِيِّ الْمُجَرَّدِ), as in: سَافَرَ زَيدٌ or سَفَرَ زَيدٌ *Zaid traveled.* Often when the verb in this Baab is used to attribute something to Allah Ta'ala, it will have this meaning, as in: قَاتَلَهُمُ اللَّهُ *Allah killed them;* عَافَاكَ اللَّهُ *May Allah grant well being to you,* and:

﴿يُخَادِعُونَ اللَّهَ وَ الَّذِينَ آمَنُوا وَ ما يَخْدَعُونَ إِلَّا أَنْفُسَهُمْ وَ ما يَشْعُرُونَ﴾

"*They (the nonbelievers) desire to deceive Allah and those who believe, and they deceive only themselves and they do not perceive.*" (Al-Baqarah 2:9)

CONJUGATION OF THE NON-SOUND AND WEAK VERB IN THE BAAB OF MUFAA'ALAH

Table 4.30 - The Active Voice Non-Sound Verb (Mahmooz): أَخَذَ

آخَذَ، يُوَاخِذُ، آخِذْ، لِيُوَاخِذْ، أُوخِذَ، يُوَاخَذُ لِيُوَاخَذْ هُوَ مُوَاخَذَةٌ و مُوَاخِذٌ و مُوَاخَذٌ

الجَمْع	المُثَنَّى	المُفْرَد		الماضِي المَعْلُوم
آخَذُوا	آخَذَا	آخَذَ	الغائِب:	
آخَذْنَ	آخَذَتَا	آخَذَتْ	الغائِبَة:	
آخَذْتُمْ	آخَذْتُمَا	آخَذْتَ	المُخاطَب:	
آخَذْتُنَّ	خَذْتُمَا	آخَذْتِ	المُخاطَبَة:	
آخَذْنَا		آخَذْتُ	المُتَكَلِّم:	

الجَمْع	المُثَنَّى	المُفْرَد		المُضارِع المَعْلُوم
يُوَاخِذُونَ	يُوَاخِذَانِ	يُوَاخِذُ	الغائِب:	
يُوَاخِذْنَ	تُوَاخِذَانِ	تُوَاخِذُ	الغائِبَة:	
تُوَاخِذُونَ	تُوَاخِذَانِ	تُوَاخِذُ	المُخاطَب:	
تُوَاخِذْنَ	تُوَاخِذَانِ	تُوَاخِذِينَ	المُخاطَبَة:	
نُوَاخِذُ		أُوَاخِذُ	المُتَكَلِّم:	

الجَمْع	المُثَنَّى	المُفْرَد		الأَمْرُ المَعْلُوم
لِيُوَاخِذُوا	لِيُوَاخِذَا	لِيُوَاخِذْ	الغائِب:	
لِيُوَاخِذْنَ	لِتُوَاخِذَا	لِتُوَاخِذْ	الغائِبَة:	
آخِذُوا	آخِذَا	آخِذْ	المُخاطَب:	
آخِذْنَ	آخِذَا	آخِذِي	المُخاطَبَة:	
لِنُوَاخِذْ		لِأُوَاخِذْ	المُتَكَلِّم:	

Table 4.31 - The Passive Voice Non-Sound Verb (Mahmooz): أخذ (أُوخِذَ، يُؤَاخَذُ)

الجَمع	المُثَنَّى	المُفرَد	الماضِي المَجْهُول
أُوخِذوا	أُوخِذا	أُوخِذَ	الغائِب:
أُوخِذْنَ	أُوخِذَتا	أُوخِذَتْ	الغائِبَة:
أُوخِذْتُم	أُوخِذْتُما	أُوخِذْتَ	المُخاطَب:
أُوخِذْتُنَّ	أُوخِذْتُما	أُوخِذْتِ	المُخاطَبَة:
أُوخِذْنا		أُوخِذْتُ	المُتَكَلِّم:

الجَمع	المُثَنَّى	المُفرَد	المُضارِع المَجْهُول
يُؤَاخَذونَ	يُؤَاخَذانِ	يُؤَاخَذُ	الغائِب:
يُؤَاخَذْنَ	تُؤَاخَذانِ	تُؤَاخَذُ	الغائِبَة:
تُؤَاخَذونَ	تُؤَاخَذانِ	تُؤَاخَذُ	المُخاطَب:
تُؤَاخَذْنَ	تُؤَاخَذانِ	تُؤَاخَذينَ	المُخاطَبَة:
نُؤَاخَذُ		أُؤَاخَذُ	المُتَكَلِّم:

الجَمع	المُثَنَّى	المُفرَد	الأَمْر المَجْهُول
لِيُؤَاخَذوا	لِيُؤَاخَذا	لِيُؤَاخَذْ	الغائِب:
لِيُؤَاخَذْنَ	لِيُؤَاخَذا	لِتُؤَاخَذْ	الغائِبَة:
لِتُؤَاخَذوا	لِتُؤَاخَذا	لِتُؤَاخَذْ	المُخاطَب:
لِتُؤَاخَذْنَ	لِتُؤَاخَذا	لِتُؤَاخَذي	المُخاطَبَة:
لِنُؤَاخَذْ		لِأُؤَاخَذْ	المُتَكَلِّم:

Table 4.32 - The Active Voice Non-Sound Verb (Mudhaa'af): حجّ

حاجَّ، يُحاجُّ، حاجِجْ، لِيُحاجِجْ، حُوجِجَ، يُحاجَجُ، لِيُحاجَجْ هُوَ مُحاجَجَةٌ (حِجاجٌ) و مُحاجِجٌ و مُحاجَجٌ

الماضِيُ المَعْلُوم	المُفْرَد	المُثَنَّى	الجَمْع
الغائب:	حاجَّ	حاجّا	حاجُّوا
الغائبة:	حاجَّتْ	حاجَّتا	حاجَجْنَ
المُخاطَب:	حاجَجْتَ	حاجَجْتُما	حاجَجْتُم
المُخاطَبة:	حاجَجْتِ	حاجَجْتُما	حاجَجْتُنَّ
المُتَكَلِّم:	حاجَجْتُ		حاجَجْنا

المُضارِعُ المَعْلُوم	المُفْرَد	المُثَنَّى	الجَمْع
الغائب:	يُحاجُّ	يُحاجّانِ	يُحاجُّونَ
الغائبة:	تُحاجُّ	تُحاجّانِ	يُحاجِجْنَ
المُخاطَب:	تُحاجُّ	تُحاجّانِ	تُحاجُّونَ
المُخاطَبة:	تُحاجِّينَ	تُحاجّانِ	تُحاجِجْنَ
المُتَكَلِّم:	أُحاجُّ		نُحاجُّ

الأَمْرُ المَعْلُوم	المُفْرَد	المُثَنَّى	الجَمْع
الغائب:	لِيُحاجِجْ	لِيُحاجّا	لِيُحاجُّوا
الغائبة:	لِتُحاجِجْ	لِتُحاجّا	لِيُحاجِجْنَ
المُخاطَب:	حاجِجْ	حاجِجا	حاجِجوا
المُخاطَبة:	حاجِجي	حاجِجا	حاجِجْنَ
المُتَكَلِّم:	لِأُحاجِجْ		لِنُحاجِجْ

Table 4.33 - The Passive Voice Non-Sound Verb (Mudhaa'af): (حُوجِجَ، يُحَاجَجُ) حَجَّ

الجَمْع	المُثَنَّى	المُفْرَد	الماضِيُ المَجْهُول
حُوجِجُوا	حُوجِجا	حُوجِجَ	الغائِب:
حُوجِجْنَ	حُوجِجتا	حُوجِجَتْ	الغائِبَة:
حُوجِجتُمْ	حُوجِجتُما	حُوجِجتَ	المُخاطَب:
حُوجِجتُنَّ	حُوجِجتُما	حُوجِجتِ	المُخاطَبة:
حُوجِجنا		حُوجِجتُ	المُتَكَلِّم:

الجَمْع	المُثَنَّى	المُفْرَد	المُضارِعُ المَجْهُول
يُحاجَجُونَ	يُحاجَجانِ	يُحاجَجُ	الغائِب:
يُحاجَجْنَ	تُحاجَجانِ	تُحاجَجُ	الغائِبَة:
تُحاجَجُونَ	تُحاجَجانِ	تُحاجَجُ	المُخاطَب:
تُحاجَجْنَ	تُحاجَجانِ	تُحاجَجِينَ	المُخاطَبة:
نُحاجَجُ		أُحاجَجُ	المُتَكَلِّم:

الجَمْع	المُثَنَّى	المُفْرَد	الأَمْرُ المَجْهُول
لِيُحاجَجُوا	لِيُحاجَجا	لِيُحاجَجْ	الغائِب:
لِيُحاجَجْنَ	لِتُحاجَجا	لِتُحاجَجْ	الغائِبَة:
لِتُحاجَجُوا	لِتُحاجَجا	لِتُحاجَجْ	المُخاطَب:
لِتُحاجَجْنَ	لِتُحاجَجا	لِتُحاجَجِي	المُخاطَبة:
لِنُحاجَجْ		لِأُحاجَجْ	المُتَكَلِّم:

Table 4.34 - The Active Voice Weak Verb (Mithaal): وفق

وافَقَ، يُوافِقُ، وافِقْ، لِيُوافِقْ، وُوفِقَ، يُوافَقُ، لِيُوافَقْ هُوَ مُوافَقَةٌ و مُوافِقٌ و مُوافَقٌ

الجَمْع	المُثَنَّى	المُفْرَد	الماضِي المَعْلُوم
وافَقُوا	وافَقا	وافَقَ	الغائِب:
وافَقْنَ	وافَقَتا	وافَقَتْ	الغائِبة:
وافَقْتُمْ	وافَقْتُما	وافَقْتَ	المُخاطَب:
وافَقْتُنَّ	وافَقْتُما	وافَقْتِ	المُخاطَبة:
وافَقْنا		وافَقْتُ	المُتَكَلِّم:

الجَمْع	المُثَنَّى	المُفْرَد	المُضارِع المَعْلُوم
يُوافِقُونَ	يُوافِقانِ	يُوافِقُ	الغائِب:
يُوافِقْنَ	تُوافِقانِ	تُوافِقُ	الغائِبة:
تُوافِقُونَ	تُوافِقانِ	تُوافِقُ	المُخاطَب:
تُوافِقْنَ	تُوافِقانِ	تُوافِقِينَ	المُخاطَبة:
نُوافِقُ		أُوافِقُ	المُتَكَلِّم:

الجَمْع	المُثَنَّى	المُفْرَد	الأَمْرُ المَعْلُوم
لِيُوافِقُوا	لِيُوافِقا	لِيُوافِقْ	الغائِب:
لِيُوافِقْنَ	لِتُوافِقا	لِتُوافِقْ	الغائِبة:
وافِقُوا	وافِقا	وافِقْ	المُخاطَب:
وافِقْنَ	وافِقا	وافِقي	المُخاطَبة:
لِنُوافِقْ		لِأُوافِقْ	المُتَكَلِّم:

Table 4.35 - The Passive Voice Weak Verb (Mithaal): (وَفَقَ، يُوفِقَ، يُوافَقُ)

الجَمع	المُثَنَّى	المُفرَد	الماضِي المَجهُول
وُوفِقُوا	وُوفِقا	وُوفِقَ	الغائِب:
وُوفِقْنَ	وُوفِقَتا	وُوفِقَتْ	الغائِبَة:
وُوفِقْتُم	وُوفِقْتُما	وُوفِقْتَ	المُخاطَب:
وُوفِقْتُنَّ	وُوفِقْتُما	وُوفِقْتِ	المُخاطَبَة:
وُوفِقْنا		وُوفِقْتُ	المُتَكَلِّم:
الجَمع	المُثَنَّى	المُفرَد	المُضارِعُ المَجهُول
يُوافَقُونَ	يُوافَقانِ	يُوافَقُ	الغائِب:
يُوافَقْنَ	تُوافَقانِ	تُوافَقُ	الغائِبَة:
تُوافَقُونَ	تُوافَقانِ	تُوافَقُ	المُخاطَب:
تُوافَقْنَ	تُوافَقانِ	تُوافَقينَ	المُخاطَبَة:
نُوافَقُ		أُوافَقُ	المُتَكَلِّم:
الجَمع	المُثَنَّى	المُفرَد	الأَمرُ المَجهُول
لِيُوافَقُوا	لِيُوافَقا	لِيُوافَقْ	الغائِب:
لِيُوافَقْنَ	لِتُوافَقا	لِتُوافَقْ	الغائِبَة:
لِتُوافَقُوا	لِتُوافَقا	لِتُوافَقْ	المُخاطَب:
لِتُوافَقْنَ	لِتُوافَقا	لِتُوافَقي	المُخاطَبَة:
لِنُوافَقْ		لِأُوافَقْ	المُتَكَلِّم:

Table 4.36 - The Active Voice Weak Verb (Ajwaf): قوم

قاوَمَ، يُقاوِمُ، قاوِمْ، لِيُقاوِمْ، قُووِمَ، يُقاوَمُ، لِيُقاوَمْ هُوَ مُقاوَمَةً و مُقاوِمٌ و مُقاوَمٌ

الجَمْع	المُثَنَّى	المُفْرَد	الماضِيُ المَعْلُوم
قاوَمُوا	قاوَما	قاوَمَ	الغائِب:
قاوَمْنَ	قاوَمَتا	قاوَمَتْ	الغائِبَة:
قاوَمْتُمْ	قاوَمْتُما	قاوَمْتَ	المُخاطَب:
قاوَمْتُنَّ	قاوَمْتُما	قاوَمْتِ	المُخاطَبَة:
قاوَمْنا		قاوَمْتُ	المُتَكَلِّم:

الجَمْع	المُثَنَّى	المُفْرَد	المُضارِعُ المَعْلُوم
يُقاوِمُونَ	يُقاوِمانِ	يُقاوِمُ	الغائِب:
يُقاوِمْنَ	تُقاوِمانِ	تُقاوِمُ	الغائِبَة:
تُقاوِمُونَ	تُقاوِمانِ	تُقاوِمُ	المُخاطَب:
تُقاوِمْنَ	تُقاوِمانِ	تُقاوِمِينَ	المُخاطَبَة:
نُقاوِمُ		أُقاوِمُ	المُتَكَلِّم:

الجَمْع	المُثَنَّى	المُفْرَد	الأَمْرُ المَعْلُوم
لِيُقاوِمُوا	لِيُقاوِما	لِيُقاوِمْ	الغائِب:
لِيُقاوِمْنَ	لِتُقاوِما	لِتُقاوِمْ	الغائِبَة:
قاوِمُوا	قاوِما	قاوِمْ	المُخاطَب:
قاوِمْنَ	قاوِما	قاوِمِي	المُخاطَبَة:
لِنُقاوِمْ		لِأُقاوِمْ	المُتَكَلِّم:

Table 4.37 - The Passive Voice Weak Verb (Ajwaf): (قوم (قُوِّمَ، يُقاوَمُ

الجَمْع	المُثَنَّى	المُفْرَد	الماضِيُ المَجْهُول
قُووِمُوا	قُووِما	قُووِمَ	الغائِب:
قُووِمْنَ	قُووِمَتا	قُووِمَتْ	الغائِبَة:
قُووِمْتُم	قُووِمْتُما	قُووِمْتَ	المُخاطَب:
قُووِمْتُنَّ	قُووِمْتُما	قُووِمْتِ	المُخاطَبَة:
قُووِمْنا		قُووِمْتُ	المُتَكَلِّم:

الجَمْع	المُثَنَّى	المُفْرَد	المُضارِعُ المَجْهُول
يُقاوَمُونَ	يُقاوَمانِ	يُقاوَمُ	الغائِب:
يُقاوَمْنَ	تُقاوَمانِ	تُقاوَمُ	الغائِبَة:
تُقاوَمُونَ	تُقاوَمانِ	تُقاوَمُ	المُخاطَب:
تُقاوَمْنَ	تُقاوَمانِ	تُقاوَمِينَ	المُخاطَبَة:
نُقاوَمُ		أُقاوَمُ	المُتَكَلِّم:

الجَمْع	المُثَنَّى	المُفْرَد	الأَمْرُ المَجْهُول
لِيُقاوَمُوا	لِيُقاوَما	لِيُقاوَمْ	الغائِب:
لِيُقاوَمْنَ	لِتُقاوَما	لِتُقاوَمْ	الغائِبَة:
لِتُقاوَمُوا	لِتُقاوَما	لِتُقاوَمْ	المُخاطَب:
لِتُقاوَمْنَ	لِتُقاوَما	لِتُقاوَمِي	المُخاطَبَة:
لِنُقاوَمْ		لِأُقاوَمْ	المُتَكَلِّم:

Table 4.38 - The Active Voice Weak Verb (Naaqis): ندو

نادَى، يُنادِي، نادِ لِيُنادِ، نُودِيَ، يُنادَى، لِيُنادَ هُوَ مُناداةٌ و مُنادٍ و مُنادَىً

الجَمع	المُثَنَّى	المُفرَد	الماضِيُ المَعلُوم
نادَوا	نادَيا	نادَى	الغائِب:
نادَيْنَ	نادَتا	نادَت	الغائِبة:
نادَيتُم	نادَيتُما	نادَيتَ	المُخاطَب:
نادَيتُنَّ	نادَيتُما	نادَيتِ	المُخاطَبة:
نادَينا		نادَيتُ	المُتَكَلِّم:

الجَمع	المُثَنَّى	المُفرَد	المُضارِعُ المَعلُوم
يُنادُونَ	يُنادِيانِ	يُنادِي	الغائِب:
يُنادِينَ	تُنادِيانِ	تُنادِي	الغائِبة:
تُنادُونَ	تُنادِيانِ	تُنادِي	المُخاطَب:
تُنادِينَ	تُنادِيانِ	تُنادِينَ	المُخاطَبة:
نُنادِي		أُنادِي	المُتَكَلِّم:

الجَمع	المُثَنَّى	المُفرَد	الأَمرُ المَعلُوم
لِيُنادُوا	لِيُنادِيا	لِيُنادِ	الغائِب:
لِيُنادِينَ	لِتُنادِيا	لِتُنادِ	الغائِبة:
نادُوا	نادِيا	نادِ	المُخاطَب:
نادِينَ	نادِيا	نادِي	المُخاطَبة:
لِنُنادِ		لِأُنادِ	المُتَكَلِّم:

Table 4.39 - The Passive Voice Weak Verb (Naaqis): (ندو (نُودِيَ، يُنادَى

الجَمع	المُثَنَّى	المُفرَد	الماضيُ المَجهُول
نُودُوا	نُودِيا	نُودِيَ	الغائب:
نُودِينَ	نُودِيَتا	نُودِيَتْ	الغائبة:
نُودِيتُم	نُودِيتُما	نُودِيتَ	المُخاطَب:
نُودِيتُنَّ	نُودِيتُما	نُودِيتِ	المُخاطَبة:
نُودِينا		نُودِيتُ	المُتَكَلِّم:

الجَمع	المُثَنَّى	المُفرَد	المُضارعُ المَجهُول
يُنادَونَ	يُنادَيانِ	يُنادَى	الغائب:
يُنادَينَ	تُنادَيانِ	تُنادَى	الغائبة:
تُنادَونَ	تُنادَيانِ	تُنادَى	المُخاطَب:
تُنادَينَ	تُنادَيانِ	نُنادَينَ	المُخاطَبة:
نُنادَى		أُنادَى	المُتَكَلِّم:

الجَمع	المُثَنَّى	المُفرَد	الأَمرُ المَجهُول
لِيُنادَوا	لِيُنادَيا	لِيُنادَ	الغائب:
لِيُنادَينَ	لِتُنادَيا	لِتُنادَ	الغائبة:
لِتُنادَوا	لِتُنادَيا	لِتُنادَ	المُخاطَب:
لِتُنادَينَ	لِتُنادَيا	لِتُنادَ	المُخاطَبة:
لِنُنادَ		لأُنادَ	المُتَكَلِّم:

Table 4.40 - The Active Voice Weak Verb (Lafeef): قوي

قَاوَى، يُقاوِي، قَاوِ، لِيُقاوِ، قُووِيَ، يُقاوَى، لِيُقاوَى، لِيُقاوَ هُوَ مُقاوَاةٌ و مُقاوٍ و مُقاوًى

الجَمْع	المُثَنَّى	المُفْرَد	الماضِي المَعْلُوم
قاوُوا	قاوَيا	قاوَى	الغائِب:
قاوَيْنَ	قاوَتا	قاوَتْ	الغائِبَة:
قاوَيْتُمْ	قاوَيْتُما	قاوَيْتَ	المُخاطَب:
قاوَيْتُنَّ	قاوَيْتُما	قاوَيْتِ	المُخاطَبَة:
قاوَيْنا		قاوَيْتُ	المُتَكَلِّم:

الجَمْع	المُثَنَّى	المُفْرَد	المُضارِع المَعْلُوم
يُقاوُونَ	يُقاوِيانِ	يُقاوِي	الغائِب:
يُقاوِينَ	تُقاوِيانِ	تُقاوِي	الغائِبَة:
تُقاوُونَ	تُقاوِيانِ	تُقاوِي	المُخاطَب:
تُقاوِينَ	تُقاوِيانِ	تُقاوِينَ	المُخاطَبَة:
نُقاوِي		أُقاوِي	المُتَكَلِّم:

الجَمْع	المُثَنَّى	المُفْرَد	الأَمْر المَعْلُوم
لِيُقاوُوا	لِيُقاوِيا	لِيُقاوِ	الغائِب:
لِتُقاوِينَ	لِتُقاوِيا	لِتُقاوِ	الغائِبَة:
قاوُوا	قاوِيا	قاوِ	المُخاطَب:
قاوِينَ	قاوِيا	قاوِي	المُخاطَبَة:
لِنُقاوِ		لِأُقاوِ	المُتَكَلِّم:

Table 4.41 - The Passive Voice Weak Verb (Lafeef): قوي (قُوِّيَ، يُقاوَى)

الجَمع	المُثَنَّى	المُفْرَد	الماضِيُ المَجْهُول
قُووُوا	قُوويا	قُوويَ	الغائب:
قُوِّينَ	قُوويَتا	قُوويَتْ	الغائبة:
قُوويتُمْ	قُوويتُما	قُوويتَ	المُخاطَب:
قُوويتُنَّ	قُوويتُما	قُوويتِ	المُخاطَبة:
قُوِّينا		قُوويتُ	المُتَكَلِّم:

الجَمع	المُثَنَّى	المُفْرَد	المُضارِعُ المَجْهُول
يُقاوَوْنَ	يُقاوَيانِ	يُقاوَى	الغائب:
يُقاوَيْنَ	تُقاوَيانِ	تُقاوَى	الغائبة:
تُقاوَوْنَ	تُقاوَيانِ	تُقاوَى	المُخاطَب:
تُقاوَيْنَ	تُقاوَيانِ	تُقاوَيْنَ	المُخاطَبة:
نُقاوَى		أُقاوَى	المُتَكَلِّم:

الجَمع	المُثَنَّى	المُفْرَد	الأَمْرُ المَجْهُول
لِيُقاوَوْا	لِيُقاوَيا	لِيُقاوَ	الغائب:
لِيُقاوَيْنَ	لِتُقاوَيا	لِتُقاوَ	الغائبة:
لِتُقاوَوْا	لِتُقاوَيا	لِتُقاوَ	المُخاطَب:
لِتُقاوَيْنَ	لِتُقاوَيا	لِتُقاوَيْ	المُخاطَبة:
لِنُقاوَ		لِأُقاوَ	المُتَكَلِّم:

▶ CONCLUDING NOTES

The *Mudhaa'af* Verb has the option of being conjugated with or without *Idghaam* as a Derivative Verb. As a Primary Verb, *Idghaam* is obligatory in certain circumstances. The verb used as an example (حَاجَّ) can be conjugated as mentioned with *Idghaam* or it can be conjugated without. In order to simplify its conjugation, we used *Idghaam* in some instances, like the Past and Present Tense Active Voice. In other instances, we conjugated the verb without *Idghaam*. Observe the pattern of conjugation with *Idhgaam*:

حَاجَّ، يُحاجُّ، حَاجَّ (أو حاجٌّ)، لِيُحاجَّ، حُوجَّ، يُحاجُّ، لِيُحاجَّ

This is the conjugation pattern without *Idghaam*:

حَاجَجَ، يُحَاجِجُ، حَاجِجْ، لِيُحَاجِجْ، حُوجِجَ، يُحَاجَجُ، لِيُحَاجَجْ

It's obvious that confusion can arise in some Seeghah, particularly the 2nd person Command Verb and the Present Tense Passive Voice. It is better, then, to avoid *Idghaam* in order to present the Seeghah in a clear manner that helps to prevent confusing the listener or reader.

SECTION FOUR

The Baab Of Ifti'aal

بابُ إِفْتِعالٍ

إِفْتَعَلَ، يَفْتَعِلُ، إِفْتَعِلْ، لِيَفْتَعِلْ، أُفْتُعِلَ، يُفْتَعَلُ، لِيُفْتَعَلْ هُوَ إِفْتِعالٌ و مُفْتَعِلٌ و مُفْتَعَلٌ

The Masdar of this *Baab* is on the pattern of إِفْتِعالٌ. The Past Tense Active Voice Verb is formed by adding the two Additional Letters Hamzah and Taa'. The Hamzah is found only in the Masdar, the Past Tense Verb and the 2nd Person Command Verb (الأَمْرُ الحاضِرُ). The Taa', on the other hand, is found in most of the derivatives of this Baab.

▶ **Ibdaal In Mazeed Fihi** الإبدالُ في المَزيدِ فيهِ

Literally, the word *Ibdaal* (الإبدالُ) means to exchange or substitute. In Tasreef, *Ibdaal* means to exchange one letter for another. A few of the *Abwaab* of the Derivative Verb have the letter Taa' (ت) as one of its Additional Letters, namely: (إِفْتِعالٌ، تَفَعُّلٌ، تَفاعُلٌ). These *Abwaab* will require *Ibdaal* under certain circumstances which will be mentioned shortly. The *Baab of Istif'aal* (إِسْتِفْعالٌ) is the exception, there is no Ibdaal although it has Taa' as an Additional Letter.

The verb group of our current discussion, the *Baab of Ifti'aal*, has the most instances *Ibdaal* of the three *Abwaab* mentioned previously. There are seven fundamental rules associated with this *Baab*, five of which are related to *Ibdaal*:

▶ SEVEN SPECIAL RULES IN THE BAAB OF IFTI'AAL: القَواعِدُ السَّبعُ الخاصُّ لِباب إفتِعالٍ

▷ Whenever one of the following four letters: (ص، ض، ط، ظ) happens to be the first Original Letter (فآءُ الكَلِمَة) of the root, the letter (ط) will replace the letter (ت) in this Baab. For example:

صبر إصطَبَرَ؛ ضرب إضطَرَبَ؛ طرد إطَّرَدَ؛ ظلم إظطَلَمَ

Note that in the third example: إطَّرَدَ, Idghaam is obligatory since the letters are the same (إطْطَرَدَ). In the last example: إظطَلَمَ, Idghaam is permissible since these two letters are similar. As a result, two other forms can be derived in addition to the form mentioned, they are: إطَّلَمَ and إظَّلَمَ. The Idghaam can be formed from either letter (ط) or (ظ).

▷ Whenever the first Original Letter is: (د، ذ، ز), the letter (د) will be substituted for the (ت), as in:

درك إدَّرَكَ؛ ذكر إدْذَكَرَ؛ زجر إزْدَجَرَ

Again, where the letters are similar, Idghaam is permissible, as in: إدْذَكَرَ إذَّكَرَ أو إدَّكَرَ

▷ Whenever the first Original Letter is a Weak Letter (الحَرفُ العِلَّةُ), the Weak Letter will be substituted with (ت) and then it will contracted (Idghaam) with the Taa' of the Baab, for example:

وحد إتَّحَدَ إتَّحَدَ؛ يسر إنْتَسَرَ إتَّسَرَ

In the last example (إتَّسَرَ), the form إيْتَسَرَ is also permissible, although rare.

▷ In most cases, the rule of the Reduction of the Hamzah (تَخْفِيفُ الهَمْزَة) is not applied in this Baab, for example: أمِنَ إِنْتَمَنَ.

One exception is the Kalimah (أخذ), in this *Baab*, the Hamzah is replaced with the letter (ت), as is the case with a Weak Letter, and *Idghaam* takes place:

إِنْتَخَذَ إِتْتَخَذَ إِتَّخَذَ

▷ If the first Original Letter is (ث), the (ت) of the *Baab* will be substituted with the (ث) and then contracted, as in: ثأر إِثْتَأَر إِثْثَأَر إِثَّأَر.

▷ Whenever one of the following twelve letters occurs as the second Original Letter, it is permissible to substitute the Taa' of the *Baab* with the same letter as that second Original Letter:

ت، ث، ج، د، ذ، ز، س، ش، ص، ض، ط، ظ

Idghaam must be made and the first Original Letter is Maftooh or Maksoor (Maftooh according to the rule *Idghaam* or Maksoor according to the rule preventing the meeting of two voweless letters. Also, this form is also found without the Hamzah as well, for example:

خصم إِخْتَصَمَ إِخْصَصَمَ إِخْصَّمَ إِخَصَّمَ

This form has also been known to be found existing without the Hamzah as well (خَصَّمَ).

▷ If the *Ajwaf* Verb in this *Baab* has the meaning of partnership, the rule of *I'laal* is not applied, for example: إِزْدَوَجَ عَلِيٌّ وَ فاطِمَةُ , as compared to: إِخْتَارَ عَلِيٌّ فاطِمَةَ.

Here are the basic patterns of the verbs in this *Baab*:

Table 4.42 - Patterns Of Baab Of Ifti'aal Active Voice Verb - Pattern Of: إِفْتَعَلَ يَفْتَعِلُ

إِفْتَعَلَ، يَفْتَعِلُ، إِفْتَعِلْ، لِيَفْتَعِلْ، يَفْتَعِلُ، أُفْتُعِلْ، لِيُفْتَعَلْ هُوَ إِفْتِعالٌ و مُفْتَعِلٌ و مُفْتَعَلٌ

الجَمْع	المُثَنَّى	المُفْرَد		الماضِي المَعلُوم
إِفْتَعَلُوا	إِفْتَعَلا	إِفْتَعَلَ	الغائِب:	
إِفْتَعَلْنَ	إِفْتَعَلَتا	إِفْتَعَلَتْ	الغائِبة:	
إِفْتَعَلْتُم	إِفْتَعَلْتُما	إِفْتَعَلْتَ	المُخاطَب:	
إِفْتَعَلْتُنَّ	إِفْتَعَلْتُما	إِفْتَعَلْتِ	المُخاطَبة:	
إِفْتَعَلْنا		إِفْتَعَلْتُ	المُتَكَلِّم:	
الجَمْع	المُثَنَّى	المُفْرَد		المُضارِع المَعلُوم
يَفْتَعِلُونَ	يَفْتَعِلانِ	يَفْتَعِلُ	الغائِب:	
يَفْتَعِلْنَ	تَفْتَعِلانِ	تَفْتَعِلُ	الغائِبة:	
تَفْتَعِلُونَ	تَفْتَعِلانِ	تَفْتَعِلُ	المُخاطَب:	
تَفْتَعِلْنَ	تَفْتَعِلانِ	تَفْتَعِلِينَ	المُخاطَبة:	
نَفْتَعِلُ		أَفْتَعِلُ	المُتَكَلِّم:	
الجَمْع	المُثَنَّى	المُفْرَد		الأَمْرُ المَعلُوم
لِيَفْتَعِلُوا	لِيَفْتَعِلا	لِيَفْتَعِلْ	الغائِب:	
لِيَفْتَعِلْنَ	لِتَفْتَعِلا	لِتَفْتَعِلْ	الغائِبة:	
إِفْتَعِلُوا	إِفْتَعِلا	إِفْتَعِلْ	المُخاطَب:	
إِفْتَعِلْنَ	إِفْتَعِلا	إِفْتَعِلِي	المُخاطَبة:	
لِنَفْتَعِلْ		لأَفْتَعِلْ	المُتَكَلِّم:	

Table 4.43 - Patterns Of Baab Of Ifti'aal Passive Voice Verb - Pattern Of: أُفْتُعِلَ يُفْتَعَلُ

الجَمْع	المُثَنَّى	المُفْرَد	المَاضِي المَجْهُول
أُفْتُعِلُوا	أُفْتُعِلَا	أُفْتُعِلَ	لغائِب:
أُفْتُعِلْنَ	أُفْتُعِلَتَا	أُفْتُعِلَتْ	الغَائِبَة:
أُفْتُعِلْتُم	أُفْتُعِلْتُما	أُفْتُعِلْتَ	المُخاطَب:
أُفْتُعِلْتُنَّ	أُفْتُعِلْتُما	أُفْتُعِلْتِ	المُخاطَبَة:
أُفْتُعِلْنا		أُفْتُعِلْتُ	المُتَكَلِّم:

الجَمْع	المُثَنَّى	المُفْرَد	المُضَارِعُ المَجْهُول
يُفْتَعَلُونَ	يُفْتَعَلانِ	يُفْتَعَلُ	الغائِب:
يُفْتَعَلْنَ	تُفْتَعَلانِ	تُفْتَعَلُ	الغَائِبَة:
تُفْتَعَلُونَ	تُفْتَعَلانِ	تُفْتَعَلُ	المُخاطَب:
تُفْتَعَلْنَ	تُفْتَعَلانِ	تُفْتَعَلِينَ	المُخاطَبَة:
نُفْتَعَلُ		أُفْتَعَلُ	المُتَكَلِّم:

الجَمْع	المُثَنَّى	المُفْرَد	الأَمْرُ المَجْهُول
لِيُفْتَعَلُوا	لِيُفْتَعَلا	لِيُفْتَعَلْ	الغائِب:
لِيُفْتَعَلْنَ	لِتُفْتَعَلا	لِتُفْتَعَلْ	الغَائِبَة:
لِتُفْتَعَلُونَ	لِتُفْتَعَلا	لِتُفْتَعَلْ	المُخاطَب:
لِتُفْتَعَلْنَ	لِتُفْتَعَلا	لِتُفْتَعَلِي	المُخاطَبَة:
لِنُفْتَعَلْ		لِأُفْتَعَلْ	المُتَكَلِّم:

▷ **Reflexive** (المُطَاوَعَةُ), meaning that the Subject accepts the affect of the action as in the Passive Voice. For example: جَمَعْتُ النَّاسَ فَاجْتَمَعُوا *I gathered the people, then, they assembled.* In the first part of the example, the Primary Verb (جَمَعْتُ) is used and the Object (النَّاسَ) receives the affect of the action (assembling). In the second part with the Derivative Verb (إِجْتَمَعُوا), the implied Subject (هُم) receives the affect of the same action. In this same manner that the Object stands in the place of the Subject when the verb is in the Passive Voice.

▷ **Partnership** (المُشارَكَةُ), as in: إِخْتَصَمَ زَيدٌ وَ بَكْرٌ *Zaid and Bakr argued.* As opposed to the method of the *Baab of Mufaa'alah* wherein the action was a partnership between the Subject and the Object, in this *Baab*, the meaning of partnership is conveyed by having more than one Subject.

▷ **Preparation** (الإِتّخاذُ), meaning to prepare in accordance with the meaning of the verb, for example: إِحْتَطَبَ زَيدٌ *Zaid prepared firewood*; إِخْتَبَزَ بَكْرٌ *Bakr prepared bread*; إِشْتَوَى *He made Kabab.*

▷ **Seeking** (الطَّلَبُ), meaning to seek an action from the Object, as in: إِكْتَدَّ زَيدٌ بَكْراً *Zaid urged Bakr.*

▷ **Effort** (الجُهْدُ), meaning that it indicates that the action is done with considerable effort or difficulty, sometimes, even exaggerated. For example: إِكْتَسَبْتُ المالَ *I worked hard for money.*

▷ **The Meaning Of The Primary Verb** (مَعْنَى الثُّلاثِيِّ المُجَرَّد), for example: جَذَبْتُ رِدآءَ زَيدٍ or إِجْتَذَبْتُ رِدآءَهُ *I pulled Zaid's cloak.*

SAMPLE CONJUGATIONS OF VERBS IN THE BAAB OF IFTI'AAL

Table 4.44 - The Active Voice Verb With Ibdaal: طرح

إطَّرَحَ، يَطَّرِحُ، إطِّرِحْ، لِيَطَّرِحْ، إطِّرَاحْ، أُطَّرِحْ، يُطَّرَحُ، لِيُطَّرَحْ هُوَ إطِّرَاحْ، مُطَّرِحْ، مُطَّرَحْ

الجَمع	المُثَنَّى	المُفرَد	الماضِيُ المَعلُوم
إطَّرَحُوا	إطَّرَحا	إطَّرَحَ	الغائِب:
إطَّرَحنَ	إطَّرَحتا	إطَّرَحتْ	الغائِبَة:
إطَّرَحتُم	إطَّرَحتُما	إطَّرَحتَ	المُخاطَب:
إطَّرَحتُنَّ	إطَّرَحتُما	إطَّرَحتِ	المُخاطَبَة:
إطَّرَحنا		إطَّرَحتُ	المُتَكَلِّم:

الجَمع	المُثَنَّى	المُفرَد	المُضارِعُ المَعلُوم
يَطَّرِحونَ	يَطَّرِحانِ	يَطَّرِحُ	الغائِب:
يَطَّرِحنَ	تَطَّرِحانِ	تَطَّرِحُ	الغائِبَة:
تَطَّرِحونَ	تَطَّرِحانِ	تَطَّرِحُ	المُخاطَب:
تَطَّرِحنَ	تَطَّرِحانِ	تَطَّرِحينَ	المُخاطَبَة:
نَطَّرِحُ		أَطَّرِحُ	المُتَكَلِّم:

الجَمع	المُثَنَّى	المُفرَد	الأَمرُ المَعلُوم
لِيَطَّرِحوا	لِيَطَّرِحا	لِيَطَّرِحْ	الغائِب:
لِيَطَّرِحنَ	لِتَطَّرِحا	لِتَطَّرِحْ	الغائِبَة:
إطَّرِحوا	إطَّرِحا	إطَّرِحْ	المُخاطَب:
إطَّرِحنَ	إطَّرِحا	إطَّرِحي	المُخاطَبَة:
لِنَطَّرِحْ		لأَطَّرِحْ	المُتَكَلِّم:

Table 4.45 - Passive Voice Verb With Ibdaal (طَرح (أُطُّرِحَ، يُطَّرَحُ)

الجَمع	المُثَنَّى	المُفرَد	الماضِي المَجْهُول
أُطُّرِحوا	أُطُّرِحا	أُطُّرِحَ	الغائِب:
أُطُّرِحنَ	أُطُّرِحتا	أُطُّرِحتْ	الغائِبة:
أُطُّرِحتُم	أُطُّرِحتما	أُطُّرِحتَ	المُخاطَب:
أُطُّرِحتُنَّ	أُطُّرِحتما	أُطُّرِحتِ	المُخاطَبة:
أُطُّرِحنا		أُطُّرِحتُ	المُتَكَلِّم:

الجَمع	المُثَنَّى	المُفرَد	المُضارِع المَجْهُول
يُطَّرَحونَ	يُطَّرَحانِ	يُطَّرَحُ	الغائِب:
يُطَّرَحنَ	يُطَّرَحانِ	تُطَّرَحُ	الغائِبة:
تُطَّرَحونَ	تُطَّرَحانِ	تُطَّرَحُ	المُخاطَب:
تُطَّرَحنَ	تُطَّرَحانِ	تُطَّرَحينَ	المُخاطَبة:
نُطَّرَحُ		أُطَّرَحُ	المُتَكَلِّم:

الجَمع	المُثَنَّى	المُفرَد	الأَمْر المَجْهُول
لِيُطَّرَحوا	لِيُطَّرَحا	لِيُطَّرَحْ	الغائِب:
لِيُطَّرَحنَ	لِيُطَّرَحا	لِتُطَّرَحْ	الغائِبة:
لِتُطَّرَحوا	لِتُطَّرَحا	لِتُطَّرَحْ	المُخاطَب:
لِتُطَّرَحنَ	لِتُطَّرَحا	لِتُطَّرَحي	المُخاطَبة:
لِنُطَّرَحْ		لِأُطَّرَحْ	المُتَكَلِّم:

Table 4.46 - The Active Voice Non-Sound Verb (Mahmooz): أَمِن

إِئْتَمَنَ، يَأْتَمِنُ، إِئْتَمِنْ، لِيَأْتَمِنْ، أُوتُمِنَ، يُؤْتَمَنُ، لِيُؤْتَمَنْ هُوَ إِئْتِمانٌ و مُؤْتَمَنٌ و مُؤْتَمِنٌ

الجَمْع	المُثَنَّى	المُفْرَد	الماضِيُ المَعْلُوم
إِئْتَمَنُوا	إِئْتَمَنا	إِئْتَمَنَ	الغائِب:
إِئْتَمَنَّ	إِئْتَمَنَتا	إِئْتَمَنَتْ	الغائِبَة:
إِئْتَمَنْتُمْ	إِئْتَمَنْتُما	إِئْتَمَنْتَ	المُخاطَب:
إِئْتَمَنْتُنَّ	إِئْتَمَنْتُما	إِئْتَمَنْتِ	المُخاطَبَة:
إِئْتَمَنّا		إِئْتَمَنْتُ	المُتَكَلِّم:

الجَمْع	المُثَنَّى	المُفْرَد	المُضارِعُ المَعْلُوم
يَأْتَمِنُونَ	يَأْتَمِنانِ	يَأْتَمِنُ	الغائِب:
يَأْتَمِنَّ	تَأْتَمِنانِ	تَأْتَمِنُ	الغائِبَة:
تَأْتَمِنُونَ	تَأْتَمِنانِ	تَأْتَمِنُ	المُخاطَب:
تَأْتَمِنَّ	تَأْتَمِنانِ	تَأْتَمِنِينَ	المُخاطَبَة:
نَأْتَمِنُ		آتَمِنُ	المُتَكَلِّم:

الجَمْع	المُثَنَّى	المُفْرَد	الأَمْرُ المَعْلُوم
لِيَأْتَمِنُوا	لِيَأْتَمِنا	لِيَأْتَمِنْ	الغائِب:
لِيَأْتَمِنَّ	لِتَأْتَمِنا	لِتَأْتَمِنْ	الغائِبَة:
إِئْتَمِنُوا	إِئْتَمِنا	إِئْتَمِنْ	المُخاطَب:
إِئْتَمِنَّ	إِئْتَمِنا	إِئْتَمِنِي	المُخاطَبَة:
لِنَأْتَمِنْ		لآتَمِنْ	المُتَكَلِّم:

Table 4.47 - Passive Voice Non-Sound Verb (Mahmooz): أمن (أُتُمِنَ، يُؤْتَمَنُ)

الجَمْع	المُثَنَّى	المُفْرَد	الماضي المَجْهول
أُوتُمِنُوا	أُوتُمِنَا	أُوتُمِنَ	الغائب:
أُوتُمِنَّ	أُوتُمِنَتَا	أُوتُمِنَتْ	الغائبة:
أُوتُمِنْتُمْ	أُوتُمِنْتُما	أُوتُمِنْتَ	المُخاطَب:
أُوتُمِنْتُنَّ	أُوتُمِنْتُما	أُوتُمِنْتِ	المُخاطَبة:
أُوتُمِنَّا		أُوتُمِنْتُ	المُتَكَلِّم:

الجَمْع	المُثَنَّى	المُفْرَد	المُضارع المَجْهول
يُؤْتَمَنُونَ	يُؤْتَمَنانِ	يُؤْتَمَنُ	الغائب:
يُؤْتَمَنَّ	تُؤْتَمَنانِ	تُؤْتَمَنُ	الغائبة:
تُؤْتَمَنُونَ	تُؤْتَمَنانِ	تُؤْتَمَنُ	المُخاطَب:
تُؤْتَمَنَّ	تُؤْتَمَنانِ	تُؤْتَمَنِينَ	المُخاطَبة:
نُؤْتَمَنُ		أُوتَمَنُ	المُتَكَلِّم:

الجَمْع	المُثَنَّى	المُفْرَد	الأمر المَجْهول
لِيُؤْتَمَنُوا	لِيُؤْتَمَنا	لِيُؤْتَمَنْ	الغائب:
لِيُؤْتَمَنَّ	لِتُؤْتَمَنا	لِتُؤْتَمَنْ	الغائبة:
لِتُؤْتَمَنُوا	لِتُؤْتَمَنا	لِتُؤْتَمَنْ	المُخاطَب:
لِتُؤْتَمَنَّ	لِتُؤْتَمَنا	لِتُؤْتَمَني	المُخاطَبة:
لِنُؤْتَمَنْ		لأُوتَمَنْ	المُتَكَلِّم:

Table 4.48 - Active Voice Non-Sound Verb (Mudhaa'af): ضرَّ

إضطَرَّ، يَضطَرُّ، إضطَرِرْ، لِيَضطَرِرْ، إضطَرِرْ، يُضطَرُّ، لِيُضطَرُّ هُوَ إضطِرَازُ هُوَ إضطَرَّ و مُضطَرٌّ

الجَمع	المُثَنَّى	المُفرَد	الماضي المَعلُوم
إضطَرُّوا	إضطَرَّا	إضطَرَّ	الغائب:
إضطَرَرنَ	إضطَرَّتا	إضطَرَّت	الغائبة:
إضطَرَرتُم	إضطَرَرتُما	إضطَرَرتَ	المُخاطَب:
إضطَرَرتُنَّ	إضطَرَرتُما	إضطَرَرتِ	المُخاطَبة:
إضطَرَرنا		إضطَرَرتُ	المُتَكَلِّم:

الجَمع	المُثَنَّى	المُفرَد	المُضارِعُ المَعلُوم
يَضطَرُّونَ	يَضطَرَّان	يَضطَرُّ	الغائب:
يَضطَرِرنَ	تَضطَرَّان	تَضطَرُّ	الغائبة:
تَضطَرُّونَ	تَضطَرَّان	تَضطَرُّ	المُخاطَب:
تَضطَرِرنَ	تَضطَرَّان	تَضطَرِّينَ	المُخاطَبة:
نَضطَرُّ		أَضطَرُّ	المُتَكَلِّم:

الجَمع	المُثَنَّى	المُفرَد	الأَمُر المَعلُوم
لِيَضطَرُّوا	لِيَضطَرَّا	لِيَضطَرِر	الغائب:
لِيَضطَرِرنَ	لِتَضطَرَّا	لِتَضطَرِر	الغائبة:
إضطَرُّوا	إضطَرَّا	إضطَرِر	المُخاطَب:
إضطَرِرنَ	إضطَرَّا	إضطَرِّي	المُخاطَبة:
لِنَضطَرِر		لِأَضطَرِر	المُتَكَلِّم:

Table 4.49 - Passive Voice Non-Sound Verb (Mudhaa'af): (ضَرَّ (أُصطُرَّ، يُضطَرُّ

الجَمع	المُثَنَّى	المُفرَد		الماضِي
أُصطُرُّوا	أُصطُرَّا	أُصطُرَّ	الغائِب:	
أُصطُرِّنَ	أُصطُرَّتا	أُصطُرَّتْ	الغائِبة:	
أُصطُرِرتُم	أُصطُرِرتُما	أُصطُرِرتَ	المُخاطَب:	
أُصطُرِرتُنَّ	أُصطُرِرتُما	أُصطُرِرتِ	المُخاطَبة:	
أُصطُرِرنا		أُصطُرِرتُ	المُتَكَلِّم:	

الجَمع	المُثَنَّى	المُفرَد		المُضارِع
يُضطَرُّونَ	يُضطَرَّانِ	يُضطَرُّ	الغائِب:	
يُضطَرِرنَ	تُضطَرَّانِ	تُضطَرُّ	الغائِبة:	
تُضطَرُّونَ	تُضطَرَّانِ	تُضطَرُّ	المُخاطَب:	
تُضطَرِرنَ	تُضطَرَّانِ	تُضطَرِّينَ	المُخاطَبة:	
نُضطَرُّ		أُضطَرُّ	المُتَكَلِّم:	

الجَمع	المُثَنَّى	المُفرَد		الأَمرُ المَعلُوم
لِيُضطَرُّوا	لِيُضطَرَّا	لِيُضطَرَر	الغائِب:	
لِيُضطَرِرنَ	لِتُضطَرَّا	لِتُضطَرَر	الغائِبة:	
لِتُضطَرُّوا	لِتُضطَرَّا	لِتُضطَرَر	المُخاطَب:	
لِتُضطَرِرنَ	لِتُضطَرَّا	لِتُضطَرِّي	المُخاطَبة:	
لِنُضطَرَر		لِأُضطَرَر	المُتَكَلِّم:	

Table 4.50 - The Active Voice Weak Verb (Mithaal): وهم

إتَّهَمَ، يَتَّهِمُ، إتِّهِمْ، إتِّهَمْ، لِيَتَّهِمْ، يُتَّهَمُ، أُتُّهِمُ، لِيُتَّهَمْ هُوَ إتِّهامٌ و مُتَّهَمٌ و مُتَّهِمٌ

الجَمع	المُثَنَّى	المُفرَد	الماضِي المَعلُوم
إتَّهَموا	إتَّهَما	إتَّهَمَ	الغائِب:
إتَّهَمنَ	إتَّهَمَتا	إتَّهَمَتْ	الغائِبَة:
إتَّهَمتُم	إتَّهَمتُما	إتَّهَمتَ	المُخاطَب:
إتَّهَمتُنَّ	إتَّهَمتُما	إتَّهَمتِ	المُخاطَبة:
إتَّهَمنا		إتَّهَمتُ	المُتَكَلِّم:

الجَمع	المُثَنَّى	المُفرَد	المُضارِعُ المَعلُوم
يَتَّهِمونَ	يَتَّهِمانِ	يَتَّهِمُ	الغائِب:
يَتَّهِمنَ	تَتَّهِمانِ	تَتَّهِمُ	الغائِبَة:
تَتَّهِمونَ	تَتَّهِمانِ	تَتَّهِمُ	المُخاطَب:
تَتَّهِمنَ	تَتَّهِمانِ	تَتَّهِمينَ	المُخاطَبة:
نَتَّهِمُ		أَتَّهِمُ	المُتَكَلِّم:

الجَمع	المُثَنَّى	المُفرَد	الأَمرُ المَعلُوم
لِيَتَّهِموا	لِيَتَّهِما	لِيَتَّهِمْ	الغائِب:
لِتَتَّهِمنَ	لِتَتَّهِما	لِتَتَّهِمْ	الغائِبَة:
إتَّهِموا	إتَّهِما	إتَّهِمْ	المُخاطَب:
إتَّهِمنَ	إتَّهِما	إتَّهِمي	المُخاطَبة:
لِنَتَّهِمْ		لِأَتَّهِمْ	المُتَكَلِّم:

Table 4.51 - The Passive Voice Weak Verb (Mithaal): (أُتُّهِم، يُتَّهَم) وهم

الجَمْع	المُثَنَّى	المُفْرد	الماضِي المَجهُول
أُتُّهِمُوا	أُتُّهِما	أُتُّهِم	الغائِب:
أُتُّهِمْنَ	أُتُّهِمَتا	أُتُّهِمَتْ	الغائِبة:
أُتُّهِمْتُمْ	أُتُّهِمْتُما	أُتُّهِمْتَ	المُخاطَب:
أُتُّهِمْتُنَّ	أُتُّهِمْتُما	أُتُّهِمْتِ	المُخاطَبة:
أُتُّهِمْنا		أُتُّهِمْتُ	المُتَكَلِّم:

الجَمْع	المُثَنَّى	المُفْرد	المُضارِعُ المَجهُول
يُتَّهَمُونَ	يُتَّهَمانِ	يُتَّهَم	الغائِب:
يُتَّهَمْنَ	تُتَّهَمانِ	تُتَّهَم	الغائِبة:
تُتَّهَمُونَ	تُتَّهَمانِ	تُتَّهَم	المُخاطَب:
تُتَّهَمْنَ	تُتَّهَمانِ	تُتَّهَمِينَ	المُخاطَبة:
نُتَّهَم		أُتَّهَم	المُتَكَلِّم:

الجَمْع	المُثَنَّى	المُفْرد	الأمْرُ المَجهُول
لِيُتَّهَمُوا	لِيُتَّهَما	لِيُتَّهَمْ	الغائِب:
لِيُتَّهَمْنَ	لِتُتَّهَما	لِتُتَّهَمْ	الغائِبة:
لِتُتَّهَمُوا	لِتُتَّهَما	لِتُتَّهَمْ	المُخاطَب:
لِتُتَّهَمْنَ	لِتُتَّهَما	لِتُتَّهَمِي	المُخاطَبة:
لِنُتَّهَم		لِأُتَّهَمْ	المُتَكَلِّم:

Table 4.52 - Active Voice Weak Verb (Ajwaf): خير

إختارَ، يَخْتارُ، إخْتَرْ، لِيَخْتَرْ، أُخْتيرَ، يُخْتارُ، لِيُخْتَرْ هُوَ إخْتيارٌ و مُخْتارٌ و مُختَارٌ

الجَمع	المُثَنَّى	المُفرَد	الماضيُّ المَعلُوم
إختاروا	إختارا	إختارَ	الغائب:
إخْتَرْنَ	إختارَتا	إختارَتْ	الغائبة:
إخْتَرْتُمْ	إخْتَرْتُما	إخْتَرْتَ	المُخاطب:
إخْتَرْتُنَّ	إخْتَرْتُما	إخْتَرْتِ	المُخاطِبة:
إخْتَرْنا		إخْتَرْتُ	المُتَكَلِّم:

الجَمع	المُثَنَّى	المُفرَد	المُضارِعُ المَعلُوم
يَخْتارُونَ	يَخْتاران	يَخْتارُ	الغائب:
يَخْتَرْنَ	تَخْتاران	تَخْتارُ	الغائبة:
تَخْتارُونَ	تَخْتاران	تَخْتارُ	المُخاطب:
تَخْتَرْنَ	تَخْتاران	تَخْتارِينَ	المُخاطِبة:
نَخْتارُ		أَخْتارُ	المُتَكَلِّم:

الجَمع	المُثَنَّى	المُفرَد	الأَمرُ المَعلُوم
لِيَخْتارُوا	لِيَخْتارا	لِيَخْتَرْ	الغائب:
لِيَخْتَرْنَ	لِتَخْتارا	لِتَخْتَرْ	الغائبة:
إخْتارُوا	إختارا	إخْتَرْ	المُخاطب:
إخْتَرْنَ	إختارا	إخْتاري	المُخاطِبة:
لِنَخْتَرْ		لِأَخْتَرْ	المُتَكَلِّم:

Table 4.53 - Passive Voice Weak Verb (Ajwaf): خير (أُختِيرَ، يُختَار)

الجَمع	المُثَنَّى	المُفرَد	الماضي المَجهول
أُختِيروا	أُختِيرا	أُختِيرَ	الغائب:
أُختِرنَ	أُختِيرَتا	أُختِيرَت	الغائبة:
أُختِرتُم	أُختِرتُما	أُختِرتَ	المُخاطَب:
أُختِرتُنَّ	أُختِرتُما	أُختِرتِ	المُخاطَبة:
أُختِرنا		أُختِرتُ	المُتَكَلِّم:

الجَمع	المُثَنَّى	المُفرَد	المُضارِع المَجهول
يُختَارونَ	يُختَاران	يُختَار	الغائب:
يُخترنَ	تُختَاران	تُختَار	الغائبة:
تُختَارونَ	تُختَاران	تُختَار	المُخاطَب:
تُخترنَ	تُختَاران	تُختَارينَ	المُخاطَبة:
نُختَار		أُختَار	المُتَكَلِّم:

الجَمع	المُثَنَّى	المُفرَد	الأمر المَجهول
لِيُختَاروا	لِيُختَارا	لِيُختَر	الغائب:
لِيُخترنَ	لِتُختَارا	لِتُختَر	الغائبة:
لِتُختَاروا	لِتُختَارا	لِتُختَر	المُخاطَب:
لِتُخترنَ	لِتُختَارا	لِتُختَاري	المُخاطَبة:
لِنُختَر		لِأُختَر	المُتَكَلِّم:

Table 4.54 - Active Voice Weak Verb (Naaqis): رَضِي

إِرْتَضَى، يَرْتَضِي، إِرْتَضِ، لِيَرْتَضِ، أُرْتُضِ، يُرْتَضَى، لِيُرْتَضَ هُوَ إِرْتِضَاءً و مُرْتَضٍ و مُرْتَضَى

الجَمع	المُثَنَّى	المُفرَد	الماضِي المَعلُوم
إِرْتَضَوا	إِرْتَضَيا	إِرْتَضَى	الغائِب:
إِرْتَضَينَ	إِرْتَضَتا	إِرْتَضَتْ	الغائِبَة:
إِرْتَضَيتُمْ	إِرْتَضَيتُما	إِرْتَضَيتَ	المُخاطَب:
إِرْتَضَيتُنَّ	إِرْتَضَيتُما	إِرْتَضَيتِ	المُخاطَبَة:
إِرْتَضَينا		إِرْتَضَيتُ	المُتَكَلِّم:

الجَمع	المُثَنَّى	المُفرَد	المُضارِعُ المَعلُوم
يَرْتَضُونَ	يَرْتَضِيان	يَرْتَضِي	الغائِب:
يَرْتَضِينَ	تَرْتَضِيان	تَرْتَضِي	الغائِبَة:
تَرْتَضُونَ	تَرْتَضِيان	تَرْتَضِي	المُخاطَب:
تَرْتَضِينَ	تَرْتَضِيان	تَرْتَضِينَ	المُخاطَبَة:
نَرْتَضِي		أَرْتَضِي	المُتَكَلِّم:

الجَمع	المُثَنَّى	المُفرَد	الأَمرُ المَعلُوم
لِيَرْتَضُوا	لِيَرْتَضِيا	لِيَرْتَضِ	الغائِب:
لِيَرْتَضِينَ	لِتَرْتَضِيا	لِتَرْتَضِ	الغائِبَة:
إِرْتَضُوا	إِرْتَضِيا	إِرْتَضِ	المُخاطَب:
إِرْتَضِينَ	إِرْتَضِيا	إِرْتَضِي	المُخاطَبَة:
لِنَرْتَضِ		لِأَرْتَضِ	المُتَكَلِّم:

Table 4.55 - Passive Voice Weak Verb (Naaqis): (رَضِي أُرْتُضِي، يُرْتَضَى)

الجَمْع	المُثَنَّى	المُفْرَد	الماضِي المَجْهُول
أُرْتُضُوا	أُرْتُضِيا	أُرْتُضِيَ	الغائِب:
أُرْتُضِينَ	أُرْتُضِيَتا	أُرْتُضِيَتْ	الغائِبَة:
أُرْتُضِيتُم	أُرْتُضِيتُما	أُرْتُضِيتَ	المُخاطَب:
أُرْتُضِيتُنَّ	أُرْتُضِيتُما	أُرْتُضِيتِ	المُخاطَبَة:
أُرْتُضِينا		أُرْتُضِيتُ	المُتَكَلِّم:

الجَمْع	المُثَنَّى	المُفْرَد	المُضارِع المَجْهُول
يُرْتَضَوْنَ	يُرْتَضَيانِ	يُرْتَضَى	الغائِب:
يُرْتَضَيْنَ	تُرْتَضَيانِ	تُرْتَضَى	الغائِبَة:
تُرْتَضَوْنَ	تُرْتَضَيانِ	تُرْتَضَى	المُخاطَب:
تُرْتَضَيْنَ	تُرْتَضَيانِ	تُرْتَضَيْنَ	المُخاطَبَة:
نُرْتَضَى		أُرْتَضَى	المُتَكَلِّم:

الجَمْع	المُثَنَّى	المُفْرَد	الأَمْر المَجْهُول
لِيُرْتَضَوْا	لِيُرْتَضَيا	لِيُرْتَضَ	الغائِب:
لِيُرْتَضَيْنَ	لِتُرْتَضَيا	لِتُرْتَضَ	الغائِبَة:
لِتُرْتَضَوْا	لِتُرْتَضَيا	لِتُرْتَضَ	المُخاطَب:
لِتُرْتَضَيْنَ	لِتُرْتَضَيا	لِتُرْتَضِيْ	المُخاطَبَة:
لِنُرْتَضَ		لِأُرْتَضَ	المُتَكَلِّم:

Table 4.56 - Active Voice Weak Verb (Lafeef): وقى

إِتَّقَى، يَتَّقِي، إِتَّقِ، لِيَتَّقِ أُتُّقِيَ، يَتَّقَى هُوَ إِتِّقَاءً و مُتَّقٍ و مُتَّقَى

الجَمْع	المُثَنَّى	المُفْرَد	الماضِي المَعْلُوم
إِتَّقَوا	إِتَّقَيا	إِتَّقَى	الغائِب:
إِتَّقَيْنَ	إِتَّقَيا	إِتَّقَتْ	الغائِبَة:
إِتَّقَيْتُمْ	إِتَّقَيْتُما	إِتَّقَيْتَ	المُخاطَب:
إِتَّقَيْتُنَّ	إِتَّقَيْتُما	إِتَّقَيْتِ	المُخاطَبَة:
إِتَّقَيْنا		إِتَّقَيْتُ	المُتَكَلِّم:

الجَمْع	المُثَنَّى	المُفْرَد	المُضارِعُ المَعْلُوم
يَتَّقُونَ	يَتَّقِيان	يَتَّقِي	الغائِب:
يَتَّقِينَ	تَتَّقِيان	تَتَّقِي	الغائِبَة:
تَتَّقُونَ	تَتَّقِيان	تَتَّقِي	المُخاطَب:
تَتَّقِينَ	تَتَّقِيان	تَتَّقِينَ	المُخاطَبَة:
نَتَّقِي		أَتَّقِي	المُتَكَلِّم:

الجَمْع	المُثَنَّى	المُفْرَد	الأَمْرُ المَعْلُوم
لِيَتَّقُوا	لِيَتَّقِيا	لِيَتَّقِ	الغائِب:
لِيَتَّقِينَ	لِتَتَّقِيا	لِتَتَّقِ	الغائِبَة:
إِتَّقُوا	إِتَّقِيا	إِتَّقِ	المُخاطَب:
إِتَّقِينَ	إِتَّقِيا	إِتَّقِي	المُخاطَبَة:
لِنَتَّقِ		لِأَتَّقِ	المُتَكَلِّم:

Table 4.57 - Passive Voice Weak Verb (Naaqis): (وَقَى (أُتَّقِيَ، يَتَّقَى

الجَمْع	المُثَنَّى	المُفْرَد	الماضِي المَجْهُول
أُتُّقُوا	أُتُّقِيَا	أُتُّقِيَ	الغائِب:
أُتُّقِينَ	أُتُّقِيَتا	أُتُّقِيَتْ	الغائِبَة:
أُتُّقِيتُمْ	أُتُّقِيتُما	أُتُّقِيتَ	المُخاطَب:
أُتُّقِيتُنَّ	أُتُّقِيتُما	أُتُّقِيتِ	المُخاطَبَة:
أُتُّقِينا		أُتُّقِيتُ	المُتَكَلِّم:

الجَمْع	المُثَنَّى	المُفْرَد	المُضارِع المَجْهُول
يُتَّقَونَ	يُتَّقَيانِ	يُتَّقَى	الغائِب:
يُتَّقَينَ	تُتَّقَيانِ	تُتَّقَى	الغائِبَة:
تُتَّقَونَ	تُتَّقَيانِ	تُتَّقَى	المُخاطَب:
تُتَّقَينَ	تُتَّقَيانِ	تُتَّقَينَ	المُخاطَبَة:
نُتَّقَى		أُتَّقَى	المُتَكَلِّم:

الجَمْع	المُثَنَّى	المُفْرَد	الأَمْر المَجْهُول
لِيُتَّقَوا	لِيُتَّقَيا	لِيُتَّقَ	الغائِب:
لِيُتَّقَينَ	لِيُتَّقَيا	لِتُتَّقَّ	الغائِبَة:
لِتُتَّقَونَ	لِتُتَّقَيا	لِتُتَّقَ	المُخاطَب:
لِتُتَّقَينَ	لِتُتَّقَيا	لِتُتَّقَيْ	المُخاطَبَة:
لِنُتَّقَ		لأُتَّقَ	المُتَكَلِّم:

SECTION FIVE

The Baab Of Infi'aal

بابُ إِنْفِعالٍ

إِنْفَعَلَ، يَنْفَعِلُ، إِنْفَعِلْ، إِنْفِعَلْ، لِيَنْفَعِلْ هُوَ إِنْفِعالٌ و مُنْفَعِلُ

There are two special letters that are added to words derived from this Baab. One is the
Conjunctive Hamzah (ا) found in the beginning of the Past Tense, the Command Verb and
the Masdar. The second letter is Noon (ن) which can be found in all derivatives from this
Baab, as in مُنْصَرِفٌ. The unique feature of this *Baab* is that the verbs derived from this *Baab*
are all intransitive (اللّازِمُ), meaning that they do not require an Object. The verb is
conjugated based on the following patterns:

Table 4.58 - Patterns Of Baab Of Infi'aal Active Voice Verb - Pattern Of: إِنْفَعَلَ يَنْفَعِلُ

إِنْفَعَلَ، يَنْفَعِلُ، إِنْفَعِلْ، لِيَنْفَعِلْ هُوَ إِفعالٌ وَ مُنْفَعِلٌ

الجَمْع	المُثَنَّى	المُفْرَد	الماضِي المَعْلُوم
إِنْفَعَلُوا	إِنْفَعَلا	إِنْفَعَلَ	الغائِب:
إِنْفَعَلْنَ	إِنْفَعَلَتا	إِنْفَعَلَتْ	الغائِبَة:
إِنْفَعَلْتُم	إِنْفَعَلْتُما	إِنْفَعَلْتَ	المُخاطَب:
إِنْفَعَلْتُنَّ	إِنْفَعَلْتُما	إِنْفَعَلْتِ	المُخاطَبَة:
إِنْفَعَلْنا		إِنْفَعَلْتُ	المُتَكَلِّم:

الجَمْع	المُثَنَّى	المُفْرَد	المُضارِع المَعْلُوم
يَنْفَعِلُونَ	يَنْفَعِلانِ	يَنْفَعِلُ	الغائِب:
يَنْفَعِلْنَ	تَنْفَعِلانِ	تَنْفَعِلُ	الغائِبَة:
تَنْفَعِلُونَ	تَنْفَعِلانِ	تَنْفَعِلُ	المُخاطَب:
تَنْفَعِلْنَ	تَنْفَعِلانِ	تَنْفَعِلِينَ	المُخاطَبَة:
نَنْفَعِلُ		أَنْفَعِلُ	المُتَكَلِّم:

الجَمْع	المُثَنَّى	المُفْرَد	الأَمْرُ المَعْلُوم
لِيَنْفَعِلُوا	لِيَنْفَعِلا	لِيَنْفَعِلْ	الغائِب:
لِيَنْفَعِلْنَ	لِتَنْفَعِلا	لِتَنْفَعِلْ	الغائِبَة:
إِنْفَعِلُوا	إِنْفَعِلا	إِنْفَعِلْ	المُخاطَب:
إِنْفَعِلْنَ	إِنْفَعِلا	إِنْفَعِلي	المُخاطَبَة:
لِنَنْفَعِلْ		لِأَنْفَعِلْ	المُتَكَلِّم:

▶ MEANING OF THE BAAB OF INFI'AAL مَعْنَى بَابِ إِنْفِعَالٍ

This *Baab* only comes in the reflexive meaning (المُطَاوَعَةُ), in other words, the action is affected upon the Subject, not the Object as is usually the case in a transitive verb. For example: صَرَفْتُهُ فَانْصَرَفَ *I spent it, then, it was spent*; قَسَمْتُهُ فَانْقَسَمَ *I divided it, then, it was divided*; كَسَرْتُ القَلَمَ فَانْكَسَرَ *I broke the pen, then, it was broken*.

The *Mahmooz* Kalimah cannot be found in this *Baab* nor the *Mithaal* or *Ajwaf*. Keeping in mind that verbs in this *Baab* are instansitive, there will be no conjugation of the Passive Voice. Here are some sample conjugations:

SAMPLE CONJUGATIONS OF NON-SOUND AND WEAK VERBS IN THE BAAB OF INFI'AAL

Table 4.59 - The Active Voice Non-Sound Verb (Mudhaa'af): ضمَّ

إنْضَمَّ، يَنْضَمُّ، إنْضَمِمْ، لِيَنْضَمِمْ هُوَ إنْضِمامٌ و مُنْضَمٌّ

الجَمْع	المُثَنَّى	المُفْرَد		الماضِي المَعْلُوم
إنْضَمُّوا	إنْضَمَّا	إنْضَمَّ	الغائِب:	
إنْضَمَمْنَ	إنْضَمَّتا	إنْضَمَّتْ	الغائِبَة:	
إنْضَمَمْتُمْ	إنْضَمَمْتُما	إنْضَمَمْتَ	المُخاطَب:	
إنْضَمَمْتُنَّ	إنْضَمَمْتُما	إنْضَمَمْتِ	المُخاطَبَة:	
إنْضَمَمْنا		إنْضَمَمْتُ	المُتَكَلِّم:	

الجَمْع	المُثَنَّى	المُفْرَد		المُضارِع المَعْلُوم
يَنْضَمُّونَ	يَنْضَمَّانِ	يَنْضَمُّ	الغائِب:	
يَنْضَمِمْنَ	تَنْضَمَّانِ	تَنْضَمُّ	الغائِبَة:	
تَنْضَمُّونَ	تَنْضَمَّانِ	تَنْضَمُّ	المُخاطَب:	
تَنْضَمِمْنَ	تَنْضَمَّانِ	تَنْضَمِّينَ	المُخاطَبَة:	
نَنْضَمُّ		أَنْضَمُّ	المُتَكَلِّم:	

الجَمْع	المُثَنَّى	المُفْرَد		الأَمْر المَعْلُوم
لِيَنْضَمُّوا	لِيَنْضَمَّا	لِيَنْضَمِمْ	الغائِب:	
لِيَنْضَمِمْنَ	لِتَنْضَمَّا	لِتَنْضَمِمْ	الغائِبَة:	
إنْضَمُّوا	إنْضَمَّا	إنْضَمِمْ	المُخاطَب:	
إضْمِمْنَ	إنْضَمَّا	إنْضَمِّي	المُخاطَبَة:	
لِنَنْضَمِمْ		لِأَنْضَمِمْ	المُتَكَلِّم:	

Table 4.60 - Active Voice Weak Verb (Naaqis): قَضَى

إِنْقَضَى، يَنْقَضِي، إِنْقَضِ، لِيَنْقَضِ هُوَ إِنْقِضَآءً و مُنْقَضٍ

الجَمْع	المُثَنَّى	المُفْرَد	الماضِيُ المَعْلُوم
إِنْقَضُوا	إِنْقَضَيا	إِنْقَضَى	الغائِب:
إِنْقَضَيْنَ	إِنْقَضَتا	إِنْقَضَتْ	الغائِبَة:
إِنْقَضَيْتُمْ	إِنْقَضَيْتُما	إِنْقَضَيْتَ	المُخاطَب:
إِنْقَضَيْتُنَّ	إِنْقَضَيْتُما	إِنْقَضَيْتِ	المُخاطَبَة:
إِنْقَضَيْنا		إِنْقَضَيْتُ	المُتَكَلِّم:

الجَمْع	المُثَنَّى	المُفْرَد	المُضارِعُ المَعْلُوم
يَنْقَضُونَ	يَنْقَضِيان	يَنْقَضِي	الغائِب:
يَنْقَضِينَ	تَنْقَضِيان	تَنْقَضِي	الغائِبَة:
تَنْقَضُونَ	تَنْقَضِيان	تَنْقَضِي	المُخاطَب:
تَنْقَضِينَ	تَنْقَضِيان	تَنْقَضِينَ	المُخاطَبَة:
نَنْقَضِي		أَنْقَضِي	المُتَكَلِّم:

الجَمْع	المُثَنَّى	المُفْرَد	الأَمْرُ المَعْلُوم
لِيَنْقَضُوا	لِيَنْقَضِيا	لِيَنْقَضِ	الغائِب:
لِيَنْقَضِينَ	لِتَنْقَضِيا	لِتَنْقَضِ	الغائِبَة:
إِنْقَضُوا	إِنْقَضِيا	إِنْقَضِ	المُخاطَب:
إِنْقَضِينَ	إِنْقَضِيا	إِنْقَضِي	المُخاطَبَة:
لِنَنْقَضِ		لِأَنْقَضِ	المُتَكَلِّم:

Table 4.61 - Active Voice Weak Verb (Lafeef): طوى

إنْطَوَى، يَنْطَوِي، إنْطَوِ، لِيَنْطَوِ هُوَ إنْطِوَاءً وَ مُنْطَوٍ

الجَمْع	المُثَنَّى	المُفْرَد	الماضِيُ المَعْلُوم
إنْطَوَوا	إنْطَوَيا	إنْطَوَى	الغائِب:
إنْطَوَيْنَ	إنْطَوَتا	إنْطَوَتْ	الغائِبَة:
إنْطَوَيْتُمْ	إنْطَوَيْتُما	إنْطَوَيْتَ	المُخاطَب:
إنْطَوَيْتُنَّ	إنْطَوَيْتُما	إنْطَوَيْتِ	المُخاطَبَة:
إنْطَوَيْنا		إنْطَوَيْتُ	المُتَكَلِّم:

الجَمْع	المُثَنَّى	المُفْرَد	المُضارِعُ المَعْلُوم
يَنْطَوُونَ	يَنْطَوِيانِ	يَنْطَوِي	الغائِب:
يَنْطَوِينَ	تَنْطَوِيانِ	تَنْطَوِي	الغائِبَة:
تَنْطَوُونَ	تَنْطَوِيانِ	تَنْطَوِي	المُخاطَب:
تَنْطَوِينَ	تَنْطَوِيانِ	تَنْطَوِينَ	المُخاطَبَة:
نَنْطَوِي		أنْطَوِي	المُتَكَلِّم:

الجَمْع	المُثَنَّى	المُفْرَد	الأَمْرُ المَعْلُوم
لِيَنْطَوُوا	لِيَنْطَوِيا	لِيَنْطَوِ	الغائِب:
لِيَنْطَوِينَ	لِتَنْطَوِيا	لِتَنْطَوِ	الغائِبَة:
إنْطَوُوا	إنْطَوِيا	إنْطَوِ	المُخاطَب:
إنْطَوِينَ	إنْطَوِيا	إنْطَوِي	المُخاطَبَة:
لِنَنْطَوِ		لِأَنْطَوِ	المُتَكَلِّم:

SECTION SIX

The Baab Of Tafa'ul

بابُ تَفَعُّلٍ

تَفَعَّلَ، يَتَفَعَّلُ، تَفَعَّلْ، لِيَتَفَعَّلْ، تَفَعَّلَ، يَتَفَعَّلُ، لِيَتَفَعَّلْ هُوَ تَفَعُّلٌ و مُتَفَعَّلٌ و مُتَفَعِّلٌ

The Masdar of this *Baab* is on the pattern of: تَفَعُّلٌ. All of the derivatives have two distinguishing features. One is the letter Taa' (ت), which occurs before the first Original Letter and the second is that the second Original Letter is doubled or *Mushaddad*. Additionally, there are four special rules applied in the *Baab of Tafa'ul*:

▷   In the Present Tense Active Voice Verb, in Seeghah 4 and 5 of the 3rd person and the 12th Seeghah of the 2nd person, it is permissible to combine the two letters Taa' in the beginning of the verb (the first Taa' being the Particle of the Present Tense and the second is the Taa' of the *Baab*). In reality, since the first letter in *Idghaam* is *Saakin*, *Idghaam* cannot occur in the very first letter of a word. One Taa', therefore, is elided. For example: تَفَعَّلُ تَتَفَعَّلُ؛ تَتَفَعَّلانِ تَفَعَّلانِ, and so forth.

▷   Whenever one of the following twelve letters: (ت، ث، ج، د، ذ، ز، س، ش، ص، ض، ط، ظ) occurs as the first Original Letter, it is permissible to substitute the Taa' of the *Baab* with the same letter as the first Original letter and then contract both into one letter. This action, however, will bring a *Saakin* letter in the beginning of the word, which is impossible. To eliminate this problem, a Hamzah is placed before the first letter so that a voweled letter can connect with the *Shaddah*. The additional Hamzah is a Conjunctive Hamzah, meaning that its vowel may be elided to facilitate pronounciaiton. Observe the transition in the following verbs:

تَثَبَّتَ ثَثَبَّتَ ثَّبَّتَ إِثَّبَّتَ وَ يَثَّبَّتُ؛   تَدَثَّرَ دَدَثَّرَ دَّثَّرَ إِدَّثَّرَ و يَدَّثَّرُ

There are a number of words in the Holy Quran which exhibit this type of *Ibdaal*, for example:

يَدَّبَّرُ (23:68) ؛ يَدَّكَّرُ (2:269) ؛ وَازَّيَّنَتْ (10:24) ؛ يَسَّمَّعُونَ (37:8) ؛ يَشَّقَّقُ (2:74)

فَأَصَّدَّقَ (63:10) ؛ يَضَّرَّعُونَ (7:94) ؛ فَاطَّهَّرُوا (5:6) ؛ الْمُدَّثِّرُ (74:1)

▷ In the instances where the *Mudhaa'af* Verb comes in this *Baab*, the third Original letter (لَامُ الكَلِمَة) may suffix the Alif Maqsoorah, as in:

ظَنَّ تَظَنَّنَ تَظَنَّى و يَتَظَنَّى

▷ In the Masdar of the *Naaqis* with Waw, the Waw will be converted to Yaa' and the letter preceding it will receive the vowel of Kasrah. The Masdar of the *Naaqis* with Yaa' will also be formed in this manner, for example:

(رجو) تَرَجَّو تَرَجِّي تَرَجِّي؛ (ولي) تَوَلَّى تَوَلِّي

The verb is conjugated according to the following patterns in the *Baab of Tafa'ul*:

Table 4.62 - Patterns Of Baab Of Tafa'ul Active Voice Verb - Pattern Of: تَفَعَّلَ يَتَفَعَّلُ

تَفَعَّلَ، يَتَفَعَّلُ، تَفَعَّلْ، لِيَتَفَعَّلْ، تُفَعَّلُ، يَتَفَعَّلُ، لِيَتَفَعَّلْ هُوَ تَفَعُّلٌ و مُتَفَعِّلٌ و مُتَفَعَّلٌ

الجَمْع	المُثَّى	المُفْرَد	الماضي المَعْلُوم
تَفَعَّلُوا	تَفَعَّلا	تَفَعَّلَ	الغائب:
تَفَعَّلْنَ	تَفَعَّلَتا	تَفَعَّلَتْ	الغائبة:
تَفَعَّلْتُمْ	تَفَعَّلْتُما	تَفَعَّلْتَ	المُخاطَب:
تَفَعَّلْتُنَّ	تَفَعَّلْتُما	تَفَعَّلْتِ	المُخاطَبة:
تَفَعَّلْنا		تَفَعَّلْتُ	المُتَكَلِّم:

الجَمْع	المُثَّى	المُفْرَد	المُضارِع المَعْلُوم
يَتَفَعَّلُونَ	يَتَفَعَّلانِ	يَتَفَعَّلُ	الغائب:
يَتَفَعَّلْنَ	تَتَفَعَّلانِ	تَتَفَعَّلُ	الغائبة:
تَتَفَعَّلُونَ	تَتَفَعَّلانِ	تَتَفَعَّلُ	المُخاطَب:
تَتَفَعَّلْنَ	تَتَفَعَّلانِ	تَتَفَعَّلِينَ	المُخاطَبة:
نَتَفَعَّلُ		أَتَفَعَّلُ	المُتَكَلِّم:

الجَمْع	المُثَّى	المُفْرَد	الأَمْر المَعْلُوم
لِيَتَفَعَّلُوا	لِيَتَفَعَّلا	لِيَتَفَعَّلْ	الغائب:
لِيَتَفَعَّلْنَ	لِتَتَفَعَّلا	لِتَتَفَعَّلْ	الغائبة:
تَفَعَّلُوا	تَفَعَّلا	تَفَعَّلْ	المُخاطَب:
تَفَعَّلْنَ	تَفَعَّلا	تَفَعَّلي	المُخاطَبة:
لِنَتَفَعَّلْ		لأَتَفَعَّلْ	المُتَكَلِّم:

Table 4.63 - Patterns Of Baab Of Tafa'ul Passive Voice Verb - Pattern Of: تُفُعِّلَ يُتَفَعَّلُ

الجَمْع	المُثَنَّى	المُفْرَد	الماضِي المَجْهُول
تُفُعِّلُوا	تُفُعِّلا	تُفُعِّلَ	الغائِب:
تُفُعِّلْنَ	تُفُعِّلَتا	تُفُعِّلَتْ	الغائِبة:
تُفُعِّلْتُم	تُفُعِّلْتُما	تُفُعِّلْتَ	المُخاطَب:
تُفُعِّلْتُنَّ	تُفُعِّلْتُما	تُفُعِّلْتِ	المُخاطَبة:
تُفُعِّلْنا		تُفُعِّلْتُ	المُتَكَلِّم:

الجَمْع	المُثَنَّى	المُفْرَد	المُضارِع المَجْهُول
يُتَفَعَّلُونَ	يُتَفَعَّلانِ	يُتَفَعَّلُ	الغائِب:
يُتَفَعَّلْنَ	تُتَفَعَّلانِ	تُتَفَعَّلُ	الغائِبة:
تُتَفَعَّلُونَ	تُتَفَعَّلانِ	تُتَفَعَّلُ	المُخاطَب:
تُتَفَعَّلْنَ	تُتَفَعَّلانِ	تُتَفَعَّلِينَ	المُخاطَبة:
نُتَفَعَّلُ		أُتَفَعَّلُ	المُتَكَلِّم:

الجَمْع	المُثَنَّى	المُفْرَد	الأَمْر المَجْهُول
لِيُتَفَعَّلُوا	لِيُتَفَعَّلا	لِيُتَفَعَّلْ	الغائِب:
لِيُتَفَعَّلْنَ	لِتُتَفَعَّلا	لِتُتَفَعَّلْ	الغائِبة:
لِتُتَفَعَّلُوا	لِتُتَفَعَّلا	لِتُتَفَعَّلْ	المُخاطَب:
لِتُتَفَعَّلْنَ	لِتُتَفَعَّلا	لِتُتَفَعَّلِي	المُخاطَبة:
لِنُتَفَعَّلْ		لأُتَفَعَّلْ	المُتَكَلِّم:

▶ **THE MEANINGS OF THE BAAB OF TAFA'UL** مَعَانِي بَابِ تَفَعُّلِ

The *Baab of Tafa'ul* has nine meanings associated with it:

▷ **Reflexive** (المُطَاوَعَةُ), for example: أَدَّبَهُ فَتَأَدَّبَ *I trained him, then, he became well mannered.* In many instances, this *Baab* will be reflexive of the *Baab of Taf'eel* (تَفْعِيل). Meaning that the Object of the verb in the *Baab of Taf'eel* will be the Subject in this *Baab*. For example, كَسَّرَ زَيْدٌ المِرْآةَ *Zaid shattered the mirror* (the word mirror being the Object as it receives the action); تَكَسَّرَتِ المِرْآةُ *The mirror was shattered* (here, the Subject is mirror and it is the recipient of the action). Mostly, verbs in this *Baab* has a reflexive meaning.

▷ **Takalluf** (التَّكَلُّفُ), meaning that with difficulty an action is being borne by someone, as in: تَشَجَّعَ *To show oneself to be brave* (with difficulty) and تَحَلَّمَ *To show oneself to be forbearing.*

▷ **Preparation** (الإِتِّخَاذُ), in the same meaning as was in the *Baab of Ifti'aal* or to take on something, for example: تَوَسَّدَ *To prepare something as a pillow,* as in: تَوَسَّدَ الحَجَرَ *The rock was made a pillow;* تَبَنَّى زَيْدٌ *Zaid adopted children.*

▷ **Seeking** (الطَّلَبُ), meaning to seek the meaning of the verb, as in: تَعَجَّلْتُ الأَمَرَ *I wanted to expedite the matter;* تَنَجَّزْتُ الوَعْدَ *I want the promise to be fulfilled.*

▷ **Gradation** (التَّدْرِيجُ), for example: تَجَرَّعَ المَآءَ *He sipped the water;* تَفَهَّمَ المَسْأَلَةَ *He understood the matter little by little.*

▷ **Avoidance** (التَجَنُّبُ), meaning that the subject avoids the meaning of the verb, as in: تَأثَّمَ *To avoid sin* and تَذَمَّمَ *To avoid blame*.

▷ **To Become** (الصَّيْرُورَةُ), meaning to come to a different state, as in: تَأيَّمَتِ المَرْأةُ *The woman became a widow*.

▷ **Complaint** (الشِّكَايَةُ), as in: تَظَلَّمَ *To complain about oppression*.

▷ **Meaning of the Primary Verb** (مَعْنَى الثُّلاثِيِّ المُجَرَّدِ), as in: بَسَمَ or تَبَسَّمَ *To smile, laugh*.

Table 4.64 - Active Voice Non-Sound Verb (Mudhaa'af): خَلَّ

تَخَلَّلَ، يَتَخَلَّلُ، تَخَلَّلْ، لِيَتَخَلَّلْ، تُخَلِّلَ، يَتَخَلَّلُ، لِيَتَخَلَّلْ هُوَ تَخَلُّلٌ و مُخَلِّلٌ و مُخَلٌّ

الجَمع	المُثَنَّى	المُفرَد	الماضِيُ المَعلُوم
تَخَلَّلُوا	تَخَلَّلا	تَخَلَّلَ	الغائِب:
تَخَلَّلْنَ	تَخَلَّلَتا	تَخَلَّلَتْ	الغائِبَة:
تَخَلَّلْتُم	تَخَلَّلْتُما	تَخَلَّلْتَ	المُخاطَب:
تَخَلَّلْتُنَّ	تَخَلَّلْتُما	تَخَلَّلْتِ	المُخاطَبَة:
تَخَلَّلْنا		تَخَلَّلْتُ	المُتَكَلِّم:

الجَمع	المُثَنَّى	المُفرَد	المُضارِعُ المَعلُوم
يَتَخَلَّلُونَ	يَتَخَلَّلانِ	يَتَخَلَّلُ	الغائِب:
يَتَخَلَّلْنَ	تَتَخَلَّلانِ	تَتَخَلَّلُ	الغائِبَة:
تَتَخَلَّلُونَ	تَتَخَلَّلانِ	تَتَخَلَّلُ	المُخاطَب:
تَتَخَلَّلْنَ	تَتَخَلَّلانِ	تَتَخَلَّلِينَ	المُخاطَبَة:
نَتَخَلَّلُ		أَتَخَلَّلُ	المُتَكَلِّم:

الجَمع	المُثَنَّى	المُفرَد	الأَمرُ المَعلُوم
لِيَتَخَلَّلُوا	لِيَتَخَلَّلا	لِيَتَخَلَّلْ	الغائِب:
لِيَتَخَلَّلْنَ	لِتَتَخَلَّلا	لِتَتَخَلَّلْ	الغائِبَة:
تَخَلَّلُوا	تَخَلَّلا	تَخَلَّلْ	المُخاطَب:
تَخَلَّلْنَ	تَخَلَّلا	تَخَلَّلِي	المُخاطَبَة:
لِنَتَخَلَّلْ		لِأَتَخَلَّلْ	المُتَكَلِّم:

Table 4.65 - Passive Voice Non-Sound Verb (Mudhaa'af): خلّ (تُخُلَّلَ، يُتَخَلَّلُ)

الجَمع	المُثَنَّى	المُفرَد	الماضي المَجهُول
تُخُلِّلُوا	تُخُلِّلا	تُخُلِّلَ	الغائب:
تُخُلِّلنَ	تُخُلِّلتا	تُخُلِّلتْ	الغائبة:
تُخُلِّلتُم	تُخُلِّلتُما	تُخُلِّلتَ	المُخاطَب:
تُخُلِّلتُنَّ	تُخُلِّلتُما	تُخُلِّلتِ	المُخاطَبة:
تُخُلِّلنا		تُخُلِّلتُ	المُتَكَلِّم:

الجَمع	المُثَنَّى	المُفرَد	المُضارع المَجهُول
يُتَخَلَّلُونَ	يُتَخَلَّلانِ	يُتَخَلَّلُ	الغائب:
يُتَخَلَّلنَ	تُتَخَلَّلانِ	تُتَخَلَّلُ	الغائبة:
تُتَخَلَّلُونَ	تُتَخَلَّلانِ	تُتَخَلَّلُ	المُخاطَب:
تُتَخَلَّلنَ	تُتَخَلَّلانِ	تُتَخَلَّلُ	المُخاطَبة:
نُتَخَلَّلُ		أُتَخَلَّلُ	المُتَكَلِّم:

الجَمع	المُثَنَّى	المُفرَد	الأمر المَجهُول
لِيُتَخَلَّلُوا	لِيُتَخَلَّلا	لِيُتَخَلَّلْ	الغائب:
لِيُتَخَلَّلنَ	لِتُتَخَلَّلا	لِتُتَخَلَّلْ	الغائبة:
لِتُتَخَلَّلُوا	لِتُتَخَلَّلا	لِتُتَخَلَّلْ	المُخاطَب:
لِتُتَخَلَّلنَ	لِتُتَخَلَّلا	لِتُتَخَلَّلي	المُخاطَبة:
لِنُتَخَلَّلْ		لِأُتَخَلَّلْ	المُتَكَلِّم:

Table 4.66 - Active Voice Weak Verb (Mithaal): وهم

تَوَهَّمَ، يَتَوَهَّمُ، تَوَهَّمْ، لِيَتَوَهَّمْ، تَوَهَّمْ، يَتَوَهَّمُ، تُوُهِّمَ، لِيَتَوَهَّمْ، يَتَوَهَّمُ هُوَ تَوَهُّمٌ و مُتَوَهِّمٌ و مُتَوَهَّمٌ

الجَمْع	المُثَنَّى	المُفْرَد		الماضِي المَعْلُوم
تَوَهَّمُوا	تَوَهَّما	تَوَهَّمَ	الغائِب:	
تَوَهَّمْنَ	تَوَهَّمَتا	تَوَهَّمَتْ	الغائِبة:	
تَوَهَّمْتُم	تَوَهَّمْتُما	تَوَهَّمْتَ	المُخاطَب:	
تَوَهَّمْتُنَّ	تَوَهَّمْتُما	تَوَهَّمْتِ	المُخاطَبة:	
تَوَهَّمْنا		تَوَهَّمْتُ	المُتَكَلِّم:	

الجَمْع	المُثَنَّى	المُفْرَد		المُضارِع المَعْلُوم
يَتَوَهَّمُونَ	يَتَوَهَّمانِ	يَتَوَهَّمُ	الغائِب:	
يَتَوَهَّمْنَ	تَتَوَهَّمانِ	تَتَوَهَّمُ	الغائِبة:	
تَتَوَهَّمُونَ	تَتَوَهَّمانِ	تَتَوَهَّمُ	المُخاطَب:	
تَتَوَهَّمْنَ	تَتَوَهَّمانِ	تَتَوَهَّمِينَ	المُخاطَبة:	
نَتَوَهَّمُ		أَتَوَهَّمُ	المُتَكَلِّم:	

الجَمْع	المُثَنَّى	المُفْرَد		الأَمْر المَعْلُوم
لِيَتَوَهَّمُوا	لِيَتَوَهَّما	لِيَتَوَهَّمْ	الغائِب:	
لِيَتَوَهَّمْنَ	لِتَتَوَهَّما	لِتَتَوَهَّمْ	الغائِبة:	
تَوَهَّمُوا	تَوَهَّما	تَوَهَّمْ	المُخاطَب:	
تَوَهَّمْنَ	تَوَهَّما	تَوَهَّمِي	المُخاطَبة:	
لِنَتَوَهَّمْ		لَأَتَوَهَّمْ	المُتَكَلِّم:	

Table 4.67 - Passive Voice Weak Verb (Mithaal): (وهم (تُوُهِّمَ، يُتَوَهَّمُ

الجَمْع	المُثَنَّى	المُفْرَد		الماضِيُ المَجْهُول
تُوُهِّموا	تُوُهِّما	تُوُهِّمَ	الغائِب:	
تُوُهِّمْنَ	تُوُهِّمَتا	تُوُهِّمَتْ	الغائِبَة:	
تُوُهِّمْتُم	تُوُهِّمْتُما	تُوُهِّمْتَ	المُخاطَب:	
تُوُهِّمْتُنَّ	تُوُهِّمْتُما	تُوُهِّمْتِ	المُخاطَبَة:	
تُوُهِّمْنا		تُوُهِّمْتُ	المُتَكَلِّم:	

الجَمْع	المُثَنَّى	المُفْرَد		المُضارِعُ المَجْهُول
يُتَوَهَّمُونَ	يُتَوَهَّمانِ	يُتَوَهَّمُ	الغائِب:	
يُتَوَهَّمْنَ	تُتَوَهَّمانِ	تُتَوَهَّمُ	الغائِبَة:	
تُتَوَهَّمُونَ	تُتَوَهَّمانِ	تُتَوَهَّمُ	المُخاطَب:	
تُتَوَهَّمْنَ	تُتَوَهَّمانِ	تُتَوَهَّمِينَ	المُخاطَبَة:	
نُتَوَهَّمُ		أُتَوَهَّمُ	المُتَكَلِّم:	

الجَمْع	المُثَنَّى	المُفْرَد		الأَمْرُ المَجْهُول
لِيُتَوَهَّموا	لِيُتَوَهَّما	لِيُتَوَهَّمْ	الغائِب:	
لِيُتَوَهَّمْنَ	لِتُتَوَهَّما	لِتُتَوَهَّمْ	الغائِبَة:	
لِتُتَوَهَّموا	لِتُتَوَهَّما	لِتُتَوَهَّمْ	المُخاطَب:	
لِتُتَوَهَّمْنَ	لِتُتَوَهَّما	لِتُتَوَهَّمي	المُخاطَبَة:	
لِنُتَوَهَّمْ		لِأُتَوَهَّمْ	المُتَكَلِّم:	

Table 4.68 - Active Voice Weak Verb (Ajwaf): بَيَّنَ

تَبَيَّنَ، يَتَبَيَّنُ، تَبَيَّنْ، لِيَتَبَيَّنْ، تُبَيِّنْ، يُتَبَيَّنَ، لِيَتَبَيَّنْ هُوَ تَبَيُّنٌ و مُتَبَيِّنٌ و مُتَبَيَّنٌ

الجَمْع	المُثَنَّى	المُفْرَد	الماضِيُّ المَعْلُوم
تَبَيَّنُوا	تَبَيَّنَا	تَبَيَّنَ	الغائِب:
تَبَيَّنَّ	تَبَيَّنَتَا	تَبَيَّنَتْ	الغائِبَة:
تَبَيَّنْتُمْ	تَبَيَّنْتُما	تَبَيَّنْتَ	المُخاطَب:
تَبَيَّنْتُنَّ	تَبَيَّنْتُما	تَبَيَّنْتِ	المُخاطَبَة:
تَبَيَّنَّا		تَبَيَّنْتُ	المُتَكَلِّم:

الجَمْع	المُثَنَّى	المُفْرَد	المُضارِعُ المَعْلُوم
يَتَبَيَّنُونَ	يَتَبَيَّنانِ	يَتَبَيَّنُ	الغائِب:
يَتَبَيَّنَّ	تَتَبَيَّنانِ	تَتَبَيَّنُ	الغائِبَة:
تَتَبَيَّنُونَ	تَتَبَيَّنانِ	تَتَبَيَّنُ	المُخاطَب:
تَتَبَيَّنَّ	تَتَبَيَّنانِ	تَتَبَيَّنِينَ	المُخاطَبَة:
نَتَبَيَّنُ		أَتَبَيَّنُ	المُتَكَلِّم:

الجَمْع	المُثَنَّى	المُفْرَد	الأَمْرُ المَعْلُوم
لِيَتَبَيَّنُوا	لِيَتَبَيَّنا	لِيَتَبَيَّنْ	الغائِب:
لِيَتَبَيَّنَّ	لَتَتَبَيَّنا	لِتَتَبَيَّنْ	الغائِبَة:
تَبَيَّنُوا	تَبَيَّنا	تَبَيَّنْ	المُخاطَب:
تَبَيَّنَّ	تَبَيَّنا	تَبَيَّنِي	المُخاطَبَة:
لِنَتَبَيَّنا		لأَتَبَيَّنْ	المُتَكَلِّم:

Table 4.69 - Passive Voice Weak Verb (Ajwaf): بين (تُبُيِّنَ، يَتَبَيَّنُ)

الجَمع	المُثَنَّى	المُفْرَد	الماضِي المَجْهُول
تُبُيِّنُوا	تُبُيِّنا	تُبُيِّنَ	الغائب:
تُبُيِّنَّ	تُبُيِّنَتا	تُبُيِّنَتْ	الغائبة:
تُبُيِّنْتُم	تُبُيِّنْتُما	تُبُيِّنْتَ	المُخاطَب:
تُبُيِّنْتُنَّ	تُبُيِّنْتُما	تُبُيِّنْتِ	المُخاطَبة:
تُبُيِّنّا		تُبُيِّنْتُ	المُتَكَلِّم:

الجَمع	المُثَنَّى	المُفْرَد	المُضارِعُ المَجْهُول
يُتَبَيَّنُونَ	يُتَبَيَّنانِ	يُتَبَيَّنُ	الغائب:
يُتَبَيَّنَّ	تُتَبَيَّنانِ	تُتَبَيَّنُ	الغائبة:
تُتَبَيَّنُونَ	تُتَبَيَّنانِ	تُتَبَيَّنُ	المُخاطَب:
تُتَبَيَّنَّ	تُتَبَيَّنانِ	تُتَبَيَّنِينَ	المُخاطَبة:
نُتَبَيَّنّا		أُتَبَيَّنُ	المُتَكَلِّم:

الجَمع	المُثَنَّى	المُفْرَد	الأَمْرُ المَجْهُول
لِيُتَبَيَّنُوا	لِيُتَبَيَّنا	لِيُتَبَيَّنْ	الغائب:
لِيُتَبَيَّنَّ	لِتُتَبَيَّنا	لِتُتَبَيَّنْ	الغائبة:
لِتُتَبَيَّنُوا	لِتُتَبَيَّنا	لِتُتَبَيَّني	المُخاطَب:
لِتُتَبَيَّنَّ	لِتُتَبَيَّنا	لِتُتَبَيَّني	المُخاطَبة:
لِنُتَبَيَّنْ		لِأُتَبَيَّنْ	المُتَكَلِّم:

Table 4.70 - Active Voice Weak Verb (Naaqis): رجو

تَرَجَّى، يَتَرَجَّى، تَرَجَّ، لِيَتَرَجَّ، تُرَجِّي، يُتَرَجَّى، لِيُتَرَجَّ هُو تَرَجٍّ و مُتَرَجٍّ و مُتَرَجَّى

الجَمع	المُثَنَّى	المُفْرَد	الماضِي المَعْلُوم
تَرَجُّوا	تَرَجَّيا	تَرَجَّى	الغائب:
تَرَجَّينَ	تَرَجَّتا	تَرَجَّتْ	الغائبة:
تَرَجَّيتُمْ	تَرَجَّيتُما	تَرَجَّيتَ	المُخاطَب:
تَرَجَّيتُنَّ	تَرَجَّيتُما	تَرَجَّيتِ	المُخاطَبة:
تَرَجَّينا		تَرَجَّيتُ	المُتَكَلِّم:

الجَمع	المُثَنَّى	المُفْرَد	المُضارِع المَعْلُوم
يَتَرَجَّوْنَ	يَتَرَجَّيانِ	يَتَرَجَّى	الغائب:
يَتَرَجَّينَ	تَتَرَجَّيانِ	تَتَرَجَّى	الغائبة:
تَتَرَجَّوْنَ	تَتَرَجَّيانِ	تَتَرَجَّى	المُخاطَب:
تَتَرَجَّينَ	تَتَرَجَّيانِ	تَتَرَجَّينَ	المُخاطَبة:
نَتَرَجَّى		أَتَرَجَّى	المُتَكَلِّم:

الجَمع	المُثَنَّى	المُفْرَد	الأَمْرُ المَعْلُوم
لِيَتَرَجَّوا	لِيَتَرَجَّيا	لِيَتَرَجَّ	الغائب:
لِيَتَرَجَّينَ	لِتَتَرَجَّيا	لِتَتَرَجَّ	الغائبة:
تَرَجَّوا	تَرَجَّيا	تَرَجَّ	المُخاطَب:
تَرَجَّينَ	تَرَجَّيا	تَرَجَّيْ	المُخاطَبة:
لِنَتَرَجَّ		لأَتَرَجَّ	المُتَكَلِّم:

Table 4.71 - Passive Voice Weak Verb (Naaqis): رجو (تُرُجِّي، يُتَرَجَّى)

الجَمْع	المُثَنَّى	المُفْرَد	الماضِي المَجْهُول
تُرُجُّوا	تُرُجِّيا	تُرُجِّيَ	الغائِب:
تُرُجِّينَ	تُرُجِّيتا	تُرُجِّيتْ	الغائِبة:
تُرُجِّيتُم	تُرُجِّيتُما	تُرُجِّيتَ	المُخاطَب:
تُرُجِّيتُنَّ	تُرُجِّيتُما	تُرُجِّيتِ	المُخاطَبة:
تُرُجِّينا		تُرُجِّيتُ	المُتَكَلِّم:

الجَمْع	المُثَنَّى	المُفْرَد	المُضارِع المَجْهُول
يُتَرَجَّونَ	يُتَرَجِّيانِ	يُتَرَجَّى	الغائِب:
يُتَرَجِّينَ	تُتَرَجِّيانِ	تُتَرَجَّى	الغائِبة:
تُتَرَجَّونَ	تُتَرَجِّيانِ	تُتَرَجَّى	المُخاطَب:
تُتَرَجِّينَ	تُتَرَجِّيانِ	تُتَرَجِّينَ	المُخاطَبة:
نُتَرَجَّى		أُتَرَجَّى	المُتَكَلِّم:

الجَمْع	المُثَنَّى	المُفْرَد	الأَمْر المَجْهُول
لِيُتَرَجَّوا	لِيُتَرَجِّيا	لِيُتَرَجَّ	الغائِب:
لِيُتَرَجِّينَ	لِتُتَرَجِّيا	لِتُتَرَجَّ	الغائِبة:
لِتُتَرَجَّوا	لِتُتَرَجِّيا	لِتُتَرَجَّ	المُخاطَب:
لِتُتَرَجِّينَ	لِتُتَرَجِّيا	لِتُتَرَجِّي	المُخاطَبة:
لِنُتَرَجَّ		لِأُتَرَجَّ	المُتَكَلِّم:

Table 4.72 - Active Voice Weak Verb (Lafeef): وَلِي

تَوَلَّى، يَتَوَلَّى، تَوَلَّ، لِيَتَوَلَّ، تُوَلِّي، يَتَوَلَّ، لِيَتَوَلَّ هُوَ تَوَلٌّ و مُتَوَلٌّ و مُتَوَلًّى

الجَمْع	المُثَنَّى	المُفْرَد	الماضي المَعْلُوم
تَوَلُّوا	تَوَلَّيا	تَوَلَّى	الغائب:
تَوَلَّيْنَ	تَوَلَّتا	تَوَلَّتْ	الغائبة:
تَوَلَّيْتُمْ	تَوَلَّيْتُما	تَوَلَّيْتَ	المُخاطَب:
تَوَلَّيْتُنَّ	تَوَلَّيْتُما	تَوَلَّيْتِ	المُخاطَبة:
تَوَلَّيْنا		تَوَلَّيْتُ	المُتَكَلِّم:

الجَمْع	المُثَنَّى	المُفْرَد	المُضارِع المَعْلُوم
يَتَوَلَّوْنَ	يَتَوَلَّيانِ	يَتَوَلَّى	الغائب:
يَتَوَلَّيْنَ	تَتَوَلَّيانِ	تَتَوَلَّى	الغائبة:
تَتَوَلَّوْنَ	تَتَوَلَّيانِ	تَتَوَلَّى	المُخاطَب:
تَتَوَلَّيْنَ	تَتَوَلَّيانِ	تَتَوَلَّيْنَ	المُخاطَبة:
نَتَوَلَّى		أَتَوَلَّى	المُتَكَلِّم:

الجَمْع	المُثَنَّى	المُفْرَد	الأَمْر المَعْلُوم
لِيَتَوَلَّوْا	لِيَتَوَلَّيا	لِيَتَوَلَّ	الغائب:
لِيَتَوَلَّيْنَ	لِتَتَوَلَّيا	لِتَتَوَلَّ	الغائبة:
تَوَلَّوْا	تَوَلَّيا	تَوَلَّ	المُخاطَب:
تَوَلَّيْنَ	تَوَلَّيا	تَوَلِّي	المُخاطَبة:
لِنَتَوَلَّ		لِأَتَوَلَّ	المُتَكَلِّم:

Table 4.73 - Passive Voice Weak Verb (Lafeef): (وَلِي (تُولِّي، يُتَوَلَّى

الجَمع	المُثَنَّى	المُفرَد	الماضِي المَجْهُول
تُوُلُّوا	تُوُلِّيا	تُوُلِّي	الغائِب:
تُوُلِّينَ	تُوُلِّيتا	تُوُلِّيتْ	الغائِبة:
تُوُلِّيتُمْ	تُوُلِّيتُما	تُوُلِّيتَ	المُخاطَب:
تُوُلِّيتُنَّ	تُوُلِّيتُما	تُوُلِّيتِ	المُخاطَبة:
تُوُلِّينا		تُوُلِّيتُ	المُتَكَلِّم:

الجَمع	المُثَنَّى	المُفرَد	المُضارِع المَجْهُول
يُتَوَلَّوْنَ	يُتَوَلَّيانِ	يُتَوَلَّى	الغائِب:
يُتَوَلَّيْنَ	تُتَوَلَّيانِ	تُتَوَلَّى	الغائِبة:
تُتَوَلَّوْنَ	تُتَوَلَّيانِ	تُتَوَلَّى	المُخاطَب:
تُتَوَلَّيْنَ	تُتَوَلَّيانِ	تُتَوَلَّيْنَ	المُخاطَبة:
نُتَوَلَّى		أُتَوَلَّى	المُتَكَلِّم:

الجَمع	المُثَنَّى	المُفرَد	الأمرُ المَجْهُول
لِيُتَوَلَّوْا	لِيُتَوَلَّيا	لِيُتَوَلَّ	الغائِب:
لِيُتَوَلَّيْنَ	لِيُتَوَلَّيا	لِتُتَوَلَّ	الغائِبة:
لِيُتَوَلَّوْا	لِتُتَوَلَّيا	لِتُتَوَلَّ	المُخاطَب:
لِتُتَوَلَّيْنَ	لِتُتَوَلَّيا	لِتُتَوَلَّيْ	المُخاطَبة:
لِنُتَوَلَّ		لِأُتَوَلَّ	المُتَكَلِّم:

SECTION SEVEN

The Baab Of Tafaa'ul

بابُ تَفاعُلٍ

تَفاعَلَ، يَتَفاعَلُ، تَفاعَلْ، لِيَتَفاعَلْ، تُفُوعِلَ، يُتَفاعَلُ، لِيُتَفاعَلْ هُوَ تَفاعَلٌ و مُتَفاعِلٌ و مُتَفاعَلٌ

In the *Baab of Tafaa'ul*, the Additional Letters are Taa' (ت) which precedes the first Original Letter and the Alif (ا) which follows the first Original Letter. As with the preceding *Baab*, this *Baab* has letter Taa' as its initial letter and there are three rules (1, 2,4) which were applied in the *Baab of Tafa'ul* (Section Six) which are also applied in this *Baab* in the same manner:

› Elision of the Taa' in particular Seeghah: تَتَضارَبُ تَضارَبُ ؛ تَتَضارَبانِ تَضارَبانِ .

› Conversion of Taa' to agree with 1st Original Letter, *Idghaam* and prefixing Hamzah to verb: تَتابَعَ تَّابَعَ إتَّابَعَ و يَتَّابَعُ؛ تَثاقَلَ ثَّاقَلَ إثَّاقَلَ .

› Changing pattern of Masdar in the *Naaqis* Kalimah to the pattern of: تَفاعِل, as in:

تَداعُو تَداعَى تَداعِي؛ تَوالُى تَوالِي

The basic pattern of conjugation for the *Baab of Tafaa'ul* can be found in the following tables:

Table 4.74 - Patterns Of Baab Of Tafaa'ul Active Voice Verb - **Pattern Of:** تَفَاعَلَ يَتَفَاعَلُ

تَفَاعَلَ، يَتَفَاعَلُ، تَفَاعَلْ، لِيَتَفَاعَلْ، تُفُوعِلَ، يُتَفَاعَلُ، لِيُتَفَاعَلْ هُوَ تَفَاعُلٌ و مُتَفَاعَلٌ و مُتَفَاعِلٌ

الماضي المَعْلُوم		المُفرَد	المُثَّى	الجَمع
الغائب:		تَفَاعَلَ	تَفَاعَلا	تَفَاعَلُوا
الغائبة:		تَفَاعَلَتْ	تَفَاعَلَتا	تَفَاعَلْنَ
المُخاطَب:		تَفَاعَلْتَ	تَفَاعَلْتُما	تَفَاعَلْتُم
المُخاطَبة:		تَفَاعَلْتِ	تَفَاعَلْتُما	تَفَاعَلْتُنَّ
المُتَكَلِّم:		تَفَاعَلْتُ		تَفَاعَلْنا

المُضارِع المَعْلُوم		المُفرَد	المُثَّى	الجَمع
الغائب:		يَتَفَاعَلُ	يَتَفَاعَلانِ	يَتَفَاعَلُونَ
الغائبة:		تَتَفَاعَلُ	تَتَفَاعَلانِ	يَتَفَاعَلْنَ
المُخاطَب:		تَتَفَاعَلُ	تَتَفَاعَلانِ	تَتَفَاعَلُونَ
المُخاطَبة:		تَتَفَاعَلِينَ	تَتَفَاعَلانِ	تَتَفَاعَلْنَ
المُتَكَلِّم:		أَتَفَاعَلُ		نَتَفَاعَلُ

الأَمْر المَعْلُوم		المُفرَد	المُثَّى	الجَمع
الغائب:		لِيَتَفَاعَلْ	لِيَتَفَاعَلا	لِيَتَفَاعَلُوا
الغائبة:		لِتَتَفَاعَلْ	لِتَتَفَاعَلا	لِيَتَفَاعَلْنَ
المُخاطَب:		تَفَاعَلْ	تَفَاعَلا	تَفَاعَلُوا
المُخاطَبة:		تَفَاعَلِي	تَفَاعَلا	تَفَاعَلْنَ
المُتَكَلِّم:		لأَتَفَاعَلْ		لِنَتَفَاعَلْ

Table 4.75 - Patterns Of Baab Of Tafaa'ul Passive Voice Verb - Pattern Of: تُفُوعِلَ يَتَفاعَلُ

الجَمع	المُثَنَّى	المُفْرَد		الماضِي المَجْهُول
تُفُوعِلُوا	تُفُوعِلا	تُفُوعِلَ	الغائِب:	
تُفُوعِلْنَ	تُفُوعِلَتا	تُفُوعِلَتْ	الغائِبَة:	
تُفُوعِلْتُم	تُفُوعِلْتُما	تُفُوعِلْتَ	المُخاطَب:	
تُفُوعِلْتُنَّ	تُفُوعِلْتُما	تُفُوعِلْتِ	المُخاطَبة:	
تُفُوعِلْنا		تُفُوعِلْتُ	المُتَكَلِّم:	

الجَمع	المُثَنَّى	المُفْرَد		المُضارِع المَجْهُول
يُتَفاعَلُونَ	يُتَفاعَلانِ	يُتَفاعَلُ	الغائِب:	
يُتَفاعَلْنَ	تُتَفاعَلانِ	تُتَفاعَلُ	الغائِبَة:	
تُتَفاعَلُونَ	تُتَفاعَلانِ	تُتَفاعَلُ	المُخاطَب:	
تُتَفاعَلْنَ	تُتَفاعَلانِ	تُتَفاعَلِينَ	المُخاطَبة:	
نُتَفاعَلُ		أُتَفاعَلُ	المُتَكَلِّم:	

الجَمع	المُثَنَّى	المُفْرَد		الأَمْر المَجْهُول
لِيُتَفاعَلُوا	لِيُتَفاعَلا	لِيُتَفاعَلْ	الغائِب:	
لِيُتَفاعَلْنَ	لِتُتَفاعَلا	لِتُتَفاعَلْ	الغائِبَة:	
لِتُتَفاعَلُوا	لِتُتَفاعَلا	لِتُتَفاعَلْ	المُخاطَب:	
لِتُتَفاعَلْنَ	لِتُتَفاعَلا	لِتُتَفاعَلِي	المُخاطَبة:	
لِنُتَفاعَلْ		لِأُتَفاعَلْ	المُتَكَلِّم:	

► THE MEANINGS OF THE BAAB OF TAFAA'UL مَعاني بابِ تَفاعُلٍ

There are five meanings associated with the Baab of Tafaa'ul:

▷ **Partnership** (المُشارَكَةُ), as in: تَضارَبَ زَيدٌ وَ عَمْرو *Zaid and Amr hit (each other)*. Often the verbs in this *Baab* come in this meaning. There are three *Abwaab* which convey the meaning of partnership (مُفاعَلَة، إِفْتِعالٌ، تَفاعُلٌ), however, only the *Baab of Mufaa'alah* is mostly transitive (المُتَعَدِّي), meaning that it requires two nouns to complete its meaning, namely the Subject (الفاعِل) which is Marfoo' and the Object (المَفْعُولُ بِهِ) which is Mansoob, as in: كاتَبَ زَيدٌ وَ بَكراً *Zaid and Bakr corresponded*.

Verbs in the other two *Abwaab* (إِفْتِعالٌ، تَفاعُلٌ), are mostly intransitive (اللّازِم) and only require one noun: the Subject (الفاعِل). The Subject can be one word, as in: إِخْتَصَمَ القَومُ *The people disputed (among themselves)* or تَضارَبَ الرَّجُلانِ *The two men struck (one another)*. Or the Subject can be two nouns, as in: تَجادَلَ زَيدٌ وَ بَكْرٌ *Zaid and Bakr quarreled* and تَضارَبَ زَيدٌ وَ بَكْرٌ *Zaid and Bakr struck one another*.

▷ **Reflexive** (المُطاوَعَةُ), this *Baab* is reflexive of the *Baab of Mufaa'alah* (مُفاعَلَة), for example: باعَدْتُهُ فَتَباعَدَ *I separated from him, then, he was separated*.

▷ **To pretend or resemble** (التَّظاهُرُ، التَّشَبُّهُ), meaning to pretend to be in the state depicted by the verb or to show a resemblance to the state, as in: تَمارَضَ *To pretend to be ill* and تَجاهَلَ *To pretend to be ignorant*.

▷ **Gradation** (التَّدْرِيج), for example: تَوارَدَ القَومُ *The people arrive (little by little)*.

▷ **The Meaning Of The Primary Verb** (مَعْنى الثُّلاثِيِّ المُجَرَّد), as in: تَعالَى اللَّهُ *Exalted be Allah*, which has the same meaning as: عَلا اللَّهُ (the Primary Verb).

SAMPLE CONJUGATIONS OF THE NON-SOUND AND WEAK VERBS IN THE BAAB OF TAFAA'UL

Table 4.76 - The Non-Sound Active Voice Verb M(duhaa'af): ضَدَّ

تَضادَّ (تَضادَدَ)، يَتَضادُّ (يَتَضادَدُ)، تَضادَدْ، لِيَتَضادَدْ هُوَ تَضادُّ و مُتَضادِدٌ

الجَمع	المُثَنَّى	المُفرَد	الماضِي المَعلُوم
تَضادُّوا	تَضادَّا	تَضادَّ	الغائِب:
تَضادَدْنَ	تَضادَّتا	تَضادَّتْ	الغائِبَة:
تَضادَدْتُم	تَضادَدْتُما	تَضادَدْتَ	المُخاطَب:
تَضادَدْتُنَّ	تَضادَدْتُما	تَضادَدْتِ	المُخاطَبَة:
تَضادَدْنا		تَضادَدْتُ	المُتَكَلِّم:

الجَمع	المُثَنَّى	المُفرَد	المُضارِع المَعلُوم
يَتَضادُّونَ	يَتَضادّانِ	يَتَضادُّ	الغائِب:
يَتَضادَدْنَ	تَتَضادّانِ	تَتَضادُّ	الغائِبَة:
تَتَضادُّونَ	تَتَضادّانِ	تَتَضادُّ	المُخاطَب:
تَتَضادَدْنَ	تَتَضادّانِ	تَتَضادّينَ	المُخاطَبَة:
نَتَضادُّ		أَتَضادُّ	المُتَكَلِّم:

الجَمع	المُثَنَّى	المُفرَد	الأَمرُ المَعلُوم
لِيَتَضادُّوا	لِيَتَضادَّا	لِيَتَضادَدْ	الغائِب:
لِيَتَضادَدْنَ	لِتَتَضادَّا	لِتَتَضادَدْ	الغائِبَة:
تَضادُّوا	تَضادّا	تَضادَدْ	المُخاطَب:
تَضادَدْنَ	تَضادّا	تَضادّي	المُخاطَبَة:
نَتَضادَدْ		أَتَضادَدْ	المُتَكَلِّم:

Table 4.77 - Active Voice Weak Verb (Mithaal): وصف

تَواصَفَ، يَتَواصَفُ، تَواصُفْ، لِيَتَواصَفْ، تُوُوصِفَ، تُوَاصَفُ، يُتَواصَفُ هُوَ تَواصَفْ لِيَتَواصَفْ و مُتَواصِفٌ و مُتَواصَفٌ

الجَمْع	المُثَنَّى	المُفْرَد	الماضي المَعْلُوم
تَواصَفوا	تَواصَفا	تَواصَفَ	الغائِب:
تَواصَفْنَ	تَواصَفَتا	تَواصَفَتْ	الغائِبة:
تَواصَفْتُمْ	تَواصَفْتُما	تَواصَفْتَ	المُخاطَب:
تَواصَفْتُنَّ	تَواصَفْتُما	تَواصَفْتِ	المُخاطَبة:
تَواصَفْنا		تَواصَفْتُ	المُتَكَلِّم:

الجَمْع	المُثَنَّى	المُفْرَد	المُضارع المَعْلُوم
يَتَواصَفونَ	يَتَواصَفانِ	يَتَواصَفُ	الغائِب:
يَتَواصَفْنَ	تَتَواصَفانِ	تَتَواصَفُ	الغائِبة:
تَتَواصَفونَ	تَتَواصَفانِ	تَتَواصَفُ	المُخاطَب:
تَتَواصَفْنَ	تَتَواصَفانِ	تَتَواصَفينَ	المُخاطَبة:
نَتَواصَفُ		أَتَواصَفُ	المُتَكَلِّم:

الجَمْع	المُثَنَّى	المُفْرَد	الأمْر المَعْلُوم
لِيَتَواصَفوا	لِيَتَواصَفا	لِيَتَواصَفْ	الغائِب:
لِيَتَواصَفْنَ	لِتَتَواصَفا	لِتَتَواصَفْ	الغائِبة:
تَواصَفوا	تَواصَفا	تَواصَفْ	المُخاطَب:
تَواصَفْنَ	تَواصَفا	تَواصَفي	المُخاطَبة:
لِنَتَواصَفْ		لِأَتَواصَفْ	المُتَكَلِّم:

Table 4.78 - Passive Voice Weak Verb (Mithaal): وصف (تُوُوصِفَ، يُتَواصَفُ)

الجَمْع	المُثَنَّى	المُفْرَد	الماضِيُ المَجْهُول
تُوُوصِفُوا	تُوُوصِفا	تُوُوصِفَ	الغائِب:
تُوُوصِفْنَ	تُوُوصِفَتا	تُوُوصِفَتْ	الغائِبَة:
تُوُوصِفْتُمْ	تُوُوصِفْتُما	تُوُوصِفْتَ	المُخاطَب:
تُوُوصِفْتُنَّ	تُوُوصِفْتُما	تُوُوصِفْتِ	المُخاطَبة:
تُوُوصِفْنا		تُوُوصِفْتُ	المُتَكَلِّم:

الجَمْع	المُثَنَّى	المُفْرَد	المُضارِعُ المَجْهُول
يُتَواصَفُونَ	يُتَواصَفانِ	يُتَواصَفُ	الغائِب:
يُتَواصَفْنَ	تُتَواصَفانِ	تُتَواصَفُ	الغائِبَة:
تُتَواصَفُونَ	تُتَواصَفانِ	تُتَواصَفُ	المُخاطَب:
تُتَواصَفْنَ	تُتَواصَفانِ	تُتَواصَفِينَ	المُخاطَبة:
نُتَواصَفُ		أُتَواصَفُ	المُتَكَلِّم:

الجَمْع	المُثَنَّى	المُفْرَد	الأَمْرُ المَجْهُول
لِيُتَواصَفُوا	لِيُتَواصَفا	لِيُتَواصَفْ	الغائِب:
لِيُتَواصَفْنَ	لِتُتَواصَفا	لِتُتَواصَفْ	الغائِبَة:
لِتُتَواصَفُوا	لِتُتَواصَفا	لِتُتَواصَفْ	المُخاطَب:
لِتُتَواصَفْنَ	لِتُتَواصَفا	لِتُتَواصَفِي	المُخاطَبة:
لِنُتَواصَفْ		لِأُتَواصَفْ	المُتَكَلِّم:

Table 4.79 - Active Voice Weak Verb (Ajwaf): نول

تَناوَلَ، يَتَناوَلُ، تَناوُلْ، لِيَتَناوَلْ، يُتَناوَلُ، تُنُووِلَ، لِيُتَناوَلْ هُوَ تَناوُلٌ و مُتَناوَلٌ و مُتَناوِلٌ

الجَمْع	المُثَنَّى	المُفْرَد	المَاضِي المَعْلُوم
تَناوَلُوا	تَناوَلا	تَناوَلَ	الغَائِب:
تَناوَلْنَ	تَناوَلَتا	تَناوَلَتْ	الغَائِبة:
تَناوَلْتُمْ	تَناوَلْتُما	تَناوَلْتَ	المُخاطَب:
تَناوَلْتُنَّ	تَناوَلْتُما	تَناوَلْتِ	المُخاطَبة:
تَناوَلْنا		تَناوَلْتُ	المُتَكَلِّم:

الجَمْع	المُثَنَّى	المُفْرَد	المُضارِعُ المَعْلُوم
يَتَناوَلُونَ	يَتَناوَلانِ	يَتَناوَلُ	الغَائِب:
يَتَناوَلْنَ	تَتَناوَلانِ	تَتَناوَلُ	الغَائِبة:
تَتَناوَلُونَ	تَتَناوَلانِ	تَتَناوَلُ	المُخاطَب:
تَتَناوَلْنَ	تَتَناوَلانِ	تَتَناوَلِينَ	المُخاطَبة:
نَتَناوَلُ		أَتَناوَلُ	المُتَكَلِّم:

الجَمْع	المُثَنَّى	المُفْرَد	الأَمْرُ المَعْلُوم
لِيَتَناوَلُوا	لِيَتَناوَلا	لِيَتَناوَلْ	الغَائِب:
لِيَتَناوَلْنَ	لِتَتَناوَلا	لِتَتَناوَلْ	الغَائِبة:
تَناوَلُوا	تَناوَلا	تَناوَلْ	المُخاطَب:
تَناوَلْنَ	تَناوَلا	تَناوَلِي	المُخاطَبة:
لِنَتَناوَلْ		لأَتَناوَلْ	المُتَكَلِّم:

Table 4.80 - Pasive Voice Weak Verb (Ajwaf): (نُوِّلَ، يُتَناوَلُ) نول

الجَمع	المُثَنَّى	المُفرَد	الماضِي المَجهُول
تُنُووِلُوا	تُنُووِلا	تُنُووِلَ	الغائِب:
تُنُووِلْنَ	تُنُووِلَتا	تُنُووِلَتْ	الغائِبَة:
تُنُووِلْتُمْ	تُنُووِلْتُما	تُنُووِلْتَ	المُخاطَب:
تُنُووِلْتُنَّ	تُنُووِلْتُما	تُنُووِلْتِ	المُخاطَبة:
تُنُووِلْنا		تُنُووِلْتُ	المُتَكَلِّم:

الجَمع	المُثَنَّى	المُفرَد	المُضارِع المَجهُول
يُتَناوَلُونَ	يُتَناوَلانِ	يُتَناوَلُ	الغائِب:
يُتَناوَلْنَ	تُتَناوَلانِ	تُتَناوَلُ	الغائِبَة:
تُتَناوَلُونَ	تُتَناوَلانِ	تُتَناوَلُ	المُخاطَب:
تُتَناوَلْنَ	تُتَناوَلانِ	تُتَناوَلِينَ	المُخاطَبة:
نُتَناوَلُ		أُتَناوَلُ	المُتَكَلِّم:

الجَمع	المُثَنَّى	المُفرَد	الأَمرُ المَجهُول
لِيُتَناوَلُوا	لِيُتَناوَلا	لِيُتَناوَلْ	الغائِب:
لِيُتَناوَلْنَ	لِتُتَناوَلا	لِتُتَناوَلْ	الغائِبَة:
لِتُتَناوَلُوا	لِتُتَناوَلا	لِتُتَناوَلْ	المُخاطَب:
لِتُتَناوَلْنَ	لِتُتَناوَلا	لِتُتَناوَلي	المُخاطَبة:
لِنُتَناوَلْ		لِأُتَناوَلْ	المُتَكَلِّم:

Table 4.81 - Active Voice Weak Verb (Naaqis): ندو

تَنادى، يَتَنادى، تَنادَ، لِيَتَنادَ هُوَ تَنادٍ و مُتَنادٍ

الجَمْع	المُثَنّى	المُفْرَد	المَاضِيُ المَعْلُوم
تَنادوا	تَنادَيا	تَنادى	الغائِب:
تَنادَيْنَ	تَنادَتا	تَنادَتْ	الغائِبة:
تَنادَيْتُمْ	تَنادَيْتُما	تَنادَيْتَ	المُخاطَب:
تَنادَيْتُنَّ	تَنادَيْتُما	تَنادَيْتِ	المُخاطَبة:
تَنادَيْنا		تَنادَيْتُ	المُتَكَلِّم:

الجَمْع	المُثَنّى	المُفْرَد	المُضارِعُ المَعْلُوم
يَتَنادَوْنَ	يَتَنادَيانِ	يَتَنادى	الغائِب:
يَتَنادَيْنَ	تَتَنادَيانِ	تَتَنادى	الغائِبة:
تَتَنادَوْنَ	تَتَنادَيانِ	تَتَنادى	المُخاطَب:
تَتَنادَيْنَ	تَتَنادَيانِ	تَتَنادَيْنَ	المُخاطَبة:
نَتَنادى		أتَنادى	المُتَكَلِّم:

الجَمْع	المُثَنّى	المُفْرَد	الأَمْرُ المَعْلُوم
لِيَتَنادوا	لِيَتَنادَيا	لِيَتَنادَ	الغائِب:
لِيَتَنادَيْنَ	لِتَتَنادَيا	لِتَتَنادَ	الغائِبة:
تَنادوا	تَنادَيا	تَنادَ	المُخاطَب:
تَنادَيْنَ	تَنادَيا	تَنادَيْ	المُخاطَبة:
لِنَتَنادَ		لأَتَنادَ	المُتَكَلِّم:

Table 4.82 - Active Voice Weak Verb (Lafeef): وفى

تَوافى، يَتَوافى، تَوافَ، لِيَتَوافَ هو تَوافٍ و مُتَوافٍ

الجَمْع	المُثَنَّى	المُفْرَد	الماضِيُ المَعْلُوم
تَوافوا	تَوافَيا	تَوافى	الغائِب:
تَوافَيْنَ	تَوافَتا	تَوافَتْ	الغائِبَة:
تَوافَيْتُمْ	تَوافَيْتُما	تَوافَيْتَ	المُخاطَب:
تَوافَيْتُنَّ	تَوافَيْتُما	تَوافَيْتِ	المُخاطَبَة:
تَوافَيْنا		تَوافَيْتُ	المُتَكَلِّم:

الجَمْع	المُثَنَّى	المُفْرَد	المُضارِعُ المَعْلُوم
يَتَوافَوْنَ	يَتَوافَيانِ	يَتَوافى	الغائِب:
يَتَوافَيْنَ	تَتَوافَيانِ	تَتَوافى	الغائِبَة:
تَتَوافَوْنَ	تَتَوافَيانِ	تَتَوافى	المُخاطَب:
تَتَوافَيْنَ	تَتَوافَيانِ	تَتَوافَيْنَ	المُخاطَبَة:
نَتَوافى		أَتَوافى	المُتَكَلِّم:

الجَمْع	المُثَنَّى	المُفْرَد	الأَمْرُ المَعْلُوم
لِيَتَوافَوا	لِيَتَوافَيا	لِيَتَوافَ	الغائِب:
لِيَتَوافَيْنَ	لِتَتَوافَيا	لِتَتَوافَ	الغائِبَة:
تَوافَوا	تَوافَيا	تَوافَ	المُخاطَب:
تَوافَيْنَ	تَوافَيا	تَوافَيْ	المُخاطَبَة:
لِنَتَوافَ		لِأَتَوافَ	المُتَكَلِّم:

SECTION EIGHT

The Baab of If'ilaal

بابُ إِفْعِلالٍ

إِفْعَلَّ، يَفْعَلُّ، إِفْعَلِلْ، لِيَفْعَلِلْ هُوَ إِفْعِلالٌ و مُفْعَلٌّ

The Additional Letters that are added in this *Baab* are Hamzah, in the Past Tense Verb, Command Verb and Masdar and the last Original Letter is doubled or *Mushaddad* in all derivative forms. Without *Idghaam*, the verb's original pattern is: إِفْعَلَلَ، يَفْعَلِلُ .

The particularity of this *Baab* is that the words derived from it are mostly in the meaning of colors and defects. Also, this *Baab* is always Intransitive. Keeping these points in mind, the *Baab of If'ilaal* will have two meanings:

▷ **To Enter The Subject Into the Basis of the Action** (دُخُولُ الفاعِلِ في مَبْدَأِ الفِعْلِ). Most often, the words will come in this meaning, as in: إِسْوَدَّ اللَّيلُ *The night blackened*; إِحْمَرَّ البُسْرُ *The unripened date became red*.

▷ **Exaggeration** (المُبالَغَة), as in: إِحْمَرَّ الحَدِيدُ *The iron became bright red.*

The patterns of conjugation for verbs in the *Baab of If'ilaal* are as follows:

إِفْعَلَّ، يَفْعَلُّ، إِفْعَلِلْ، لِيَفْعَلِلْ هُوَ إِفْعِلالٌ و مُفْعَلٌّ

الجَمْع	المُثَنَّى	المُفْرَد	الماضِي المَعْلُوم
إِفْعَلُّوا	إِفْعَلّا	إِفْعَلَّ	الغَائِب:
إِفْعَلَلْنَ	إِفْعَلَّتا	إِفْعَلَّتْ	الغَائِبة:
إِفْعَلَلْتُم	إِفْعَلَلْتُما	إِفْعَلَلْتَ	المُخاطَب:
إِفْعَلَلْتُنَّ	إِفْعَلَلْتُما	إِفْعَلَلْتِ	المُخاطَبة:
إِفْعَلَلْنا		إِفْعَلَلْتُ	المُتَكَلِّم:

الجَمْع	المُثَنَّى	المُفْرَد	المُضارِع المَعْلُوم
يَفْعَلُّونَ	يَفْعَلّانِ	يَفْعَلُّ	الغَائِب:
يَفْعَلِلْنَ	تَفْعَلّانِ	تَفْعَلُّ	الغَائِبة:
تَفْعَلُّونَ	تَفْعَلّانِ	تَفْعَلُّ	المُخاطَب:
تَفْعَلِلْنَ	تَفْعَلّانِ	تَفْعَلِّينَ	المُخاطَبة:
نَفْعَلُّ		أَفْعَلُّ	المُتَكَلِّم:

الجَمْع	المُثَنَّى	المُفْرَد	الأَمْر المَعْلُوم
لِيَفْعَلُّوا	لِيَفْعَلّا	لِيَفْعَلِلْ	الغَائِب:
لِيَفْعَلِلْنَ	لِتَفْعَلّا	لِتَفْعَلِلْ	الغَائِبة:
إِفْعَلُّوا	إِفْعَلّا	إِفْعَلِلْ	المُخاطَب:
إِفْعَلِلْنَ	إِفْعَلّا	إِفْعَلِّي	المُخاطَبة:
لِنَفْعَلِلْ		لِأَفْعَلِلْ	المُتَكَلِّم:

SAMPLE CONJUGATION OF A WEAK VERB IN THE BAAB OF IF'ILAAL

Table 4.84 - Active Voice Non-Sound Verb (Ajwaf): عوج

إِعْوَجَّ، يَعْوَجُّ، إِعْوِجْجْ، لِيَعْوَجِجْ هُوَ إِعْوِجاجٌ و مُعْوَجٌّ

الجَمْع	المُثَنَّى	المُفْرَد	الماضِي المَعْلُوم
إِعْوَجُّوا	إِعْوَجَّا	إِعْوَجَّ	الغائِب:
إِعْوَجْجْنَ	إِعْوَجَّتا	إِعْوَجَّتْ	الغائِبة:
إِعْوَجْجْتُمْ	إِعْوَجْجْتُما	إِعْوَجْجْتَ	المُخاطَب:
إِعْوَجْجْتُنَّ	إِعْوَجْجْتُما	إِعْوَجْجْتِ	المُخاطَبة:
إِعْوَجْجْنا		إِعْوَجْجْتُ	المُتَكَلِّم:

الجَمْع	المُثَنَّى	المُفْرَد	المُضارِعُ المَعْلُوم
يَعْوَجُّونَ	يَعْوَجَّانِ	يَعْوَجُّ	الغائِب:
يَعْوَجْجْنَ	تَعْوَجَّانِ	تَعْوَجُّ	الغائِبة:
تَعْوَجُّونَ	تَعْوَجَّانِ	تَعْوَجُّ	المُخاطَب:
تَعْوَجْجْنَ	تَعْوَجَّانِ	تَعْوَجِّينَ	المُخاطَبة:
نَعْوَجُّ		أَعْوَجُّ	المُتَكَلِّم:

الجَمْع	المُثَنَّى	المُفْرَد	الأَمْرُ المَعْلُوم
لِيَعْوَجُّوا	لِيَعْوَجَّا	لِيَعْوَجِجْ	الغائِب:
لِيَعْوَجْجْنَ	لِتَعْوَجَّا	لِتَعْوَجِجْ	الغائِبة:
إِعْوَجُّوا	إِعْوَجَّا	إِعْوَجِجْ	المُخاطَب:
إِعْوَجْجْنَ	إِعْوَجَّا	إِعْوَجِّي	المُخاطَبة:
لِنَعْوَجِجْ		لأَعْوَجِجْ	المُتَكَلِّم:

SECTION NINE

The Baab Of Istif'aal

بابُ إِستِفْعالٍ

إِستَفْعَلَ، يَستَفْعِلُ، إِستَفْعِلْ، لِيَستَفْعِلْ، إِستَفْعِلَ، يُستَفْعَلُ، أُستَفْعِلُ، لِيُستَفْعَلْ هُوَ إِستِفْعالٌ و مُستَفْعِلٌ و مُستَفْعَلٌ

As many as three Additional Letters are added in this pattern, namely Hamzah (إ), Seen (س) and Taa' (ت). The Hamzah is conjunctive and is found in the Past Tense, Command Verb and Masdar while the letters Seen and Taa' are found in all of its derivatives.

Here are the basic conjugation patterns for the *Baab of Istif'aal*:

Table 4.85 - Patterns Of Baab Of Istif'aal Active Voice Verb - Pattern Of: إِسْتَفْعَلَ يَسْتَفْعِلُ

إِسْتَفْعَلَ، يَسْتَفْعِلُ، إِسْتَفْعِلْ، لِيَسْتَفْعِلْ، أُسْتَفْعِلُ، يُسْتَفْعَلُ، لِيُسْتَفْعَلْ هُوَ إِسْتَفْعَلَ و مُسْتَفْعِلٌ و مُسْتَفْعَلٌ

الجَمْع	المُثَنَّى	المُفْرَد		الماضِي المَعْلُوم
إِسْتَفْعَلُوا	إِسْتَفْعَلَا	إِسْتَفْعَلَ	الغائِب:	
إِسْتَفْعَلْنَ	إِسْتَفْعَلَتَا	إِسْتَفْعَلَتْ	الغائِبَة:	
إِسْتَفْعَلْتُمْ	إِسْتَفْعَلْتُمَا	إِسْتَفْعَلْتَ	المُخَاطَب:	
إِسْتَفْعَلْتُنَّ	إِسْتَفْعَلْتُمَا	إِسْتَفْعَلْتِ	المُخَاطَبَة:	
إِسْتَفْعَلْنَا		إِسْتَفْعَلْتُ	المُتَكَلِّم:	

الجَمْع	المُثَنَّى	المُفْرَد		المُضارِع المَعْلُوم
يَسْتَفْعِلُونَ	يَسْتَفْعِلَانِ	يَسْتَفْعِلُ	الغائِب:	
يَسْتَفْعِلْنَ	تَسْتَفْعِلَانِ	تَسْتَفْعِلُ	الغائِبَة:	
تَسْتَفْعِلُونَ	تَسْتَفْعِلَانِ	تَسْتَفْعِلُ	المُخَاطَب:	
تَسْتَفْعِلْنَ	تَسْتَفْعِلَانِ	تَسْتَفْعِلِينَ	المُخَاطَبَة:	
نَسْتَفْعِلُ		أَسْتَفْعِلُ	المُتَكَلِّم:	

الجَمْع	المُثَنَّى	المُفْرَد		الأَمْر المَعْلُوم
لِيَسْتَفْعِلُوا	لِيَسْتَفْعِلَا	لِيَسْتَفْعِلْ	الغائِب:	
لِيَسْتَفْعِلْنَ	لِتَسْتَفْعِلَا	لِتَسْتَفْعِلْ	الغائِبَة:	
إِسْتَفْعِلُوا	إِسْتَفْعِلَا	إِسْتَفْعِلْ	المُخَاطَب:	
إِسْتَفْعِلْنَ	إِسْتَفْعِلَا	إِسْتَفْعِلِي	المُخَاطَبَة:	
لِنَسْتَفْعِلْ		لِأَسْتَفْعِلْ	المُتَكَلِّم:	

Table 4.86 - Patterns Of Baab Of Istif'aal Passive Voice Verb - Pattern Of: أُستُفْعِلَ يُستَفْعَلُ

الجَمْع	المُثَنَّى	المُفْرَد		المَاضِيُ المَجْهُول
أُستُفْعِلُوا	أُستُفْعِلا	أُستُفْعِلَ	الغَائِب:	
أُستُفْعِلْنَ	أُستُفْعِلَتا	أُستُفْعِلَتْ	الغَائِبَة:	
أُستُفْعِلْتُم	أُستُفْعِلْتُما	أُستُفْعِلْتَ	المُخَاطَب:	
أُستُفْعِلْتُنَّ	أُستُفْعِلْتُما	أُستُفْعِلْتِ	المُخَاطَبَة:	
أُستُفْعِلْنا		أُستُفْعِلْتُ	المُتَكَلِّم:	

الجَمْع	المُثَنَّى	المُفْرَد		المُضَارِعُ المَجْهُول
يُستَفْعَلُونَ	يُستَفْعَلانِ	يُستَفْعَلُ	الغَائِب:	
يُستَفْعَلْنَ	تُستَفْعَلانِ	تُستَفْعَلُ	الغَائِبَة:	
تُستَفْعَلُونَ	تُستَفْعَلانِ	تُستَفْعَلُ	المُخَاطَب:	
تُستَفْعَلْنَ	تُستَفْعَلانِ	تُستَفْعَلِينَ	المُخَاطَبَة:	
نُستَفْعَلُ		أُستَفْعَلُ	المُتَكَلِّم:	

الجَمْع	المُثَنَّى	المُفْرَد		الأَمْرُ المَجْهُول
لِيُستَفْعَلُوا	لِيُستَفْعَلا	لِيُستَفْعَلْ	الغَائِب:	
لِيُستَفْعَلْنَ	لِتُستَفْعَلا	لِتُستَفْعَلْ	الغَائِبَة:	
لِتُستَفْعَلُوا	لِتُستَفْعَلا	لِتُستَفْعَلْ	المُخَاطَب:	
لِتُستَفْعَلْنَ	لِتُستَفْعَلا	لِتُستَفْعَلي	المُخَاطَبَة:	
لِنُستَفْعَلْ		لأُستَفْعَلْ	المُتَكَلِّم:	

▶ THE MEANINGS OF THE BAAB OF ISTIF'AAL مَعاني باب إِسْتِفْعالٍ

The *Baab of Istif'aal* has seven meanings:

▷ **Seeking** (الطَّلَبُ), which is the meaning which most words in this *Baab* are found to have. For example: أَسْتَغْفِرُ اللَّهَ *I seek Allah's forgiveness*; إِسْتَنْصَرَ *To seek help*. The words in this meaning are transitive although the Primary Verb may be intransitive, as in: إِسْتَخْرَجْتُ المَعْدِنَ *I removed minerals*.

▷ **Transformation** (التَّحَوُّلُ), as in: إِسْتَحْجَرَ الطِّينُ *The clay turned to stone*.

▷ **An Attribute Is Found In The Object**(وُجودُ صِفَةٍ في المَفْعولِ), such as: إِسْتَعْظَمْتُ الأَمْرَ, *I found the matter to be great*.

▷ **The Object Is Depicted With An Attribute** (المَفْعُلُ مُتَّصِفٌ بِصِفَةٍ), as in: إِسْتَخْلَفَ عَلِيًّا *He made Ali his successor*.

▷ **To feign an action** sometimes with difficulty (التَّكَلُّفُ), as in: إِسْتَجَرَأَ *To try to act bravely*.

▷ **Reflexive**(المُطاوَعَةُ), as in: أَرَحْتُ زَيداً فَاسْتَراحَ *I let Zaid rest, then, he was rested*.

▷ **The Meaning Of The Primary Verb** (مَعْنَى الثُّلاثِيِّ المُجَرَّدِ), like: إِسْتَقَرَّ or قَرَّ.

Here are some sample conjugations of verbs in the Baab of Istif'aal:

SAMPLE CONJUGATION OF NON-SOUND & WEAK VERBS IN THE BAAB OF ISTIF'AAL

Table 4.87 - Active Voice Non-Sound Verb (Mudhaa'af): حقَّ

إِسْتَحَقَّ، يَسْتَحِقُّ، إِسْتِحْقْ، لِيَسْتَحْقِقْ، لِيَسْتَحَقَّ، أُسْتُحِقَّ، يُسْتَحَقُّ، لِيُسْتَحَقَّ هُوَ إِسْتِحْقَاقٌ و مُسْتَحِقٌّ و مُسْتَحَقٌّ

الجَمْع	المُثَنَّى	المُفْرَد		الماضِيُ المَعْلُوم
إِسْتَحَقُّوا	إِسْتَحَقَّا	إِسْتَحَقَّ	الغائِب:	
إِسْتَحْقَقْنَ	إِسْتَحَقَّتا	إِسْتَحَقَّتْ	الغائِبَة:	
إِسْتَحْقَقْتُمْ	إِسْتَحْقَقْتُما	إِسْتَحْقَقْتَ	المُخاطَب:	
إِسْتَحْقَقْتُنَّ	إِسْتَحْقَقْتُما	إِسْتَحْقَقْتِ	المُخاطَبَة:	
إِسْتَحْقَقْنا		إِسْتَحْقَقْتُ	المُتَكَلِّم:	

الجَمْع	المُثَنَّى	المُفْرَد		المُضارِعُ المَعْلُوم
يَسْتَحِقُّونَ	يَسْتَحِقَّانِ	يَسْتَحِقُّ	الغائِب:	
يَسْتَحْقِقْنَ	تَسْتَحِقَّانِ	تَسْتَحِقُّ	الغائِبَة:	
تَسْتَحِقُّونَ	تَسْتَحِقَّانِ	تَسْتَحِقُّ	المُخاطَب:	
تَسْتَحْقِقْنَ	تَسْتَحِقَّانِ	تَسْتَحِقِّينَ	المُخاطَبَة:	
نَسْتَحِقُّ		أَسْتَحِقُّ	المُتَكَلِّم:	

الجَمْع	المُثَنَّى	المُفْرَد		الأَمْرُ المَعْلُوم
لِيَسْتَحِقُّوا	لِيَسْتَحِقَّا	لِيَسْتَحْقِقْ	الغائِب:	
لِيَسْتَحْقِقْنَ	لِتَسْتَحِقَّا	لِتَسْتَحْقِقْ	الغائِبَة:	
إِسْتَحِقُّوا	إِسْتَحِقَّا	إِسْتَحْقِقْ	المُخاطَب:	
إِسْتَحْقِقْنَ	إِسْتَحِقَّا	إِسْتَحِقِّي	المُخاطَبَة:	
لِنَسْتَحِقْ		لِأَسْتَحْقِقْ	المُتَكَلِّم:	

Table 4.88 - Active Voice Non-Sound Verb: حقَّ (أُسْتُحِقَّ، يُسْتَحَقُّ)

الجَمع	المُثَنَّى	المُفْرَد	الماضِيُ المَجْهُول
أُسْتُحِقُّوا	أُسْتُحِقَّا	أُسْتُحِقَّ	الغائِب:
أُسْتُحِقِقْنَ	أُسْتُحِقَّتا	أُسْتُحِقَّتْ	الغائِبة:
أُسْتُحْقِقْتُم	أُسْتُحْقِقْتُما	أُسْتُحْقِقْتَ	المُخاطَب:
أُسْتُحْقِقْتُنَّ	أُسْتُحْقِقْتُما	أُسْتُحْقِقْتِ	المُخاطَبة:
أُسْتُحْقِقْنا		أُسْتُحْقِقْتُ	المُتَكَلِّم:

الجَمع	المُثَنَّى	المُفْرَد	المُضارِعُ المَجْهُول
يُسْتَحَقُّونَ	يُسْتَحَقَّانِ	يُسْتَحَقُّ	الغائِب:
يُسْتَحْقَقْنَ	تُسْتَحَقَّانِ	تُسْتَحَقُّ	الغائِبة:
تُسْتَحَقُّونَ	تُسْتَحَقَّانِ	تُسْتَحَقُّ	المُخاطَب:
تُسْتَحْقَقْنَ	تُسْتَحَقَّانِ	تُسْتَحَقِّينَ	المُخاطَبة:
نُسْتَحَقُّ		أُسْتَحَقُّ	المُتَكَلِّم:

الجَمع	المُثَنَّى	المُفْرَد	الأَمْرُ المَجْهُول
لِيُسْتَحَقُّوا	لِيُسْتَحَقَّا	لِيُسْتَحْقَقْ	الغائِب:
لِيُسْتَحْقَقْنَ	لِتُسْتَحَقَّا	لِتُسْتَحْقَقْ	الغائِبة:
لِتُسْتَحَقُّوا	لِتُسْتَحَقَّا	لِتُسْتَحْقَقْ	المُخاطَب:
لِتُسْتَحْقَقْنَ	لِتُسْتَحَقَّا	لِتُسْتَحَقِّي	المُخاطَبة:
لِنُسْتَحْقَقْ		لأُسْتَحْقَقْ	المُتَكَلِّم:

Table 4.89 - Active Voice Weak Verb (Mithaal): وعب

إِسْتَوْعَبَ، يَسْتَوْعِبُ، إِسْتَوْعِبْ، لِيَسْتَوْعِبْ، لِيَسْتَوْعِبْ، أُسْتَوْعِبَ، يُسْتَوْعَبُ، لِيُسْتَوْعَبْ هُوَ إِسْتِيعَابٌ و مُسْتَوْعِبٌ و مُسْتَوْعَبٌ

الجَمع	المُثَنَّى	المُفْرد	الماضِي المَعْلُوم
إِسْتَوْعَبوا	إِسْتَوْعَبا	إِسْتَوْعَبَ	الغائِب:
إِسْتَوْعَبْنَ	إِسْتَوْعَبَتا	إِسْتَوْعَبَتْ	الغائِبَة:
إِسْتَوْعَبْتُمْ	إِسْتَوْعَبْتُما	إِسْتَوْعَبْتَ	المُخاطَب:
إِسْتَوْعَبْتُنَّ	إِسْتَوْعَبْتُما	إِسْتَوْعَبْتِ	المُخاطَبَة:
إِسْتَوْعَبْنا		إِسْتَوْعَبْتُ	المُتَكَلِّم:

الجَمع	المُثَنَّى	المُفْرد	المُضارِعُ المَعْلُوم
يَسْتَوْعِبونَ	يَسْتَوْعِبانِ	يَسْتَوْعِبُ	الغائِب:
يَسْتَوْعِبْنَ	تَسْتَوْعِبانِ	تَسْتَوْعِبُ	الغائِبَة:
تَسْتَوْعِبونَ	تَسْتَوْعِبانِ	تَسْتَوْعِبُ	المُخاطَب:
تَسْتَوْعِبْنَ	تَسْتَوْعِبانِ	تَسْتَوْعِبينَ	المُخاطَبَة:
نَسْتَوْعِبُ		أَسْتَوْعِبُ	المُتَكَلِّم:

الجَمع	المُثَنَّى	المُفْرد	الأَمْرُ المَعْلُوم
لِيَسْتَوْعِبوا	لِيَسْتَوْعِبا	لِيَسْتَوْعِبْ	الغائِب:
لِيَسْتَوْعِبْنَ	لِتَسْتَوْعِبا	لِتَسْتَوْعِبْ	الغائِبَة:
إِسْتَوْعِبوا	إِسْتَوْعِبا	إِسْتَوْعِبْ	المُخاطَب:
إِسْتَوْعِبْنَ	إِسْتَوْعِبا	إِسْتَوْعِبي	المُخاطَبَة:
لِنَسْتَوْعِبْ		لِأَسْتَوْعِبْ	المُتَكَلِّم:

Table 4.90 - Passive Voice Weak Verb (Mithaal): (وَعب (أُسْتُوعِب، يُسْتَوعَبُ

الجَمع	المُثَنَّى	المُفرَد	المَاضِي المَجهُول
أُسْتُوعِبوا	أُسْتُوعِبا	أُسْتُوعِبَ	الغائب:
أُسْتُوعِبنَ	أُسْتُوعِبتا	أُسْتُوعِبَتْ	الغائبة:
أُسْتُوعِبتُم	أُسْتُوعِبتُما	أُسْتُوعِبتَ	المُخاطَب:
أُسْتُوعِبتُنَّ	أُسْتُوعِبتُما	أُسْتُوعِبتِ	المُخاطَبة:
أُسْتُوعِبنا		أُسْتُوعِبتُ	المُتَكَلِّم:

الجَمع	المُثَنَّى	المُفرَد	المُضارعُ المَجهُول
يُسْتَوعَبونَ	يُسْتَوعَبانِ	يُسْتَوعَبُ	الغائب:
يُسْتَوعَبنَ	تُسْتَوعَبانِ	تُسْتَوعَبُ	الغائبة:
تُسْتَوعَبونَ	تُسْتَوعَبانِ	تُسْتَوعَبُ	المُخاطَب:
تُسْتَوعَبنَ	تُسْتَوعَبانِ	تُسْتَوعَبينَ	المُخاطَبة:
نُسْتَوعَبْ		أُسْتَوعَبْ	المُتَكَلِّم:

الجَمع	المُثَنَّى	المُفرَد	الأَمْر المَجهُول
لِيُسْتَوعَبوا	لِيُسْتَوعَبا	لِيُسْتَوعَبْ	الغائب:
لِيُسْتَوعَبنَ	لِتُسْتَوعَبا	لِتُسْتَوعَبْ	الغائبة:
لِتُسْتَوعَبوا	لِتُسْتَوعَبا	لِيُسْتَوعَبْ	المُخاطَب:
لِتُسْتَوعَبنَ	لِتُسْتَوعَبا	لِتُسْتَوعَبي	المُخاطَبة:
لِنُسْتَوعَبْ		لأُسْتَوعَبْ	المُتَكَلِّم:

Table 4.91 - Active Voice Weak Verb (Ajwaf): طوع

إِسْتَطَاعَ، يَسْتَطِيعُ، إِسْتَطِعْ، لِيَسْتَطِعْ، إِسْتَطَاعْ، يُسْتَطِيعُ، أُسْتُطِيعَ، لِيُسْتَطَعْ هُوَ إِسْتَطَاعَةٌ و مُسْتَطِيعٌ و مُسْتَطَاعٌ

الجَمْع	المُثَنَّى	المُفْرَد		الماضِي المَعْلُوم
إِسْتَطَاعُوا	إِسْتَطَاعا	إِسْتَطَاعَ	الغائِب:	
إِسْتَطَعْنَ	إِسْتَطَاعَتا	إِسْتَطَاعَتْ	الغائِبَة:	
إِسْتَطَعْتُم	إِسْتَطَعْتُما	إِسْتَطَعْتَ	المُخاطَب:	
إِسْتَطَعْتُنَّ	إِسْتَطَعْتُما	إِسْتَطَعْتِ	المُخاطَبَة:	
إِسْتَطَعْنا		إِسْتَطَعْتُ	المُتَكَلِّم:	

الجَمْع	المُثَنَّى	المُفْرَد		المُضارِعُ المَعْلُوم
يَسْتَطِيعُونَ	يَسْتَطِيعانِ	يَسْتَطِيعُ	الغائِب:	
يَسْتَطِعْنَ	تَسْتَطِيعانِ	تَسْتَطِيعُ	الغائِبَة:	
تَسْتَطِيعُونَ	تَسْتَطِيعانِ	تَسْتَطِيعُ	المُخاطَب:	
تَسْتَطِعْنَ	تَسْتَطِيعانِ	تَسْتَطِيعِينَ	المُخاطَبَة:	
نَسْتَطِيعُ		أَسْتَطِيعُ	المُتَكَلِّم:	

الجَمْع	المُثَنَّى	المُفْرَد		الأَمْرُ المَعْلُوم
لِيَسْتَطِيعُوا	لِيَسْتَطِيعا	لِيَسْتَطِعْ	الغائِب:	
لِيَسْتَطِعْنَ	لِتَسْتَطِيعا	لِتَسْتَطِعْ	الغائِبَة:	
إِسْتَطِيعُوا	إِسْتَطِيعا	إِسْتَطِعْ	المُخاطَب:	
إِسْتَطِعْنَ	إِسْتَطِيعا	إِسْتَطِيعِي	المُخاطَبَة:	
لِنَسْتَطِعْ		لِأَسْتَطِعْ	المُتَكَلِّم:	

Table 4.92 - Passive Voice Weak Verb (Ajwaf): (أُسْتُطِيعَ، يُسْتَطَاعُ) طوع

الجَمع	المُثَنَّى	المُفْرَد		الماضِي المَجْهُول
أُسْتُطِيعُوا	أُسْتُطِيعا	أُسْتُطِيعَ	الغائِب:	
أُسْتُطِعْنَ	أُسْتُطِيعَتا	أُسْتُطِيعَتْ	الغائِبة:	
أُسْتُطِعْتُم	أُسْتُطِعْتُما	أُسْتُطِعْتَ	المُخاطَب:	
أُسْتُطِعْتُنَّ	أُسْتُطِعْتُما	أُسْتُطِعْتِ	المُخاطَبة:	
أُسْتُطِعْنا		أُسْتُطِعْتُ	المُتَكَلِّم:	

الجَمع	المُثَنَّى	المُفْرَد		المُضارِعُ المَجْهُول
يُسْتَطاعُونَ	يُسْتَطاعانِ	يُسْتَطاعُ	الغائِب:	
يُسْتَطَعْنَ	تُسْتَطاعانِ	تُسْتَطاعُ	الغائِبة:	
تُسْتَطاعُونَ	تُسْتَطاعانِ	تُسْتَطاعُ	المُخاطَب:	
تُسْتَطَعْنَ	تُسْتَطاعانِ	تُسْتَطاعِينَ	المُخاطَبة:	
نُسْتَطاعُ		أُسْتَطاعُ	المُتَكَلِّم:	

الجَمع	المُثَنَّى	المُفْرَد		الأَمرُ المَجْهُول
لِيُسْتَطاعُوا	لِيُسْتَطاعا	لِيُسْتَطَعْ	الغائِب:	
لِيُسْتَطَعْنَ	لِتُسْتَطاعا	لِتُسْتَطَعْ	الغائِبة:	
لِتُسْتَطاعُوا	لِتُسْتَطاعا	لِتُسْتَطَعْ	المُخاطَب:	
لِتُسْتَطَعْنَ	لِتُسْتَطاعا	لِتُسْتَطاعِي	المُخاطَبة:	
لِنُسْتَطَعْ		لِأُسْتَطَعْ	المُتَكَلِّم:	

Table 4.93 - Active Voice Weak Verb (Naaqis): ثنى

إِسْتَثْنَى، يَسْتَثْنِي، إِسْتَثْنِ، لِيَسْتَثْنِ، يُسْتَثْنَى، لِيُسْتَثْنَى، يُسْتَثْنِي، أُسْتُثْنِ، أُسْتُثْنِيَ هُوَ إِسْتِثْنَاءً و مُسْتَثْنٍ و مُسْتَثْنًى

الجَمْع	المُثَنَّى	المُفْرَد		الماضِيُ المَعْلُوم
إِسْتَثْنَوا	إِسْتَثْنَيا	إِسْتَثْنَى	الغَائِب:	
إِسْتَثْنَيْنَ	إِسْتَثْنَتا	إِسْتَثْنَتْ	الغَائِبَة:	
إِسْتَثْنَيْتُمْ	إِسْتَثْنَيْتُما	إِسْتَثْنَيْتَ	المُخَاطَب:	
إِسْتَثْنَيْتُنَّ	إِسْتَثْنَيْتُما	إِسْتَثْنَيْتِ	المُخَاطَبَة:	
إِسْتَثْنَيْنا		إِسْتَثْنَيْتُ	المُتَكَلِّم:	

الجَمْع	المُثَنَّى	المُفْرَد		المُضَارِعُ المَعْلُوم
يَسْتَثْنُونَ	يَسْتَثْنِيانِ	يَسْتَثْنِي	الغَائِب:	
يَسْتَثْنِينَ	تَسْتَثْنِيانِ	تَسْتَثْنِي	الغَائِبَة:	
تَسْتَثْنُونَ	تَسْتَثْنِيانِ	تَسْتَثْنِي	المُخَاطَب:	
تَسْتَثْنِينَ	تَسْتَثْنِيانِ	تَسْتَثْنِينَ	المُخَاطَبَة:	
نَسْتَثْنِي		أَسْتَثْنِي	المُتَكَلِّم:	

الجَمْع	المُثَنَّى	المُفْرَد		الأَمْرُ المَعْلُوم
لِيَسْتَثْنُوا	لِيَسْتَثْنِيا	لِيَسْتَثْنِ	الغَائِب:	
لِيَسْتَثْنِينَ	لِتَسْتَثْنِيا	لِتَسْتَثْنِ	الغَائِبَة:	
إِسْتَثْنُوا	إِسْتَثْنِيا	إِسْتَثْنِ	المُخَاطَب:	
إِسْتَثْنِينَ	إِسْتَثْنِيا	إِسْتَثْنِي	المُخَاطَبَة:	
لِنَسْتَثْنِ		لِأَسْتَثْنِ	المُتَكَلِّم:	

Table 4.94 - Passive Voice Weak Verb (Naaqis): (أُسْتُثْنِيَ، يُسْتَثْنَى) ثنى

الجَمع	المُثَنَّى	المُفْرَد	الماضي المَجْهُول
أُسْتُثْنُوا	أُسْتُثْنِيا	أُسْتُثْنِيَ	الغائب:
أُسْتُثْنِينَ	أُسْتُثْنِيتا	أُسْتُثْنِيتْ	الغائبة:
أُسْتُثْنِيتُم	أُسْتُثْنِيتُما	أُسْتُثْنِيتَ	المُخاطَب:
أُسْتُثْنِيتُنَّ	أُسْتُثْنِيتُما	أُسْتُثْنِيتِ	المُخاطَبة:
أُسْتُثْنِينا		أُسْتُثْنِيتُ	المُتَكَلِّم:

الجَمع	المُثَنَّى	المُفْرَد	المُضارِع المَجْهُول
يُسْتَثْنُونَ	يُسْتَثْنَيانِ	يُسْتَثْنَى	الغائب:
يُسْتَثْنَينَ	تُسْتَثْنَيانِ	تُسْتَثْنَى	الغائبة:
تُسْتَثْنَونَ	تُسْتَثْنَيانِ	تُسْتَثْنَى	المُخاطَب:
تُسْتَثْنَينَ	تُسْتَثْنَيانِ	تُسْتَثْنَينَ	المُخاطَبة:
نُسْتَثْنَى		أُسْتَثْنَى	المُتَكَلِّم:

الجَمع	المُثَنَّى	المُفْرَد	الأَمْر المَجْهُول
لِيُسْتَثْنَوا	لِيُسْتَثْنَيا	لِيُسْتَثْنَ	الغائب:
لِيُسْتَثْنَينَ	لِتُسْتَثْنَيا	لِتُسْتَثْنَ	الغائبة:
لِتُسْتَثْنَوا	لِتُسْتَثْنَيا	لِتُسْتَثْنَ	المُخاطَب:
لِتُسْتَثْنَينَ	لِتُسْتَثْنَيا	لِتُسْتَثْنَي	المُخاطَبة:
لِنُسْتَثْنَ		لَأُسْتَثْنَ	المُتَكَلِّم:

Table 4.95 - Active Voice Weak Verb (Lafeef): وفى

إِستَوْفَى، يَسْتَوْفِي، إِستَوْفِ، لِيَسْتَوْفِ، لِيَسْتَوْفَى، يُسْتَوْفِي، أُستُوفِيَ، إِستِيفَاءً مُسْتَوْفٍ و مُسْتَوْفًى

الجَمع	المُثَنَّى	المُفرَد		الماضِي المَعلُوم
إِستَوْفَونَ	إِستَوْفَيا	إِستَوْفَى	الغائِب:	
إِستَوْفَينَ	إِستَوْفَتا	إِستَوْفَتْ	الغائِبة:	
إِستَوْفَيتُم	إِستَوْفَيتُما	إِستَوْفَيتَ	المُخاطَب:	
إِستَوْفَيتُنَّ	إِستَوْفَيتُما	إِستَوْفَيتِ	المُخاطَبة:	
إِستَوْفَينا		إِستَوْفَيتُ	المُتَكَلِّم:	

الجَمع	المُثَنَّى	المُفرَد		المُضارِعُ المَعلُوم
يَسْتَوْفُونَ	يَسْتَوْفِيان	يَسْتَوْفِي	الغائِب:	
يَسْتَوْفِينَ	تَسْتَوْفِيان	تَسْتَوْفِي	الغائِبة:	
تَسْتَوْفُونَ	تَسْتَوْفِيان	تَسْتَوْفِي	المُخاطَب:	
تَسْتَوْفِينَ	تَسْتَوْفِيان	تَسْتَوْفِينَ	المُخاطَبة:	
نَسْتَوْفِي		أُسْتَوْفِي	المُتَكَلِّم:	

الجَمع	المُثَنَّى	المُفرَد		الأَمْرُ المَعلُوم
لِيَسْتَوْفُوا	لِيَسْتَوْفِيا	لِيَسْتَوْفِ	الغائِب:	
لِيَسْتَوْفِينَ	لِتَسْتَوْفِيا	لِتَسْتَوْفِ	الغائِبة:	
إِستَوْفُوا	إِستَوْفِيا	إِستَوْفِ	المُخاطَب:	
إِستَوْفِينَ	إِستَوْفِيا	إِستَوْفِي	المُخاطَبة:	
لِنَسْتَوْفِ		لِأَسْتَوْفِ	المُتَكَلِّم:	

Table 4.96 - Passive Voice Weak Verb (Lafeef): (أُسْتُوفِيَ، يُسْتَفَى) وفى

الجَمْع	المُثَنَّى	المُفْرَد	الماضِي المَجْهُول
أُسْتُوفُوا	أُسْتُوفِيا	أُسْتُوفِيَ	الغائِب:
أُسْتُوفِينَ	أُسْتُوفِيتا	أُسْتُوفِيتْ	الغائِبَة:
أُسْتُوفِيتُمْ	أُسْتُوفِيتُما	أُسْتُوفِيتَ	المُخاطَب:
أُسْتُوفِيتُنَّ	أُسْتُوفِيتُما	أُسْتُوفِيتِ	المُخاطَبَة:
أُسْتُوفِينا		أُسْتُوفِيتُ	المُتَكَلِّم:

الجَمْع	المُثَنَّى	المُفْرَد	المُضارِع المَجْهُول
يُسْتَوْفَونَ	يُسْتَوْفِيانِ	يُسْتَوْفَى	الغائِب:
يُسْتَوْفَينَ	تُسْتَوْفِيانِ	تُسْتَوْفَى	الغائِبَة:
تُسْتَوْفَونَ	تُسْتَوْفِيانِ	تُسْتَوْفَى	المُخاطَب:
تُسْتَوْفَينَ	تُسْتَوْفِيانِ	تُسْتَوْفَينَ	المُخاطَبَة:
نُسْتَوْفَى		أُسْتَوْفَى	المُتَكَلِّم:

الجَمْع	المُثَنَّى	المُفْرَد	الأَمْر المَجْهُول
لِيُسْتَوْفَوا	لِيُسْتَوْفَيا	لِيُسْتَوْفَ	الغائِب:
لِتُسْتَوْفَينَ	لِتُسْتَوْفَيا	لِتُسْتَوْفَ	الغائِبَة:
لِتُسْتَوْفَوا	لِتُسْتَوْفَيا	لِتُسْتَوْفَ	المُخاطَب:
لِتُسْتَوْفَينَ	لِتُسْتَوْفَيا	لِتُسْتَوْفَيْ	المُخاطَبَة:
لِنُسْتَوْفَ		لِأُسْتَوْفَ	المُتَكَلِّم:

► CONCLUDING NOTES

▷   The Masdar of the *Ajwaf* Kalimah in this *Baab* is similar to the *Baab of If'aal* in that the second Original Letter (i.e. the Weak Letter) is removed after applying the rules of *I'laal* and the Feminine Taa' (ة) is added at the end of the word in place of the dropped letter, for example: إِسْتِقْوَام إِسْتِقَامَة .

▷ The *Mudhaa'af* Kalimah (حي-), when put in this *Baab*, it is permissible to take the vowel on the second Original Letter and put on the letter preceding it and then remove the second Original Letter, for example: إِسْتَحْيَى إِسْتَحَى . It is conjugated in the following manner:

إِسْتَحَى، يَسْتَحِي، إِسْتَحِ، لِيَسْتَحِ، أُسْتُحِي، يُسْتَحَى، لِيُسْتَحَى هُوَ إِسْتِحَاءٌ، مُسْتَحٍ و مُسْتَحَىً

Its normal conjugation is as follows:

إِسْتَحْيَى، يَسْتَحْيِي، إِسْتَحْيِ، لِيَسْتَحْيِ، أُسْتُحْيِي، يُسْتَحْيَى، لِيُسْتَحْيَى

هُوَ إِسْتِحْيَاءٌ و مُسْتَحْيِي و مُسْتَحْيَىً

SECTION TEN

The Baab Of If'eelaal

بابُ إِفْعِيلالٍ

إِفْعَلَّ، يَفْعَلُّ، إِفْعالِلْ، لِيَفْعالِلْ هُوَ إِفْعِيلالٌ و مُفْعَلٌّ

The Additional Letters added in this *Baab* is the Hamzah which is prefixed before the first Original Letter in the Past Tense, the Command Verb and the Masdar. The second letter is the Alif which occurs after the second Original Letter in all of its forms except the Masdar. The particularity of this *Baab* is that most words come in the meaning of colors and defects and all verbs are intransitive. It often will exaggerate the meaning of the *Baab* of If'ilaal (إِفْعِلال) and/or express that meaning in degrees, for example: إِحْمارَّ الحَدِيدُ *The iron gradually became very red.* Without *Idghaam* or contraction of the last Original Letter, the verbs original pattern is: إِفْعالَلَ، يَفْعالِلُ.

In general, the verb in this *Baab* is conjugated as follows:

Table 4.97 - Patterns Of Baab Of If'ilaal Active Voice Verb - Pattern Of: إفْعالَّ يَفْعالُّ

إفْعالَّ، يَفْعالُّ، إفْعالِلْ، لِيَفْعالِلْ هُوَ إفْعِيلالٌ و مُفْعالٌّ

الجَمع	المُثَنَّى	المُفْرَد	الماضي المَعْلوم
إفْعالُّوا	إفْعالّا	إفْعالُّ	الغائب:
إفْعالَلْنَ	إفْعالَّتا	إفْعالَّتْ	الغائبة:
إفْعالَلْتُمْ	إفْعالَلْتُما	إفْعالَلْتَ	المُخاطَب:
إفْعالَلْتُنَّ	إفْعالَلْتُما	إفْعالَلْتِ	المُخاطَبة:
إفْعالَلْنا		إفْعالَلْتُ	المُتَكَلِّم:

الجَمع	المُثَنَّى	المُفْرَد	المُضارِع المَعْلوم
يَفْعالُّونَ	يَفْعالّانِ	يَفْعالُّ	الغائب:
يَفْعالِلْنَ	تَفْعالّانِ	تَفْعالُّ	الغائبة:
تَفْعالُّونَ	تَفْعالّانِ	تَفْعالُّ	المُخاطَب:
تَفْعالِلْنَ	تَفْعالّانِ	تَفْعالِّينَ	المُخاطَبة:
نَفْعالُّ		أَفْعالُّ	المُتَكَلِّم:

الجَمع	المُثَنَّى	المُفْرَد	الأَمْر المَعْلوم
لِيَفْعالُّوا	لِيَفْعالّا	لِيَفْعالِلْ	الغائب:
لِيَفْعالِلْنَ	لِتَفْعالّا	لِتَفْعالِلْ	الغائبة:
إفْعالُّوا	إفْعالّا	إفْعالِلْ	المُخاطَب:
إفْعالِلْنَ	إفْعالّا	إفْعالِّي	المُخاطَبة:
لِنَفْعالِلْ		لأَفْعالِلْ	المُتَكَلِّم:

SAMPLE CONJUGATION OF A WEAK VERB IN THE BAAB OF IF'EELAAL

Table 4.98 - Active Voice Weak Verb (Ajwaf): بيض

إبْيَاضٌ، يَبْيَاضُ، إبْيَاضْ، إبْيَاضْ، لِيَبْيَاضْ هُوَ إبْيِيَاضٌ و مُبْيَاضٌّ

الجَمْع	المُثَنَّى	المُفْرَد	الماضِي المَعْلُوم
إبْيَاضُّوا	إبْيَاضَّا	إبْيَاضَّ	الغَائِب:
إبْيَاضَضْنَ	إبْيَاضَّتا	إبْيَاضَّتْ	الغَائِبَة:
إبْيَاضَضْتُمْ	إبْيَاضَضْتُما	إبْيَاضَضْتَ	المُخاطَب:
إبْيَاضَضْتُنَّ	إبْيَاضَضْتُما	إبْيَاضَضْتِ	المُخاطَبَة:
إبْيَاضَضْنا		إبْيَاضَضْتُ	المُتَكَلِّم:

الجَمْع	المُثَنَّى	المُفْرَد	المُضارِعُ المَعْلُوم
يَبْيَاضُّونَ	يَبْيَاضَّانِ	يَبْيَاضُّ	الغَائِب:
يَبْيَاضِضْنَ	تَبْيَاضَّانِ	تَبْيَاضُّ	الغَائِبَة:
تَبْيَاضُّونَ	تَبْيَاضَّانِ	تَبْيَاضُّ	المُخاطَب:
تَبْيَاضِضْنَ	تَبْيَاضَّانِ	تَبْيَاضِّينَ	المُخاطَبَة:
نَبْيَاضُّ		أَبْيَاضُّ	المُتَكَلِّم:

الجَمْع	المُثَنَّى	المُفْرَد	الأَمْرُ المَعْلُوم
لِيَبْيَاضُّوا	لِيَبْيَاضّا	لِيَبْيَاضِضْ	الغَائِب:
لِيَبْيَاضِضْنَ	لِتَبْيَاضّا	لِتَبْيَاضِضْ	الغَائِبَة:
إبْيَاضُّوا	إبْيَاضّا	إبْيَاضِضْ	المُخاطَب:
إبْيَاضِضْنَ	إبْيَاضّا	إبْيَاضِّي	المُخاطَبَة:
لِنَبْيَاضِضْ		لأَبْيَاضِضْ	المُتَكَلِّم:

SECTION ELEVEN

The Uncommon Abwaab

الأَبْوابُ غَيرُ المَشْهُور

The Uncommon *Abwaab* are fifteen *Abwaab* which are only rarely found in usage in these times. Mostly, their meaning comes in the meaning of emphasis (التَّأْكِيدُ) or exaggeration (المُبالَغَةُ). Here is a list of these *Abwaab* with an example:

Table 4.99 - The Uncommon Abwaab

(١) باب فَوْعَلَة (فَوْعَلَ يُفَوْعِلُ فَوْعَلَة) نحو: (حقل) حَوْقَلَ يُحَوْقِلُ حَوْقَلَةٌ (To become elderly)

(٢) باب فَيْعَلَة (فَيْعَلَ يُفَيْعِلُ فَيْعَلَة) نحو: (شطن) شَيْطَنَ يُشَيْطِنُ شَيْطَنَةٌ (To be evil, devilish)

(٣) باب فَعْنَلَة (فَعْنَلَ يُفَعْنِلُ فَعْنَلَة) نحو: (قلس) قَلْنَسَ يُقَلْنِسُ قَلْنَسَةٌ (To wear a Fez or Kufi)

(٤) باب فَعْوَلَة (فَعْوَلَ يُفَعْوِلُ فَعْوَلَة) نحو: (جهر) جَهْوَرَ يُجَهْوِرُ جَهْوَرَةٌ (To raise the voice)

(٥) باب فَعْلَلَة (فَعْلَلَ يُفَعْلِلُ فَعْلَلَة) نحو: (شمل) شَمْلَلَ يُشَمْلِلُ شَمْلَلَةٌ (To go quickly)

(٦) باب فَعْلاة (فَعْلى يُفَعْلِي فَعْلاة) نحو: (قلس) قَلْسى يُقَلْسِي قَلْسَاةٌ (To wear a Fez or Kufi)

(٧) باب تَمَفْعُل (تَمَفْعَلَ يَتَمَفْعَلُ تَمَفْعُل) نحو: (ركز) تَمَرْكَزَ يَتَمَرْكَزُ تَمَرْكُزٌ

(To become established)

(٨) باب تَفَوْعُل (تَفَوْعَلَ يَتَفَوْعَلُ تَفَوْعُل) نحو: (جرب) تَجَوْرَبَ يَتَجَوْرَبُ تَجَوْرُبٌ

(To wear socks)

---

٩) باب تَفْئِعُل (تَفْئِعَلَ يَتَفْئِعَلُ تَفْئِعُل) نحو: (شطن) تَشَيْطَنَ يَتَشَيْطَنُ تَشَيْطُنٌ (To be evil, bad)

١٠) باب تَفَعْلُل (تَفَعْلَلَ يَتَفَعْلَلُ تَفَعْلُل) نحو: (جلب) تَجَلْبَبَ يَتَجَلْبَبُ تَجَلْبُبٌ (To wear a robe)

١١) باب تَفَعْوُل (تَفَعْوَلَ يَتَفَعْوَلُ تَفَعْوُل) نحو: (رهك) تَرَهْوَكَ يَتَرَهْوَكُ تَرَهْوُك (To walk trembling)

١٢) باب إِفْعِنْلال (إِفْعَنْلَلَ يَفْعَنْلِلُ إِفْعِنْلال) نحو: (قعس) إِقْعَنْسَسَ يَقْعَنْسِسُ إِقْعِنْساسٌ

(To prevent)

١٣) باب إِفْعِنْلاء (إِفْعَنْلى يَفْعَنْلِي إِفْعِنْلاء) نحو: (سلق) إِسْلَنْقى يَسْلَنْقِي إِسْلِنْقاءٌ

(To sleep on the back)

١٤) باب إِفْعِوّال (إِفْعَوَّلَ يَفْعَوَّلُ إِفْعِوّال) نحو: (جلز) إِجْلِوَّزَ يَجْلِوَّزُ إِجْلِوّازٌ

(To fasten, stick together)

١٥) باب إِفْعِيعال (إِفْعَوْعَلَ يَفْعَوْعِلُ إِفْعِيعال) نحو: (حلا) إِحْلَوْلى يَحْلَوْلِي إِحْلِيلاءٌ

(To be sweet)

CHAPTER FIVE

THE FOUR LETTER VERB
الفعل الرباعي

INTRODUCTION

The Four Letter Verb (الفِعْلُ الرُّباعِيُّ) is similar to the Three Letter Verb (الفِعْلُ الثُّلاثِيُّ) in nearly all matters, except that the Four Letter Verbs are far fewer in number. As such, every Four Letter Verb is either a *Primary Verb* (الرُّباعِيُّ المُجَرَّدُ) or a *Derivative Verb* (الرُّباعِيُّ المَزِيدُ فِيهِ). The Primary and Derivative Verbs are either in the Active Voice or the Passive Voice and both the Active Voice and the Passive Voice have three divisions: the Past Tense, the Present Tense and the Command Verb.

With regards to the conjugation of the Four Letter Verb, it is also the same as the Three Letter Verb. The Seeghah of both the Past and Present Tense Verbs are formed according to the same rules as was mentioned for the Three Letter Primary and Derivative Verbs. The Four Letter Primary Verb has only one *Baab* while its Derivative Verb has three *Abwaab*.

SECTION ONE

The Four Letter Primary Verb

الفِعْلُ الرُّباعِيُّ المُجَرَّد

There is only one *Baab* for the Four Letter Primary Verb. The Past Tense Verb is only on the pattern of: فَعْلَلَ and the Present Tense Verb is on the pattern of: يُفَعْلِلُ. The Masdar is on the pattern of: فَعْلَلَةٌ. It may also found on the pattern of فِعْلالٌ, as in:

دَحْرَجَ، يُدَحْرِجُ، دَحْرَجَةٌ، دِحْراجٌ؛   زَلْزَلَ، يُزَلْزِلُ، زَلْزَلَةٌ، زِلْزالٌ

Note that the *Particle of the Present Tense* (حَرْفُ المُضارِع) is voweled with Dhammah. Also, Hamzah is not used used in the formation of the Command Verb due to the fact that the first Original Letter is voweled in the Present Tense.

Four Letter Verbs are comprised exclusively of sound letters in modern Arabic. Four Letter Verbs also include the *Mudhaa'af* or doubled lettered verb. Howerver, these doubled letters are not found side by side. Rather, they are repeated in sequence, as in: زَلْزَلَ، قَهْقَهَ، قَلْقَلَ.

Here is the complete conjugation pattern of the Four Letter Primary Verb:

Table 5.1 - Pattern Of The Active Voice Four Letter Verb On The Pattern Of: فَعْلَلَ يُفَعْلِلُ

فَعْلَلَ، يُفَعْلِلُ، فَعْلِلْ، لِيُفَعْلِلْ، فُعْلِلَ، يُفَعْلَلُ، لِيُفَعْلَلْ هُوَ فَعْلَلَةً (فِعْلالٌ) و مُفَعْلِلٌ و مُفَعْلَلٌ

الجَمع	المُثَنَّى	المُفْرَد	الماضِيُ المَعلُوم
فَعْلَلُوا	فَعْلَلَا	فَعْلَلَ	الغائِب:
فَعْلَلْنَ	فَعْلَلَتَا	فَعْلَلَتْ	الغائِبَة:
فَعْلَلْتُم	فَعْلَلْتُما	فَعْلَلْتَ	المُخاطَب:
فَعْلَلْتُنَّ	فَعْلَلْتُما	فَعْلَلْتِ	المُخاطَبَة:
فَعْلَلْنا		فَعْلَلْتُ	المُتَكَلِّم:

الجَمع	المُثَنَّى	المُفْرَد	المُضارِعُ المَعلُوم
يُفَعْلِلُونَ	يُفَعْلِلانِ	يُفَعْلِلُ	الغائِب:
يُفَعْلِلْنَ	تُفَعْلِلانِ	تُفَعْلِلُ	الغائِبَة:
تُفَعْلِلُونَ	تُفَعْلِلانِ	تُفَعْلِلُ	المُخاطَب:
تُفَعْلِلْنَ	تُفَعْلِلانِ	تُفَعْلِلِينَ	المُخاطَبَة:
نُفَعْلِلُ		أُفَعْلِلُ	المُتَكَلِّم:

الجَمع	المُثَنَّى	المُفْرَد	الأَمْرُ المَعلُوم
لِيُفَعْلِلُوا	لِيُفَعْلِلا	لِيُفَعْلِلْ	الغائِب:
لِيُفَعْلِلْنَ	لِتُفَعْلِلا	لِتُفَعْلِلْ	الغائِبَة:
فَعْلِلُوا	فَعْلِلا	فَعْلِلْ	المُخاطَب:
فَعْلِلْنَ	فَعْلِلا	فَعْلِلي	المُخاطَبَة:
لِنُفَعْلِلْ		لأُفَعْلِلْ	المُتَكَلِّم:

Table 5.2 - Pattern Of The Passive Voice Four Letter Verb On The Pattern Of: فُعْلِلَ يُفَعْلَلُ

الجَمع	المُثَنَّى	المُفرَد	الماضِيُ المَجهُول
فُعْلِلُوا	فُعْلِلا	فُعْلِلَ	الغائِب:
فُعْلِلْنَ	فُعْلِلَتا	فُعْلِلَتْ	الغائِبَة:
فُعْلِلْتُم	فُعْلِلْتُما	فُعْلِلْتَ	المُخاطَب:
فُعْلِلْتُنَّ	فُعْلِلْتُما	فُعْلِلْتِ	المُخاطَبَة:
فُعْلِلْنا		فُعْلِلْتُ	المُتَكَلّم:

الجَمع	المُثَنَّى	المُفرَد	المُضارِعُ المَجهُول
يُفَعْلَلُونَ	يُفَعْلَلانِ	يُفَعْلَلُ	الغائِب:
يُفَعْلَلْنَ	تُفَعْلَلانِ	تُفَعْلَلُ	الغائِبَة:
تُفَعْلَلُونَ	تُفَعْلَلانِ	تُفَعْلَلُ	المُخاطَب:
تُفَعْلَلْنَ	تُفَعْلَلانِ	تُفَعْلَلِينَ	المُخاطَبَة:
نُفَعْلَلُ		أُفَعْلَلُ	المُتَكَلّم:

الجَمع	المُثَنَّى	المُفرَد	الأَمْرُ المَجهُول
لِيُفَعْلَلُوا	لِيُفَعْلَلا	لِيُفَعْلَلْ	الغائِب:
لِيُفَعْلَلْنَ	لِتُفَعْلَلا	لِتُفَعْلَلْ	الغائِبَة:
لِتُفَعْلَلُوا	لِتُفَعْلَلا	لِتُفَعْلَلْ	المُخاطَب:
لِتُفَعْلَلْنَ	لِتُفَعْلَلا	لِتُفَعْلَلِي	المُخاطَبَة:
لِنُفَعْلَلْ		لأُفَعْلَلْ	المُتَكَلّم:

SAMPLE CONJUGATION OF FOUR LETTER PRIMARY VERB

Table 5.3 - Active Voice Sound Verb ترجم

تَرْجَمَ، يُتَرْجِمُ، تَرْجِمْ، لِيُتَرْجِمْ، تُرْجِمَ، يُتَرْجَمُ، تَرْجِمْ، لِيُتَرْجَمْ هُوَ تَرْجَمَةً و مُتَرْجِمٌ و مُتَرْجَمٌ

الماضِيُ المَعْلُوم		المُفْرَد	المُثَنَّى	الجَمْع
الغائِب:		تَرْجَمَ	تَرْجَما	تَرْجَمُوا
الغائِبَة:		تَرْجَمَتْ	تَرْجَمَتا	تَرْجَمْنَ
المُخاطَب:		تَرْجَمْتَ	تَرْجَمْتُما	تَرْجَمْتُم
المُخاطَبَة:		تَرْجَمْتِ	تَرْجَمْتُما	تَرْجَمْتُنَّ
المُتَكَلِّم:		تَرْجَمْتُ		تَرْجَمْنا

المُضارِعُ المَعْلُوم		المُفْرَد	المُثَنَّى	الجَمْع
الغائِب:		يُتَرْجِمُ	يُتَرْجِمانِ	يُتَرْجِمُونَ
الغائِبَة:		تُتَرْجِمُ	تُتَرْجِمانِ	يُتَرْجِمْنَ
المُخاطَب:		تُتَرْجِمُ	تُتَرْجِمانِ	تُتَرْجِمُونَ
المُخاطَبَة:		تُتَرْجِمُ	تُتَرْجِمانِ	تُتَرْجِمْنَ
المُتَكَلِّم:		أُتَرْجِمُ		نُتَرْجِمُ

الأَمْرُ المَعْلُوم		المُفْرَد	المُثَنَّى	الجَمْع
الغائِب:		لِيُتَرْجِمْ	لِيُتَرْجِما	لِيُتَرْجِمُوا
الغائِبَة:		لِتُتَرْجِمْ	لِتُتَرْجِما	لِيُتَرْجِمْنَ
المُخاطَب:		تَرْجِمْ	تَرْجِما	تَرْجِمُوا
المُخاطَبَة:		تَرْجِمي	تَرْجِما	تَرْجِمْنَ
المُتَكَلِّم:		لأُتَرْجِمْ		لِنُتَرْجِمْ

ترجم (تُرجِمَ ، يُتَرْجَمُ) Table 5.4 - Passive Voice Sound Verb

الجَمْع	المُثَنَّى	المُفْرَد	الماضي المَجْهُول
تُرجِمُوا	تُرجِما	تُرجِمَ	الغائِب:
تُرجِمْنَ	تُرجِمَتا	تُرجِمَتْ	الغائِبَة:
تُرجِمْتُم	تُرجِمْتُما	تُرجِمْتَ	المُخاطَب:
تُرجِمْتُنَّ	تُرجِمْتُما	تُرجِمْتِ	المُخاطَبَة:
تُرجِمْنا		تُرجِمْتُ	المُتَكَلِّم:

الجَمْع	المُثَنَّى	المُفْرَد	المُضارِعُ المَجْهُول
يُتَرْجَمُونَ	يُتَرْجَمانِ	يُتَرْجَمُ	الغائِب:
يُتَرْجَمْنَ	تُتَرْجَمانِ	تُتَرْجَمُ	الغائِبَة:
تُتَرْجَمُونَ	تُتَرْجَمانِ	تُتَرْجَمُ	المُخاطَب:
تُتَرْجَمْنَ	تُتَرْجَمانِ	تُتَرْجَمِينَ	المُخاطَبَة:
نُتَرْجَمُ		أُتَرْجَمُ	المُتَكَلِّم:

الجَمْع	المُثَنَّى	المُفْرَد	الأَمْرُ المَجْهُول
لِيُتَرْجَمُوا	لِيُتَرْجَما	لِيُتَرْجَمْ	الغائِب:
لِيُتَرْجَمْنَ	لِتُتَرْجَما	لِتُتَرْجَمْ	الغائِبَة:
لِتُتَرْجَمُوا	لِتُتَرْجَما	لِتُتَرْجَمْ	المُخاطَب:
لِتُتَرْجَمْنَ	لِتُتَرْجَما	لِتُتَرْجَمِي	المُخاطَبَة:
لِنُتَرْجَمْ		لأُتَرْجَمْ	المُتَكَلِّم:

SECTION TWO

The Four Letter Derivative Verb

الفِعْلُ الرُّباعِيُّ المَزيدُ فيهِ

Like the three letter Derivative Verb, the four letter Derivative Verb is formed by adding Additional Letters to the letters found in the Primary Verb.

The three Abwaab of the Four Letter Derivative Verb are as follows:

▶ THE BAAB OF TAFA'LUL بابُ تَفَعْلُلٍ

تَفَعْلَلَ، يَتَفَعْلَلُ، تَفَعْلَلْ، لِيَتَفَعْلَلْ، تَفَعْلَلَ بِهِ، يَتَفَعْلَلُ بِهِ، لِيَتَفَعْلَلْ بِهِ هُوَ تَفَعْلُلٌ و مُتَفَعْلِلٌ و مُتَفَعْلَلٌ بِهِ

This verb resembles the Three Letter Derivative Verb: *Tafa'ul* (تَفَعُّلٌ). Its Additional Letter is the letter Taa' (ت) which is prefixed before the first Original Letter and appears in all derivatives forms. The rules which are applied to that *Baab* with respect to the assimilation of the letter Taa' will also apply to this *Baab*. This *Baab* is reflexive in its meaning in relation to the Primary Verb. The Primary verb (دَحْرَجَ), for example, means to roll something while the Derivative Verb (تَدَحْرَجَ) means to be rolled, as in: دَحْرَجَ بَكْرٌ الكُرَةَ *Bakr rolled the ball*; تَدَحْرَجَ الكُرَةُ *The ball rolled*.

▶ THE BAAB OF IF'INLAAL باب إِفْعِنْلالٍ

إِفْعَنْلَلَ، يَفْعَنْلِلُ، إِفْعَنْلِلْ، لِيَفْعَنْلِلْ، أُفْعَنْلِلُ بِهِ، يُفْعَنْلَلُ بِهِ، لِيُفْعَنْلَلْ بِهِ هُوَ إِفْعِنْلالٌ و مُفْعَنْلِلٌ و مُفْعَنْلَلٌ بِهِ

There are two Additional Letters in this *Baab*, Hamzah, which appears in the Past Tense forms, the Command Verb and the Masdar. Also, the letter Noon (ن) is found following the first Original Letter and it exists in all of its forms.

The meaning of this *Baab* is also reflexive of the Primary Verb, as in: حَرْجَمَ *To gather;* تَحَرْجَمَ *To be gathered.*

▶ THE BAAB OF IF'ILLAAL باب إِفْعِلالٍّ

إِفْعَلَّلَ، يَفْعَلِّلُ، إِفْعَلِّلْ، لِيَفْعَلِّلْ، أُفْعَلِّلُ بِهِ، يُفْعَلَّلُ بِهِ، لِيُفْعَلَّلْ بِهِ هُوَ إِفْعِلالٌّ و مُفْعَلِّلٌ و مُفْعَلَّلٌ بِهِ

The meaning which is associated with this Baab is emphasis (التَّأْكِيدُ) and exaggeration (المُبالَغَةُ).

CHAPTER SIX

The States Of The Verb

أحوال الفعل

For the sake of our examination of the verb's states, we will divide our discussion into the following three sections:

- The time-related states of the verb. Wherein the verb's meaning may be understood within the context of time, like past tense and present tense.

- The grammatical states of the verb. Some verbs are effected by certain particles which alter the grammatical state or *I'raab* of the verb.

- The interrogative and emphatic states of the verb. The effect, in meaning of interrogative particles and emphatic states of verbs.

SECTION ONE

Time Related States Of The Verb

أَحوالُ الفِعْلِ الزَّمانيُ

▶ THE STATES OF THE PAST TENSE VERB أَحوالُ الفِعْلِ الماضيٍ

When considering the Past Tense Verbs from the point of view of their meaning, they will be one of the following four states:

▷ **THE PAST PERFECT** (الماضيٍ المُطْلَقُ)

This is the simple past tense, for example: ذَهَبَ زَيدٌ *Zaid left*. The Past Perfect is negated in two ways:

› With the *Particles of Negation* (الحَرْفُ النَّفْي) that are found preceding the Past Perfect Verb thereby making it negative, they are two: (ما) and (لا), which are known as: (ما و لا النَّفْي), for example: ما ذَهَبَ زَيدٌ or لا ذَهَبَ زَيدٌ *Zaid did not leave*.

› By preceding the Verb with the *Particle of Negation* (لَمْ). The parculiarity of this Particle, however, is that the form of the Past Tense is substituted with the same Seeghah of the Present Tense Verb and the the Present Tense is transformed into the state of Jazm (these states of the verb will be discussed shortly). For example: ذَهَبَ زَيدٌ *Zaid left*; لَمْ يَذْهَبْ زَيدٌ *Zaid did not leave*.

▷ **THE PAST IMPERFECT** (الماضِيُ التَّقْلِيُّ)

The Past Imperfect indicates that an action occured in the past in such a manner that its effect remains until the present time. The Past Imperfect is formed by combining Past Perfect with the Particle (قَدْ), as in:

﴿يَـأَيُّها النَّاسُ قَدْ جَآءَكُمُ الحَقُّ مِنْ رَبِّكُمْ﴾

"O people! Indeed there has come to you the truth from your Lord"

[Yunus 10:108]

Here it is understood that the coming of truth from Allah Ta'ala is not an event limited to a specific time in the past. Rather, it is an on going process upto this present time and continuous in the future as well.

The negation of the Past Imperfect is made with the Particle (لَمَّا). It too uses the form of the Present Tense and transforms the verb to the state of Jazm, for example:

﴿... قُلْ لَمْ تُؤْمِنُوا وَ لِـكِنْ قُولُوا أَسْلَمْنا وَ لَمَّا يَدْخُلِ الإِيمانُ فِي قُلُوبِكُمْ...﴾

"...Say: You do not believe but say: We submit; and faith has not yet entered into your hearts..." [Al-Hujaraat 49:14].

The negation of the Past Imperfect negates the action from the past until the present in the same manner that the effect of the action exists from the past to the present. Note that when the Particle (لَمَّا) is used preceding a Past Tense Verb, its meaning is *'when'* as in:

﴿وَ لَمَّا جَآءَهُمْ كِتابٌ مِنْ عِنْدِ اللَّهِ مُصَدِّقٌ لِما مَعَهُمْ﴾

"And when there came to them a book from Allah verifying that which they have..." [al-Baqarah 2:89]

▷ **THE REMOTE PAST** (الماضِيُ البَعِيدُ)

The Remote Past indicates that an action has been realized, however, its effect does not remain. This Past Tense Verb is combined with the verb (كانَ), as in:

﴿تَجْرِي بِأَعْيُنِنا ۚ جَزَاءً لِمَنْ كانَ كُفِرَ﴾

"Sailing, before Our eyes, a reward for him who was denied." [al-Qamar 54:14]

Sometimes, either before or after the verb (كانَ), the Particle (قَدْ) is also used, as in:

إِبْرَاهِيمُ قَدْ كانَ دَفَنَ فِي الفِلِسْطِينَ   *Ibrahim (AS) was buried in Palestine*

At times, a noun may be found separating the verb (كانَ) and the Past Tense Verb, as in:

كانَ إِبْرَاهِيمُ دَفَنَ فِي الفِلِسْطِينَ

▷ **THE PAST CONTINUOUS** (الماضِيُ الإِسْتِمْرارِي)

It indicates the occurrence of a continuous action whose origin begins in the past. This verb is formed by combing the Present Tense Verb with the verb (كانَ). For example:

﴿فَمَنْ كانَ يَرْجُوا لِقَاءَ رَبِّهِ فَلْيَعْمَلْ عَمَلاً صالِحاً﴾

"...Therefore, whomever hopes to meet his Lord, he should do good deeds..."
[al-Kahf 18:110]

Sometimes, one or more words will separate the verb (كانَ) and the Present Tense Verb, as in:

﴿كانُوا قَلِيلاً مِنَ اللَّيلِ ما يَهْجَعُونَ﴾

"They were sleeping but a little in the night" [az-Zariaat 51:17]

The Past Continuous is negated by preceding the Particle of Negation (ما) before the verb (كانَ), as in: ما كانَ زَيدٌ يَذْهَبُ *Zaid was not leaving*; زَيدٌ وَ بَكْرٌ ما كانا يَذْهَبانِ *Zaid and Bakr were not leaving*. Or by preceding the Particle of Negation (لا) before the Present tense verb, as in:

﴿كانُوا لا يَتَناهَوْنَ عَنْ مُنْكَرٍ فَعَلُوهُ﴾

"They used not to forbid each other the hateful things (which) they did..."
[Al-Ma'idah 5:79].

The Past Tense Verb which is negated is termed (الماضِيُ المَنْفِيُ).

SECTION TWO

THE STATES OF THE PRESENT TENSE VERB

أَحْوالُ الفِعْلِ المُضارِع

The Present Tense Verb (المُضارِع), without modification, has the following five states and particularities:

- The Present Tense Verb can be used to indicated the Present Tense (الحالُ) or the Future Tense (المُسْتَقْبَلُ).

- It can indicate the positive (المُثْبَتُ), meaning that it indicates upon the occurrence of an action, as opposed to negating the occurrence of an action.

- It is in the state of Raf' (الرَّفْعُ) or that the verb is Marfoo' (المَرْفُوعُ).

- The meaning of the verb can be attributive (الخَبَري) wherein the attribute (الخَبَرُ) is given in order that a certain meaning is realized, as in: طالَ الزَّمانُ *Time was lengthened.*

- The meaning of the Verb is generally simple without emphasis (بِدُونِ التَّأْكِيدِ).

These meanings are associated with the Present Tense Verb that is unaffected by any Particle or *Harf*. At times, however, a Particle will precede the Present Tense Verb that will change its meaning and remove some of the particularities mentioned above. These Particles affect the meanings that correspond to the above mentioned states and particularities:

1) The Particles Of Designation (أَحرُفُ التَّعيينِ)

2) The Particle of Negation (أَحرُفُ النَّفي)

3) The Particles of Jazm and Nasb (حرُوفُ الجَزْمِ وَ النَصْبِ)

4) The Interrogative Particles (أَحرُفُ الإِستِفْهامِ) and

5) The Particles of Emphasis (أَحرُفُ التَّأْكيدِ)

These Particles transform the Present Tense Verb into particular states thereby signifying particular meanings.

The Present Tense Verb will become associated exclusively with the Present or Future Tense (الحالُ وَ المُستَقْبلُ) with the Particles of Designation. When combined with the Particle of Negation, the Present Tense Verb becomes negative (المُضارعُ المَنْفي).

With the Particle of Jazm, the Verb becomes Majzoom (المُضارعُ المَجزُومُ) or in the state of Jazm. With the Particle of Nasb, the Verb becomes Mansoob (المُضارعُ المَنْصُوبُ) or in the state of Nasb. With the Interrogative Particle, the meaning of the Verb becomes interogative (المُضارعُ الإِستِفْهامي), as opposed to attributive. With a Particle of Emphasis attached, the Verb becomes emphatic (المُضارعُ المَؤَّكَدُ). Each of these will be explained in its own review:

▷ **THE PRESENT AND FUTURE TENSE VERB** (الحالُ وَ المُستَقْبَلُ)

Whenever the Particle *Lam* (لامُ التَّأْكِيدِ) voweled with Fathah (لَ) is prefixed to the Present Tense Verb, its meaning is generally restricted to the Present Tense (الحالُ), for example: ﴿إِنَّكُمْ لَتَقُولُونَ قَوْلاً عَظِيماً﴾ "Surely you utter a grieveous saying." [al-Israa' 17:40].

If the Particle *Seen* voweled with Fathah (سَ) or the Particle *Sawfa* (سَوفَ) precede a Present Tense Verb, the Verb becomes particular to the Future Tense (المُستَقْبَلُ), for example:

﴿وَ قُلِ الحَمْدُ لِلَّهِ سَيُرِيكُمْ آيتِهِ فَتَعْرِفُونَها﴾

"And say: Praise be to Allah, He will show you his signs so that you shall recognized them." [an-Naml 27:93]

The Particle *Seen* (سَ) indicates the near future while the Particle *Sawfa* signifies the distant future, as in:

﴿سَوفَ يُؤْتِ اللَّهُ المُؤْمِنِينَ أَجْراً عَظِيماً﴾

"And Allah will grant the believers a mighty reward." [an-Nisaa' 4:146]

From this perspective, these Particles are called *Ahruf at-Ta'yeen* because they designate the Present Tense or Future Tense. They are also called *Ahruf at-Tanfees* (أَحْرُفُ التَّنْفِيسِ). *Tanfees* is in the meaning of vast, spacious. The Particle *Lam* with Fathah (لَ) has another division which will come shortly.

▷ **THE PRESENT TENSE NEGATED VERB** (المُضَارِعُ المَنْفِي)

The *Particles of Negation* are (ما) and (لا). They precede the Present Tense Verb and negate its meaning, as:

﴿وَ مَا يُضِلُّ بِهِ إِلَّا الْفَاسِقِينَ﴾

"...He (Allah) does not cause to err by it (any) except the transgressors."
[al-Baqarah 2:26]

﴿وَ لَكِنَّ أَكْثَرَ النَّاسِ لَا يَشْكُرُونَ﴾

"...But most people are not grateful." [al-Baqarah 2:243]

These two *Particles of Negation* are not specific to the Present Tense Verb as they are also used to negate the Past Tense Verb.

▷ **PRESENT TENSE VERB IN THE STATE OF JAZM**(المُضَارِعُ المَجْزُومُ)

The Particles which give the state of Jazm to the Present Tense Verb are:

لَمْ، لَمَّا، لَامُ الأَمْرِ، لَاءُ النَّهِي، الأَدَاتُ الشَّرْطِيَّة

The Particles of Jazm precede the Present Tense Verb making it Majzoom or in the state of Jazm. When the Present Tense Verb becomes Majzoom, the signs of Raf' that are normally exhibited in the verb must be omitted. In five Seeghah (1,4,7,13,14), Dhammah on the third Original Letter is omitted as the sign of Raf'. In Seeghah (2,5,8,11), of the Dual and Seeghah (3,9) of the Masculine Plural and Seeghah (10), the 2nd Person Feminine Singular, the *Noon of I'raab* (النُّونُ الإِعْرَابِي) is omitted as a sign of Raf'. In the *Naaqis* Verb in Seeghah (1,4,7,13,14) the third Original Letter itself (لَامُ الكَلِمَة) is removed. In the *Ajwaf* Verb, in seven Seeghah (1,4,6,7,12,13,14), the second Original Letter is removed (due to the meeting of two voweless letters). *Mudhaa'af* in the state of Jazm is the same as the Command Verb. Examine the following verbs in the state of Jazm:

Table 6.1 - Sound Verb In The State Of Jazm: ضرب

الجَمْع	المُثَنَّى	المُفْرَد	المُضارِعُ المَجْزُوم
لَمْ يَضْرِبُوا	لَمْ يَضْرِبا	لَمْ يَضْرِبْ	الغائِب:
لَمْ يَضْرِبْنَ	لَمْ تَضْرِبا	لَمْ تَضْرِبْ	الغائِبَة:
لَمْ تَضْرِبُوا	لَمْ تَضْرِبا	لَمْ تَضْرِبْ	المُخاطَب:
لَمْ تَضْرِبْنَ	لَمْ تَضْرِبا	لَمْ تَضْرِبِي	المُخاطَبَة:
لَمْ نَضْرِبْ		لَمْ أَضْرِبْ	المُتَكَلِّم:

Table 6.2 - Ajwaf Verb In The State Of Jazm: قول

الجَمْع	المُثَنَّى	المُفْرَد	المُضارِعُ المَجْزُوم
لَمْ يَقُولُوا	لَمْ يَقُولا	لَمْ يَقُلْ	الغائِب:
لَمْ يَقُلْنَ	لَمْ تَقُولا	لَمْ تَقُلْ	الغائِبَة:
لَمْ تَقُولُوا	لَمْ تَقُولا	لَمْ تَقُلْ	المُخاطَب:
لَمْ تَقُلْنَ	لَمْ تَقُولا	لَمْ تَقُولي	المُخاطَبَة:
لَمْ نَقُلْ		لَمْ أَقُلْ	المُتَكَلِّم:

Table 6.3 - Naaqis Verb In The State Of Jazm: دعو

الجَمْع	المُثَنَّى	المُفْرَد	المُضارِعُ لِمَجْزُوم
لَمْ يَدْعُوا	لَمْ يَدْعُوا	لَمْ يَدْعُ	الغائِب:
لَمْ يَدْعُونَ	لَمْ تَدْعُوا	لَمْ تَدْعُ	الغائِبة:
لَمْ تَدْعُوا	لَمْ تَدْعُوا	لَمْ تَدْعُ	المُخاطَب:
لَمْ تَدْعُونَ	لَمْ تَدْعُوا	لَمْ تَدْعِي	المُخاطَبة:
لَمْ نَدْعُ		لَمْ أَدْعُ	المُتَكَلِّم:

The remaining Particles of Jazm have the same effect upon the verb as illustrated above. The Passive Voice Verb is the same as the Active Voice Verb. In addition to the Particle's affect on the *I'raab* of the Present Tense Verb, they also change the meaning of the Present Tense Verb. The signification of each Particle is as follows:

The Particles (لَمْ) and (لَمَّا) actually negate the Past Tense Verb, however, they use the form of the Present Tense Verb to do so. The first is simple negation of the past while the latter is negation of the past up to the present. For example:

﴿أَ لَمْ تَعْلَمْ أَنَّ اللَّهَ على كُلِّ شَيءٍ قَدِيرٌ﴾

"Do you not know that Allah has power over all things?" [al-Baqarah 2:106]

$$﴿أَمْ حَسِبْتُمْ أَنْ تَدْخُلُوا الْجَنَّةَ وَ لَمَّا يَعْلَمِ اللَّهُ الَّذِينَ جَاهَدُوا مِنْكُمْ وَ يَعْلَمَ الصَّابِرِينَ﴾$$

"*Do you think that you will enter the garden while Allah has not yet known those who strive hard from among you, and (He has not yet) known the patient?*"

[Aali 'Imran 3:142]

These two Particles are also known as: (لَمْ وَ لَمَّا الْجَحَدِ), the Particles of *Jahd*.

The Particle (لَامُ الأَمْرِ) or the *Lam* of the Command Verb changes the meaning of the Present Tense Verb from attributive (خَبَرِي) to dictative (إِنْشَائِي) in which the meaning is to seek to complete an action, as in:

$$﴿فَلْيَعْبُدُوا رَبَّ هذا الْبَيْتِ﴾$$

"*So let them serve the Lord of this House.*" [al-Quraysh 106:3]

The Present Tense Verb which is attached to the *Lam* of the Command Verb is called *Fi'l Al-Amr* (الْفِعْلُ الأَمْرِ). As mentioned in the concluding notes of Chapter One, Section Two, it is permissible for the *Lam* of the Command Verb to be *Saakin* when preceded by either (و) or (ف), otherwise, it is vowelled with Kasrah.

The Particle (لَاءُ النَّهْيِ) or the *Particle of Prohibition* also transforms the meaning of the verb from attributive to dictative, however, in the meaning of seeking that an action not be performed, like:

$$﴿وَ لَا تَتَّبِعُوا أَهْوَاءَ قَوْمٍ قَدْ ضَلُّوا مِنْ قَبْلُ وَ أَضَلُّوا كَثِيراً﴾$$

"*And do not follow the low desires of people who went astray before and led many astray..*" [al-Maa'idah 5:77]

The verb utilizing the *Particle of Prohibition* is called *Fi'l An-Nahy* (الفِعلُ النَّهِي).
Only the fact that it produces the state of Jazm in the Present Tense Verb
distinguishes the *Particle of Prohibition* from the *Particle of Negation* (لاءُ النَّفِي).

The *Conditional Particles* (أَداتُ الشَّرطِيَةِ) are of two kind, some of which give the
verb the meaning of the future and others which give the meaning of the past.
The first type are Particles like (إِنْ) and the second type are Particles like (لَوْ). For
example:

﴿قُلْ إِنْ تُخْفُوا ما في صُدُورِكُمْ أَوْ تُبْدُوهُ يَعْلَمْهُ اللَّهُ﴾

"Say: Whether you hide what is in your hearts or manifest it, Allah knows it..."

[Aali 'Imraan 3:29]

﴿لَوْ يُؤَاخِذُهُمْ بِما كَسَبُوا لَعَجَّلَ لَهُمُ العَذابَ﴾

*"...Were He to punish them for what they earn, He would certainly have hastened
the chastisement for them..."* [al-Kahf 18:58]

Most of the *Conditional Particles* are associated with the Present Tense Verb,
although a few are also associated with the Past Tense Verb. The Particles which
govern the verb in the state of Jazm are collectively known **'Awaamil Al-Jazm**
(الجَوازِمُ) or simply, the **Jawaazim** (عوامِلُ الجَزْمِ).

▷ THE PRESENT TENSE MANSOOB VERB (المُضارِعُ المَنْصُوبُ)

The *Particles of Nasb* (أَحْرُفُ النَّصْبِ) are: أَنْ، لَنْ، كَيْ، إِذَنْ. Whenever one of these Particles are entered upon the Present Tense Verb, the verb will change from the state of Raf' to the state of Nasb. The change in the state of the verb will be reflected in the I'raab of the Present Tense Verb.

As previously mentioned, when the Present Tense Verb changes from the state of Raf' to another state, the signs of *I'raab* for Raf' must be removed. The signs of the state of Raf' are Dhammah and the *Noon of I'raab* (النُّونُ الإِعْرابِي). When one of these *Particles of Nasb* governs the Present Tense Verb, its government (عامِلٌ) upon the verb is indicated by a change in the signs of *I'raab*. The signs of Raf' are removed and replaced by the signs of Nasb.

As a result, in the Seeghah (1,4,7,13,14), the third Original Letter becomes Maftooh (changed from Dhammah to Fathah). In the Duals (Seeghah 2,5,8,11); Masculine Plurals (Seeghah 3,9) and the 2nd Person Feminine Singular (Seeghah 10), the *Noon of I'raab* (the sign of Raf') is omitted from the verb.

Therefore, the signs of Nasb are either Fathah (الفَتْحَةُ) or the removal of the *Noon Of I'raab* (حَذْفُ النُّونِ الإِعْرابِي). Observe the Sound and Weak Mansoob verb in the following charts:

Table 6.4 - The Sound Mansoob Verb: ضرب

المُضارِعُ المَنْصُوب	المُفْرَد	المُثَنَّى	الجَمْع
الغائِب:	أَنْ يَضْرِبَ	أَنْ يَضْربا	أَنْ يَضْرِبُوا
الغائِبَة:	أَنْ تَضْرِبَ	أَنْ تَضْربا	أَنْ يَضْرِبْنَ
المُخاطَب:	أَنْ تَضْرِبَ	أَنْ تَضْربا	أَنْ تَضْرِبُوا
المُخاطَبَة:	أَنْ تَضْرِبي	أَنْ تَضْربا	أَنْ تَضْرِبْنَ
المُتَكَلِّم:	أَنْ أَضْرِبَ		أَنْ نَضْرِبَ

In the Weak Verbs, the Mansoob Verb is similar to the Sound Verb. However, in the *Naaqis* Verb, which is usually *Saakin* at its end, will display Fathah as a sign of Nasb in only two situations. The first being in the *Naaqis* Verb with Waaw. The second being the *Naaqis* Verb with Yaa' (not Alif Maqsoorah). As mentioned previously, when the vowel preceding the Weak Letter is Kasrah, the Weak Letter will be Yaa' and when the vowel is Fathah, the Weak Letter will be Alif Maqsoorah. Therefore, it is possible to display Fathah as a sign of Nasb only in the *Naaqis* with Yaa'. Otherwise, the Alif Maqsoorah will have the signs of Nasb estimated as the Alif is always *Saakin*. Observe the following chart:

Table 6.5 - The Naaqis With Yaa' Mansoob Verb: رمي

المُضارِعُ المَنْصُوب	المُفْرَد	المُثَنَّى	الجَمْع
الغائِب:	أَنْ يَرْمِيَ	أَنْ يَرْمِيا	أَنْ يَرْمُوا
الغائِبَة:	أَنْ تَرْمِيَ	أَنْ تَرْمِيا	أَنْ يَرْمِينَ
المُخاطَب:	أَنْ تَرْمِيَ	أَنْ تَرْمِيا	أَنْ تَرْمُوا
المُخاطَبَة:	أَنْ تَرْمِي	أَنْ تَرْمِيا	أَنْ تَرْمِينَ
المُتَكَلِّم:	أَنْ أَرْمِيَ		أَنْ نَرْمِيَ

All of the *Particles of Nasb* will affect the Present Tense Verb in this same manner, whether the verb be in the Active Voice or the Passive Voice. The *Particles of Nasb* are used exclusively with Present Tense verb.

The *Particles of Nasb* also have their effect upon the meaning of the Present Tense Verb. The Particle (أَنْ) can give the Present Tense Verb the meaning of the Masdar or an infinitive meaning. This *Particle of Nasb* when combined with the Present Tense Verb is equivalent to the Verb's Masdar, as in: يَسُرُّنِي أَنْ يَصْدُقَ *It pleases me that he is truthful*; يَسُرُّنِي صِدْقُهُ *His truthfulness pleases me* (while both can be interpreted in the second meaning). See the following verse:

﴿أَرَدْتُ أَنْ أَعِيبَها﴾

"*I wished that I should damage it...*" [Al-Kahf 18:79]

Meaning: أَرَدْتُ عَيبَها *I wished its damage*.

The Particle (لَنْ) is a particle of emphatic negation that makes the Present Tense particular to the Future Tense, as in:

﴿فَإِنْ لَمْ تَفْعَلُوا وَ لَنْ تَفْعَلُوا...﴾ "*If you do it not and never shall you do it...*"

(Al-Baqarah 2:24)

The Particle (كَيْ) establishes the cause in the Present Tense Verb for that action which precedes it in the sentence, as in the verse:

﴿فَرَدَدْنَاهُ إِلَى أُمِّهِ كَيْ تَقَرَّ عَيْنَها﴾

"*So We gave him back to his mother that her eye might be refreshed...*"

(Al-Qasas 28:13)

Meaning that the Present Tense (تَقَرَّ) verb gives the reason why the Prophet Musa (AS) was returned to his mother (i.e., to refresh her eyes or please her).

The Particle (إِذَنْ) establishes the Present Tense Verb as a reply to a statement or a conclusion, for example:

﴿إِنَّكُمْ إِذاً مِثْلُهُمْ﴾

"Surely, then, you would be like them." [an-Nisaa' 4:140]

SECTION THREE

THE INTERROGATIVE AND EMPHATIC VERB

الفِعْلُ الإِسْتِفْهامِيُّ و المُؤَكَّدُ

▶ **THE INTERROVATIVE VERB** الفِعْلُ الإِسْتِفْهامِيُّ

The *Particles of Interrogation* are (الهَمْزَةُ) and (هَلْ). Whenever one of these particles are found preceding the Present Tense Verb, its meaning is changed from attributive (خَبَرِي) to dictative (إِنْشَائِي) in this case, asking a question. With the particle (هَلْ), in addition to the meaning just mentioned, it also has the effect of making the verb particular to the Future Tense.

The *Particles of Interrogation* have no literal effect upon verbs, meaning that the verb does not change from the state of Raf', as in: ﴿هَلْ يُهْلَكُ إِلَّا القَوْمُ الظَّالِمِينَ﴾ "...*Will anyone be destroyed except the unjust people?*" [al-An'am 6:47]. Allah Ta'ala asks the question:

﴿أَ تَأْمُرُونَ النَّاسَ بِالبِرِّ و تَنْسَوْنَ أَنْفُسَكُمْ﴾

"*Do you enjoin men to be good and neglect your own souls?...*"

[Al-Baqarah 2:44]

One difference between the two Particles in regards to their usage is that the Particle (هَلْ) is commonly used for that question whose reply will either be yes or no.

Among the *Particles of Emphasis* (أَحرُفُ التَّأْكِيدِ) is the letter Noon that is suffixed to the Present Tense Verb. The *Emphatic Noon* (النُّونُ التَّأْكِيدُ), as it is called, is of two types: the first is the *Heavy Noon of Emphasis* (النُّونُ التَّأْكِيدُ الثَّقِيلَةُ), in which the Noon is *Mushaddad* or doubled, and the second is called the *Light Noon of Emphasis* (النُّونُ التَّأْكِيدُ الخَفِيفَةُ), in which the Noon is *Saakin*.

The *Emphatic Noon* is suffixed to the end of the Present Tense Active and Passive Voice Verbs making them emphatic and exclusive for the Future Tense. Emphasis with the *Heavy Noon* is found more often than the *Light Noon*.

The *Heavy Noon* (النُّونُ الثَّقِيلَةُ) can be found attached to all Seeghah in the Present Tense, however, the *Light Noon* (النُّونُ الخَفِيفَةُ) cannot be attached to the Seeghah of the Duals and Feminine Plurals. Due to this, it is only formed in eight Seeghah (1,3,4,7,9,10,13,14). The *Heavy Noon* is Maftooh except in the Seeghah of the Duals and Feminine Plurals, where it is Maksoor. Observer the *Emphatic Noon* in the following Tables:

Table 6.6 - Present Tense Verb With Heavy Noon Of Emphasis

الجَمع	المُثَنَّى	المُفرَد	المُضارِع المُؤكَّد
يَفْعَلُنَّ	يَفْعَلانِّ	يَفْعَلَنَّ	الغائِب:
يَفْعَلْنانِّ	تَفْعَلانِّ	تَفْعَلَنَّ	الغائِبَة:
تَفْعَلُنَّ	تَفْعَلانِّ	تَفْعَلَنَّ	المُخاطَب:
تَفْعَلْنانِّ	تَفْعَلانِّ	تَفْعَلِنَّ	المُخاطَبة:
نَفْعَلَنَّ		أَفْعَلَنَّ	المُتَكَلِّم:

Table 6.7 - Present Tense Verb With Light Noon Of Emphasis

الجَمْع	المُثَنَّى	المُفْرَد	المُضارع المُؤَكَّد
يَفْعَلَنْ		يَفْعَلَنْ	الغائِب:
		تَفْعَلَنْ	الغائِبَة:
تَفْعَلَنْ		تَفْعَلَنْ	المُخاطَب:
		تَفْعَلِنْ	المُخاطِبَة:
نَفْعَلَنْ		أَفْعَلَنْ	المُتَكَلِّم:

The obvious affects which the *Emphatic Noon* has on the Present Tense Verb can be summarized as follows:

› In Seeghah (1,4,7,13,14), the third Original Letter becomes Maftooh. If this letter is the Weak Alif, it is changed to Yaa', as in: يَرْضَى يَرْضَيَنْ، يَرْضَيَنْ .

› In the Seeghah of the Duals (2,5,8,11), the *Emphatic Noon* is Maksoor and *Mushaddad*:

يَضْرِبانِّ، يَرْضَيانِّ، يَدْعُوانِّ

› In the Seeghah of the Masculine Plurals (3,9) and the 2nd Person Feminine Singular (10), the Waw and the Yaa' (the pronouns of the Subject) are omitted unless the vowel before the Pronoun is Fathah. When the Waw and Yaa' are omitted, they will be substituted with an appropriate vowel, meaning that Dhammah will be substituted for Waaw and Kasrah will be substituted for Yaà:

يَضْرِبُونَ يَضْرِبُنَّ؛ تَضْرِبِينَ تَضْرِبِنَّ

▸ In the Seeghah of the Feminine Plural (6,12), to avoid conflicts between the Noon of the Feminine Plural and the *Emphatic Noon*, the letter Alif is inserted between the Noon of the Feminine Plural and the *Emphatic Noon* becomes Maksoor, as in:

يَضْرِبْنَ يَضْرِبْنانِّ

Refer to the following tables for conjugation of Sound and Weak Verbs with the *Emphatice Noon*:

Table 6.8 - Present Tense Sound Verb With Emphatic Noon: ضرب

المُضارِعُ المُؤَكَّد	المُفْرَد	المُثَنَّى	الجَمْع
الغائب:	يَضْرِبَنَّ	يَضْرِبانِّ	يَضْرِبْنَّ
الغائبة:	تَضْرِبَنَّ	تَضْرِبانِّ	يَضْرِبْنانِّ
المُخاطَب:	تَضْرِبَنَّ	تَضْرِبانِّ	تَضْرِبْنَّ
المُخاطَبَة:	تَضْرِبِنَّ	تَضْرِبانِّ	تَضْرِبْنانِّ
المُتَكَلِّم:	أَضْرِبَنَّ		نَضْرِبَنَّ

Table 6.9 - Present Tense Weak Verb With Emphatic Noon: دعو

المُضارِعُ المُؤَكَّد	المُفْرَد	المُثَنَّى	الجَمْع
الغائب:	يَدْعُوَنَّ	يَدْعُوانِّ	يَدْعُنَّ
الغائبة:	تَدْعُوَنَّ	تَدْعُوانِّ	يَدْعُونانِّ
المُخاطَب:	تَدْعُوَنَّ	تَدْعُوانِّ	تَدْعُنَّ
المُخاطَبَة:	تَدْعِنَّ	تَدْعُوانِّ	تَدْعُونانِّ
المُتَكَلِّم:	أَدْعُوَنَّ		نَدْعُوَنَّ

Table 6.10 - Present Tense Weak Verb With Emphatic Noon: خشى

الجَمْع	المُثَنَّى	المُفْرَد	المُضارِعُ المُؤَكَّد
يَخْشَوُنَّ	يَخْشَيانِّ	يَخْشَيَنَّ	الغائِب:
يَخْشَيْنانِّ	تَخْشَيانِّ	تَخْشَيَنَّ	الغائِبَة:
تَخْشَوُنَّ	تَخْشَيانِّ	تَخْشَيَنَّ	المُخاطَب:
تَخْشَيْنانِّ	تَخْشَيانِّ	تَخْشَيِنَّ	المُخاطَبَة:
نَخْشَيَنَّ		أَخْشَيَنَّ	المُتَكَلِّم:

The *Noon of Emphasis* is often found suffixed to the Command Verb (الفِعْلُ الأَمْر). The apparent effect of the *Noon of Emphasis* can be seen in the Command Verb of *Ajwaf*. In the Seeghah (1,4,7,13,14) where the Weak Letter had been removed in order to prevent two *Saakin* letters from meeting, the Weak Letter will return. With the addition of the *Noon of Emphasis*, this conflict no longer exists. Likewise, in *Naaqis*, the third Original Letter (which was removed in the Command Verb) is present in the Command Verb with the *Noon of Emphasis*. Observe the Command Verbs with the *Heavy Noon of Emphasis* in the following tables:

Table 6.11 - The Command Verb With The Emphatic Noon

الجَمْع	المُثَنَّى	المُفْرَد	المُضارِعُ المُؤَكَّد
لِيَضْرِبُنَّ	لِيَضْرِبانِّ	لِيَضْرِبَنَّ	الغائِب:
لِيَضْرِبْنانِّ	لِتَضْرِبانِّ	لِتَضْرِبَنَّ	الغائِبَة:
لِتَضْرِبُنَّ	لِتَضْرِبانِّ	لِتَضْرِبَنَّ	المُخاطَب:
لِتَضْرِبْنانِّ	لِتَضْرِبانِّ	لِتَضْرِبِنَّ	المُخاطَبَة:
لِنَضْرِبَنَّ		لأَضْرِبَنَّ	المُتَكَلِّم:

Similarly, the particle (لاءُ النَّهْي) can also be found with verbs having the *Noon of Emphasis* attached to them. Since it is also one of the *Jawaazim*, it is formed in the same manner as the Command Verb in all respects. In addition, the Particle (لامُ التَّأْكِيد) is also used frequently with the *Noon of Emphasis*. However, since this Particle does not exert any government upon the Present Tense Verb, it is simply prefixed without any change to the verb.

CHAPTER SEVEN

THE ARTIFICIAL VERB,
THE NON-INFLECTIVE VERB
AND THE VERBAL NOUN

الفعل الصناعي و الفعل غير المتصرف
و إسم الفعل

To conclude the first part of this book, we will examine three miscellaneous categories related to the verb.

SECTION ONE

The Artificial Verb

الفِعْلُ الصَّناعِي

The *Artificial Verb* is a verb that is either derived from a *Substantive Noun*, non-Masdar noun (الإِسمُ الجامِدُ) or derived from a noun or verbal sentence based on one of the existing patterns of verbs.

In the first group, those that are taken from the Substantive Noun, the condition exists that the verb comprises all of the Original Letters of the noun. Mostly, it is on one of the patterns of the *Abwaab* of the Derivative Noun (either three letter or four letter). For example:

Table 7.1 - A List Of Artificial Verbs

المَعنى	إسمُهُ	الفعل الصناعي	
To be morning	صُبحٌ	أصبَحَ	(١)
To be evening	مَسَاءٌ (مسو)	أمسى	(٢)
To adopt a son	إبنٌ (بن)	تَبَنّى	(٣)
To grow a gland	غَدٌّ	أغَدَّ	(٤)
To be desolate	قَفْرَةٌ، قَفْرٌ	أقْفَرَ	(٥)
To put on a coat of mail	دِرْعٌ	أدَرَعَ ، إدَّرَعَ	(٦)
To strike s.o. with a sword	سَيفٌ	سافَ أو تَسَيَّفَ	(٧)
To be swung (a sword)	سَيفٌ	تَسَايفَ ، سايَفَ	(٨)
To bake bread	خُبزٌ	إخْتَبَزَ	(٩)
To gather firewood	حطَبٌ	إحتَطَبَ	(١٠)
To be mixed with pepper	فُلْفُلٌ	فَلْفَلَ	(١١)
To become a female camel	ناقَةٌ	إسْتَنْوَقَ	(١٢)
To shiver	قَشْعَرٌّ	إقْشَعَرَّ	(١٣)
To give the color of saffron	عُصْفُرٌ	عَصْفَرَ	(١٤)
To blacken	أسوَدُ	إسوَدَّ	(١٥)

For further clarity, we will use each of the Artificial Verbs in a sentence:

Zaid awoke in the morning in Egypt	أَصْبَحَ زَيدٌ في مِصْرَ	(١
The battle entered into the evening	أَمسى القَتالُ	(٢
Ali adopted Muhammad as a son	تَبَنّى عَلِيٌ مُحَمَّداً	(٣
The camel grew a gland	أَغَدَّ البَعيرُ	(٤
The city became desolate	أَقْفَرَ البَلَدُ	(٥
He put on armour as a shield for his chest	إِدَّرَعَهُ جُنَّةً لِصَدْرِه	(٦
He struck him with his sword with one intense strike	تَسَيَّفَهُ ضَرْبَةً شَديدَةً	(٧
The Iraqis and Iranians swungs swords at each other	سايَفَ العِراقِيُّ وَ الإِيرانِيُّ	(٨
My mother prepared bread morning and evening	إِنْخَبَزَتْ أُمِّي صَباحاً وَ مَساءً	(٩
Umar gathered firewood	إِحْتَطَبَ عُمَرُ	(١٠
The meal was spicy (peppery)	فَلْفَلَ الطَّعامُ	(١١
The (male) camel became female	إِسْتَنْوَقَ الجَمَلُ	(١٢
His skin trembled with fear	إِقْشَعَرَّ جِلْدُهُ مِنَ الخَوفِ	(١٣
The well-water became saffron colored	عَضْفَرَ مآءُ البِئْرِ	(١٤
The night blackened from the rain	إِسْوَدَّ اللَّيْلُ مِنَ المَطَرِ	(١٥

In this same manner are words found in the verses of the Glorious Quran and in honorable traditions:

﴿فَسُبْحَانَ اللَّهِ حِينَ تُمْسُونَ وَ حِينَ تُصْبِحُونَ﴾

"Therefore, Glory be to Allah when you enter upon the time of the evening and when you enter upon the time of the morning..." [Ar-Rum 30:17]

« كُلُّ مَوْلُودٍ يُولَدُ عَلى الفِطْرَةِ حَتَّى يَكُونَ أَبَواهُ يُهَوِّدانِهِ وَ يُنَصِّرانِهِ وَ يُمَجِّسانِهِ »

"Every child born, is born with a (pure) nature, until his parents makes him jewish or makes him Christian or makes him Majoosi." Prophet Muhammad (S)
Biharul-Anwar, Vol.2, Pg. 88]

In the second group, or those that verbs taken from noun or verb sentences, there is one condition that the verb is taken from one or more letters of all the sentence or majority of the words of the sentence and that the letters are combined in a manner that it appears as a verb until the contents of the sentence are expained. Mostly, it will be on the pattern of a four letter Primary Verb, like:

المَعْنى	الجُملَة	الفعل الصناعي	
In the name of Allah...	بِسمِ اللَّهِ الرَّحمنِ الرَّحيمِ	بَسمَلَ	(١)
Praise is for Allah	الحَمْدُ لِلَّهِ	حَمْدَلَ	(٢)
There's no strength & power except with Allah	لا حَوْلَ وَ لا قُوَّةَ إِلاَّ بِاللَّهِ	حَوْقَلَ	(٣)
Allah suffices me	حَسْبِيَ اللَّهُ	حَسْبَلَ	(٤)
Glorified is Allah	سُبْحانَ اللَّهِ	سَبْحَلَ	(٥)
May Allah make me your sacrifice	جَعَلَنِي اللَّهُ فِداكَ	جَعْفَلَ	(٦)
May Allah lengthen your stay (life)	أَطالَ اللَّهُ بَقاءَكَ	طَلْبَقَ	(٧)

SECTION TWO

Non-Inflective Verbs

الفِعْلُ غَيْرُ المُتَصَرِّف

Until now, we have focused almost entirely on fully *Inflective Verbs* (الفِعْلُ المُتَصَرِّفُ).
Inflective Verbs are verbs which have forms for the past tense, present tense and command
verb. Each form of the verb has the full fourteen Seeghah representing the complete verbal
conjugation. When one of these forms are absent in a verb, it is referred to as an
Non-Inflective Verb (الفِعْلُ غَيْرُ المُتَصَرِّفِ).

Non-Inflective Verbs are of four types:

▷ **VERBS THAT HAVE NO COMMAND VERB**

The following verbs are considered to be of this type:

زَالَ يَزالُ، بَرِحَ يَبرَحُ، فَتِي يَفتُو، إِنْفَكَّ يَنْفَكُّ، كادَ يَكادُ، أَوْشَكَ يُوشِكُ، طَفِقَ يَطفَقُ

The first four verbs (زَالَ، بَرِحَ، فَتِي، إِنْفَكَّ) have various meanings that signify a sense
of certainty. These verbs are commonly found negated by the Particle (ما) denoting
strength and continuity. The next two verbs (كادَ، أَوْشَكَ) have the meaning of
becoming near or close to performing an action while the last (طَفِقَ) has the
meaning of beginning something. Observe the following sentences:

قال الصادق (ع): «ما زالَ طَعامُ رَسُولِ اللّهِ الشَّعِيرُ حَتَّى قَبَضَهُ اللّهُ إِلَيهِ عَن إِنسٍ»

Imam Ja'far As-Saadiq (AS) said: "*Barley continued to be the food of the Messenger
of Allah until Allah took him unto Himself away from mankind.*"

قال أمير المؤمنين (ع): «التَّعَبُّدُ عَلى غَيرِ فَقهٍ كَحِمارِ الطَّاحونةِ يَدُورُ وَ لا يَبرَحُ»

Amir al-Mu'mineen (AS) said: *"The object of worship without understanding is like a donkey of the mill, it goes around and does not stop."*

قال رسول الله (ص): «إنِّي أوشَكَ أن أُدعى فَأُجيبُ...»

The Messenger of Allah (S) said: *"I will soon be summoned and I will answer..."*

▷ **THE VERBS WHICH HAVE NO PRESENT TENSE OR COMMAND VERB**

These verbs are found used only in the Past Tense form when used in the given meaning, they are:

1) تَبارَكَ   *Blessed* (as used in relation to Allah)

﴿تَبارَكَ الَّذي نَزَّلَ الفُرقانَ على عَبدِهِ لِيَكونَ لِلعالَمينَ نَذيراً﴾

"Blessed is He who sent down the criterion (between truth and falsehood) upon His servant that he may be a warner to nations." [al-Furqan 25:1]

2) خَلا، عَدا   *Except* (used in the meaning of إسِتثنآء)

قالَ أميرُ المُؤمِنينَ (ع): «النّاسُ وُلدُ آدَم ما خَلا يأجوجَ وَ مأجوجَ»

Amir al-Mu'mineen (AS) said: *"Man is the offspring of Adam except Gog and Magog.* [Bihar v. 6, pg. 314, Chp. 1, No. 23]

3) شَدَّ   *To become difficult*

قال أمير المؤمنين (ع): «لا تَجزَعَنَّ وَ شَدَّ لِلتَّرحيلِ إنَّ ابنَ آمِنةٍ مُحَمَّداً رَجُلٌ صَدوقٌ»

Amir al-Mu'mineen (AS) said: *"Don't fret and be troubled by the departure (from Medinah). Surely, the son of Aminah is Muhammad, an honest man."* [Bihar v. 38, pg. 291. chp. 66. No. 1]

4) طالَ   *A later time*

5) كَثُرَ   **To be abundant, plentiful**

«مَن كَثُرَ كَلامُهُ كَثُرَ مَلامُهُ»

Amir al-Mu'mineen (AS) said: *"He who is excessive in his speech will be excessive in his blameworthiness."* [Girar al-Hikam, No. 7849]

6) قَلَّ   **To be little, insignificant**

7) لَيِسَ   **It is not** (used to negate noun sentences)

﴿إِنَّهُ لَيْسَ لَهُ سُلْطَانٌ عَلَى الَّذِينَ آمَنُوا وَ عَلى رَبِّهِمْ يَتَوَكَّلُونَ﴾

"Surely he has no authority over those who believe and rely on their Lord."

[an-Nahl 16:99]

8) دامَ   **To be continuous.** This verb is usually found accompanied by the Particle (ما) known as: (ما الوَقْتِيَّة).

﴿خالِدِينَ فِيها ما دامَتِ السَّماواتُ وَ الأَرْضُ﴾

"Abiding therein as long as the heavens and earth endure." [Yunus 11:107]

9) عَسَى، حَرى، إِخْلَوْلَقَ   These three verbs express various degrees of hope.

﴿عَسَى اللَّهُ أَنْ يَتُوبَ عَلَيْهِمْ﴾

"Maybe Allah will turn toward them (Mercifully)." [at-Taubah 9:102]

10) أَنْشَأَ، جَعَلَ، أَخَذَ، عَلِقَ These four have the meaning of beginning or initiating an action

﴿وَ جَعَلَ لِلَّهِ أَنْداداً لِيُضِلَّ عَنْ سَبِيلِهِ﴾

"And he (Shaytan) sets up rivals with Allah that he may cause (man) to stray off from His path." [az-Zumar 39:8]

11) قَرُبَ To be near

فَلَمَّا قَرُبَ أَجَلُهُ أَوحى اللَّهُ إِلَيهِ تَعالى إِنِّي رافِعُكَ إِلى السَّمآءِ

"And when (Idris') time had drawn near, Allah, the Exalted, revealed to him (that) surely I will raise you to the heaven." [Bihar, v. 11, pg. 264, chp. 8, N0. 14]

12) بِئْسَ، سآءَ To be bad, indecent (These are called the Verbs Of Blame).

﴿وَ مَأْواهُمُ النَّارُ وَ بِئْسَ مَثْوى الظَّالِمِينَ﴾

"Their abode is the fire and evil is the abode of the unjust." [Aali 'Imran 3:151]

13) نِعْمَ، حَبَّ These two verbs signify being pleased (They are called the Verbs of Praise)

﴿حَسْبُنا اللَّهُ وَ نِعْمَ الوَكِيلُ﴾

"Allah is sufficient for us and most excellent is the Protector."

Additionally, verbs used in the form of contracts (العُقُود) are without Present Tense forms or Command Verbs. For example: بِعْتُ هذا دِيناراً I have sold this for a Dinaar; زَوَّجْتُكَ نَفْسِي I have married myself to you.

▷ VERBS WHICH HAVE NO PRESENT TENSE

They are verbs on the pattern of أَفْعَلَ and أَفْعِلْ. These are the two patterns of the Verbs Surprise or Ta'ajjub (الفِعْلُ التَّعَجُّب). The first verb always appears after the Particle of Interrogation (ما), as in: ما أَحْسَنَ زَيداً *How good Zaid is!*, and preceding a Mansoob Noun. The second verb will appear before a noun made Majroor by a Particle, as in: أَحْسِنْ بِزَيدٍ *Zaid did well!*.

Note: The second Original Letter (عَيْنُ الكَلِمَةِ), in both patterns of the Verb of Suprise, does not undergo any alteration or I'laal nor any contraction (Idghaam), for example:

يا بُنَيَّ ما أَطْيَبَ رِيحُكَ ! "*O my son, How lovely is your fragrance !*

▷ THE VERBS WHICH HAVE NO PAST TENSE NOR PRESENT TENSE

This group of verbs are only in the form of the Command Verb. They are:

1) تَعالَ   *Come!*   ﴿تَعالُوا قاتِلُوا في سَبِيلِ اللَّهِ﴾ "*Come fight in Allah's way*" [3:168]

2) هاتِ   *Bring!* ﴿هاتُوا بُرهانَكُم إِنْ كُنْتُم صادِقِينَ﴾ "*Bring your proof if you are truthful*" [2:111]

3) هآءِ   *Take!*

4) هَيِّ   *Hurry!*

5) هَبْ   *Suppose!*

The Indeclineable Verb is arrived at through derivation. It does not have a Masdar.

SECTION THREE

The Verbal Noun

إِسمُ الفِعْلِ

The Verbal Noun is a word that has the meaning and effect of a verb but it doesn't have the pattern of a verb. Or it may exhibit signs that are particular to the noun, like Tanween, as in: أُفٍ.

The Verbal Noun has three categories:

› Those Verbal Nouns that have the meaning of the Past Tense Verb, like: هَيْهاتَ *How preposterous!, What an idea!*. As in: ﴿هَيْهاتَ هَيْهاتَ لِما تُوعَدُونَ﴾ "*Far, far is that which you are threatened with.*" [23:36]

› Those Verbal Nouns that have the meaning of the Present Tense Verb, as in: أُفٍّ *Woe to you!*, as in: ﴿أُفٍّ لَكُمْ وَ لِما تَعْبُدُونَ مِنْ دُونِ اللَّهِ﴾ "*Woe on you and on what you serve besides Allah.*" [21:67]

› Those Verbal Nouns that have the meaning of the Command Verb, like: صَهِ *Quiet!*.

The Verbal Noun is commonly used to exaggerate the meaning for which it used. It will be examined in greater depth in the second part of this book which is devoted exclusively to the Noun.

With this, our discussion of the verb is complete.

الموجز

في التصريف

AL-MUJAZ

A Summary Of Tasreef

APPENDIX A

INDEX OF TABLES

Made in the USA
Monee, IL
11 April 2025